Ogilvy on Advertising

LE 4 SEPTEMBRE J'ENLEVE LE BAS.

After we paint the car we paint the paint.

The man in the Hathaway shirt

AMERICAN MEN are beginning to realize that it is ridiculous to buy good suits and then spoil the effect by wearing an ordinary, mass-produced shirt. Hence the growing popularity of HATHAWAY shirts, which are in a class by themselves.

HATHAWAY shirts wear infinitely longer—a matter of years. They make you look younger and more distinguished, because of the subtle way HATHAWAY cut collars. The whole shirt is tailored more generously, and is therefore more comfortable. The tails are longer, and stay in your trousers. The buttons are mother-of-pearl. Even the stitching has an ante-bellum elegance about it.

Above all, HATHAWAY make their shirts of remarkable *fabrics*, collected from the four corners of the earth—Viyella, and Aertex, from England, woolen taffeta from Scotland, Sea Island cotton from the West Indies, hand-woven madras from India, broadcloth from Manchester, linen batiste from Paris, hand-blocked silks from England, exclusive cottons from the best weavers in America. You will get a

great deal of quiet satisfaction out of wearing shirts which are in such impeccable taste.

HATHAWAY shirts are made by a small company of dedicated craftsmen in the little town of Waterville, Maine. They have been at it, man and boy, for one hundred and twenty years.

At better stores everywhere, or write C. F. HATHAWAY, Waterville, Maine. In New York, telephone OX 7-5566. Prices from $5.95 to $20.00.

goodness on tap

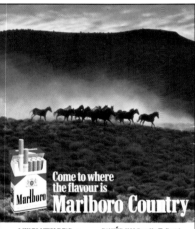

Come to where the flavour is Marlboro Country

LOW TO MIDDLE TAR As defined by H.M. Govt. DANGER. H.M. Govt. Health Depts'.
WARNING: CIGARETTES CAN SERIOUSLY DAMAGE YOUR HEALTH

JAMAICA

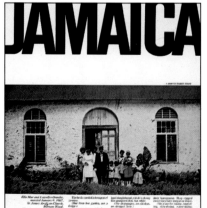

Ella Mae and Lucellen Chandler, married January 9, 1947, St. James Angelic an Church, Morant Bay. They honeymooned in Jamaica.

Pablo Casals is coming home — to Puerto Rico

THIS SIMPLE ROOM is in his mother's home at Mayaguez. The first concert Casals ever gave in Puerto Rico was from the balcony of this house last year—just beyond the fanlight.

While his mother's kinsmen listened from the street, Casals played her lullaby, smoked his pipe and wept.

The back of that armchair bears an inscription in Casals' own handwriting. "Este es mi sillón." This is my rocking chair.

Here are gentle thoughts from the world's greatest cellist—on Puerto Rico, the sea and himself:

"The first time I was aware that I was alive, I heard the sound of the sea. Before, I would have said that the most beautiful sea was the one I had in front of my Spanish house. But now I must confess that the sea I am looking at this moment is even more beautiful."

Of his plans for the future, Pablo Casals had this to say:

"The natural thing that occurs to me, is to come back to Puerto Rico and to do for this country everything within my power. I will be back for the festival I have planned for this coming Spring."

PUERTO RICO'S GREAT NEW MUSIC FESTIVAL IN SAN JUAN

The Casals Festival in San Juan opens on April 22nd and will continue through May 8th. Pablo Casals will conduct or perform at each of twelve concerts.

The Festival Orchestra brings together fifty-four of the world's most talented musicians. Principal performers include: Mieczyslaw Horszowski, Eugene Istomin, Milton Katims,

Jesus Maria Sanromá, Alexander Schneider, Rudolf Serkin, Gérard Souzay, Maria Stader, Isaac Stern, Joseph Szigeti.

Two chamber music concerts will feature the Budapest String Quartet.

For further details, write Festival Casals, P. O. Box 1831, San Juan, Puerto Rico, or to 15 West 44th Street, New York 17, N. Y.

©1957 Commonwealth of Puerto Rico, 329 Fifth Avenue, New York 17, N. Y.

Living room of the house where Casals' mother was born—in Mayaguez, Puerto Rico's third largest city. Photograph by Elliott Erwitt.

Ogilvy on Advertising

David Ogilvy

PRION

First published in the UK by Pan Books Ltd and Orbis
Publishing Ltd, and in the United States by Crown
Publishers, Inc., in 1983

This edition published in 2007 by
Prion
an imprint of the
Carlton Publishing Group
20 Mortimer Street
London
W1T 3JW

Reprinted in 2010

A catalogue record for this book is available from the
British Library

ISBN 978-1-85375-615-3

Printed and bound in Thailand

Contents

1 Overture

'Let us march against Philip'

I do not regard advertising as entertainment or an art form, but as a medium of information. When I write an advertisement, I don't want you to tell me that you find it 'creative.' I want you to find it so interesting that you *buy the product*. When Aeschines spoke, they said, 'How well he speaks.' But when Demosthenes spoke, they said, 'Let us march against Philip.'

In my *Confessions of an Advertising Man*, published in 1963, I told the story of how Ogilvy & Mather came into existence, and set forth the principles on which our early success had been based. What was then little more than a creative boutique in New York has since become one of the four biggest advertising agencies in the world, with 140 offices in 40 countries. Our principles seem to work.

But I am now so old that a French magazine lists me as the only survivor among a group of men who, they aver, contributed to the Industrial Revolution – alongside Adam Smith, Edison, Karl Marx, Rockefeller, Ford and Keynes. Does old age disqualify me from writing about advertising in today's world? Or could it be that perspective helps a man to separate the eternal verities of advertising from its passing fads?

When I set up shop on Madison Avenue in 1949, I assumed that advertising would undergo several major changes before I retired. So far, there has been only *one* change that can be called major: television has emerged as the most potent medium for selling most products.

Yes, there have been other changes and I shall describe them, but their significance has been exaggerated by pundits in search of trendy labels. For example, the concept of brand images, which I popularized in 1953, was not really new; Claude Hopkins had described it 20 years before. The so-called Creative Revolution, usually ascribed to Bill Bernbach and myself in the fifties, could equally well have been ascribed to N.W. Ayer and Young & Rubicam in the thirties.

Meanwhile, most of the advertising techniques which worked when I wrote *Confessions of an Advertising Man* still work today. Consumers still buy products whose advertising promises them value for money, beauty, nutrition, relief from suffering, social status and so on. All over the world.

In saying this, I run the risk of being denounced by the idiots who hold that any advertising technique which has been in use for more than two years is *ipso facto* obsolete. They excoriate slice-of-life commercials, demonstrations and talking heads, turning a blind eye to the fact that these techniques still make the cash register ring. If they have read Horace, they will say that I am *difficilis, querulus, laudator temporis acti. Se*

'I run the risk of being denounced by the idiots who hold that any advertising technique which has been in use for more than two years is *ipso facto* obsolete.'

*puero, castigator, censorque minorum.** So what? There have always been noisy lunatics on the fringes of the advertising business. Their stock-in-trade includes ethnic humor, eccentric art direction, contempt for research, and their self-proclaimed genius. They are seldom found out, because they gravitate to the kind of clients who, bamboozled by their rhetoric, do not hold them responsible for sales results. Their campaigns find favor at cocktail parties in New York, San Francisco and London but are taken less seriously in Chicago. In the days when I specialized in posh campaigns for *The New Yorker*, I was the hero of this coterie, but when I graduated to advertising in mass media and wrote a book which extolled the value of research, I became its devil. I comfort myself with the reflection that I have sold more merchandise than all of them put together.

'I *hate* rules'

I am sometimes attacked for imposing 'rules.' Nothing could be further from the truth. I *hate* rules. All I do is report on how consumers react to different stimuli. I may say to a copywriter, 'Research shows that commercials with celebrities are below average in persuading people to buy products. Are you *sure* you want to use a celebrity?' Call that a *rule*? Or I may say to an art director, 'Research suggests that if you set the copy in black type on a white background, more people will read it than if you set it in white type on a black background.' A *hint*, perhaps, but scarcely a rule.

In 18th-century England, a family of obstetricians built a huge practice by delivering babies with a lower rate of infant and maternal mortality than their competitors. They had a secret – and guarded it jealously, until an inquisitive medical student climbed onto the roof of their delivering room, looked through the skylight and saw the forceps they had invented. The secret was out, to the benefit of all obstetricians and their patients. Today's obstetricians do not keep their discoveries secret, they publish them. I am grateful to my partners for allowing me to publish mine. But I should add that the occasional *opinions* expressed in this book do not necessarily reflect the collegial opinions of the agency which employs me.

This is not a book for readers who think they already know all there is to be known about advertising. It is for young hopefuls – and veterans who are still in search of ways to improve their batting average at the cash register.

I write only about aspects of advertising I know from my own experience. That is why this book contains nothing about media, cable television or advertising in Japan.

If you think it is a lousy book, you should have seen it before my partner Joel Raphaelson did his best to de-louse it. *Bless you, Joel.*

David Ogilvy

---

*Testy, a grumbler, inclined to praise the way of the world when he was a boy, to play the critic and to be a censor of the new generation.

2   How to produce advertising that sells

Pretend you started work this morning in my agency, and that you have dropped by my office to ask for advice. I will start with some generalities about how to go about your work. In later chapters I will give you more specific advice on producing advertisements for magazines, newspapers, television and radio. I ask you to forgive me for oversimplifying some complicated subjects, and for the dogmatism of my style – the dogmatism of brevity. We are both in a hurry.

The first thing I have to say is that you may not realize the magnitude of difference between one advertisement and another. Says John Caples, the doyen of direct response copywriters:

> 'I have seen one advertisement actually sell not twice as much, not three times as much, but 19½ times as much as another. Both advertisements occupied the same space. Both were run in the same publication. Both had photographic illustrations. Both had carefully written copy. The difference was that one used the right appeal and the other used the wrong appeal.'*

The wrong advertising can actually *reduce* the sales of a product. I am told that George Hay Brown, at one time head of marketing research at Ford, inserted advertisements in every other copy of the *Reader's Digest*. At the end of the year, the people who had *not* been exposed to the advertising had bought more Fords than those who had.

In another survey it was found that consumption of a certain brand of beer was lower among people who remembered its advertising than those who did not. The brewer had spent millions of dollars on advertising which *un-sold* his beer.

I sometimes wonder if there is a tacit conspiracy among clients, media and agencies to avoid putting advertising to such acid tests. Everyone involved has a vested interest in prolonging the myth that *all* advertising increases sales to some degree. It doesn't.

Tested Advertising Methods by John Caples. Prentice-Hall, 1975

The Rolls-Royce Silver Cloud—$13,995

"At 60 miles an hour the loudest noise in this new Rolls-Royce comes from the electric clock"

What __makes__ Rolls-Royce the best car in the world? "There is really no magic about it— it is merely patient attention to detail," says an eminent Rolls-Royce engineer.

1. "At 60 miles an hour the loudest noise comes from the electric clock," reports the Technical Editor of THE MOTOR. Three mufflers tune out sound frequencies—acoustically.

2. Every Rolls-Royce engine is run for seven hours at full throttle before installation, and each car is test-driven for hundreds of miles over varying road surfaces.

3. The Rolls-Royce is designed as an *owner-driven* car. It is eighteen inches shorter than the largest domestic cars.

4. The car has power steering, power brakes and automatic gear-shift. It is very easy to drive and to park. No chauffeur required.

5. The finished car spends a week in the final test-shop, being fine-tuned. Here it is subjected to 98 separate ordeals. For example, the engineers use a *stethoscope* to listen for axle-whine.

6. The Rolls-Royce is guaranteed for three years. With a new network of dealers and parts-depots from Coast to Coast, service is no problem.

7. The Rolls-Royce radiator has never changed, except that when Sir Henry Royce died in 1933 the monogram RR was changed from red to black.

8. The coachwork is given five coats of primer paint, and hand rubbed between each coat, before *nine* coats of finishing paint go on.

9. By moving a switch on the steering column, you can adjust the shock-absorbers to suit road conditions.

10. A picnic table, veneered in French walnut, slides out from under the dash. Two more swing out behind the front seats.

11. You can get such optional extras as an Espresso coffee-making machine, a dictating machine, a bed, hot and cold water for washing, an electric razor or a telephone.

12. There are three separate systems of power brakes, two hydraulic and one mechanical. Damage to one will not affect the others. The Rolls-Royce is a very *safe* car—and also a very *lively* car. It cruises serenely at eighty-five. Top speed is in excess of 100 m.p.h.

13. The Bentley is made by Rolls-Royce. Except for the radiators, they are identical motor cars, manufactured by the same engineers in the same works. People who feel diffident about driving a Rolls-Royce can buy a Bentley.

PRICE. The Rolls-Royce illustrated in this advertisement – f.o.b. principal ports of entry—costs **$13,995.**

If you would like the rewarding experience of driving a Rolls-Royce or Bentley, write or telephone to one of the dealers listed on opposite page. Rolls-Royce Inc., 10 Rockefeller Plaza, New York 20, N. Y. CIrcle 5-1144.

Left Before I wrote this – the most famous of all automobile ads – I did my homework. It ran only in two newspapers and two magazines, at a cost of $25,000. The following year, Ford based their multi-million dollar campaign on the claim that their car was even quieter than a Rolls.

Below I resigned the Rolls-Royce account when they sent five hundred defective cars to the United States. Two years later we took Mercedes, and sent a team to interview their engineers in Stuttgart. From this sprang a campaign of long factual advertisements which increased sales from 10,000 cars a year to 40,000.

Below right When I got a margarine account, I was under the impression that margarine was made from coal. *Ten days reading the literature taught me otherwise.*

Do your homework

You don't stand a tinker's chance of producing successful advertising unless you start by doing your homework. I have always found this extremely tedious, but there is no substitute for it.

First, study the product you are going to advertise. The more you know about it, the more likely you are to come up with a big idea for selling it. When I got the Rolls-Royce account, I spent three weeks reading about the car and came across a statement that 'at sixty miles an hour, the loudest noise comes from the electric clock.' This became the headline, and it was followed by 607 words of factual copy.

Later, when I got the Mercedes account, I sent a team to the Daimler-Benz headquarters in Stuttgart. They spent three weeks taping interviews with the engineers. From this came a campaign of long, factual advertisements which increased Mercedes sales in the United States from 10,000 cars a year to 40,000.

When I was asked to do the advertising for Good Luck margarine, I was under the impression that margarine was made from *coal*. But ten days' reading enabled me to write a factual advertisement which worked.

Same thing with Shell gasoline. A briefing from the client revealed something which came as a surprise to me; that gasoline has several ingredients, including Platformate, which increases mileage. The

You give up things when
you buy the Mercedes-Benz 230S. Things like
rattles, rust, and shabby workmanship.

A challenge to women who would never dream of serving margarine

Lever Brothers defy you to tell the difference between
GOOD LUCK margarine and you-know-what

Save 50¢ a Pound

Suddenly DOVE makes soap old-fashioned!

New bath and toilet bar <u>creams</u> your skin while you bathe.

DOVE is <u>one-quarter cleansing cream</u>. It leaves your skin soft and smooth–without the dry feeling caused by soap.

DOVE

Dove is <u>good</u> for your skin

Above I positioned Dove as a toilet bar for women with dry skin, and used a promise which had won in test: 'Dove creams your skin while you bathe.'

Right Robert Townsend, the eccentric head of Avis, asked me to do his advertising. When conflict with another client forced me to refuse, Doyle Dane Bernbach created one of the most powerful campaigns in the history of advertising. 'When you're only Number 2, you try harder. Or else.' This diabolical positioning made life miserable for Hertz, who was Number 1.
Opposite *Doyle Dane Bernbach positioned Volkswagen as a protest against Detroit, thereby making the Beetle a cult among non-conformists. The copywriter was Julian Koenig, the art director Helmut Krone. Sales of the car went up to 500,000 cars a year.*

resulting campaign helped to reverse a seven-year decline in Shell's share-of-market.

If you are too lazy to do this kind of homework, you may occasionally *luck* into a successful campaign, but you will run the risk of skidding about on what my brother Francis called 'the slippery surface of irrelevant brilliance.'

Your next chore is to find out what kind of advertising your competitors have been doing for similar products, and with what success. This will give you your bearings.

Now comes research among consumers. Find out how they think about your kind of product, what language they use when they discuss the subject, what attributes are important to them, *and what promise would be most likely to make them buy your brand.*

If you cannot afford the services of professionals to do this research, do it yourself. Informal conversations with half-a-dozen housewives can sometimes help a copywriter more than formal surveys in which he does not participate.

Positioning

Now consider how you want to 'position' your product. This curious verb is in great favor among marketing experts, but no two of them agree what it means. My own definition is 'what the product does, and who it is for.' I could have positioned Dove as a detergent bar for men with dirty hands, but chose instead to position it as a toilet bar for women with dry skin. This is still working 25 years later.

In Norway, the SAAB car had no measurable profile. We positioned it as a car for *winter*. Three years later it was voted the *best* car for Norwegian winters.

To advertise a car that looked like an orthopedic boot would have defeated me. But Bill Bernbach and his merry men positioned Volkswagen as a protest against the vulgarity of Detroit cars in those days, thereby making the Beetle a cult among those Americans who eschew conspicuous consumption.

When you're only No. 2, you try harder. Or else.

Little fish have to keep moving all of the time. The big ones never stop picking on them.

Avis knows all about the problems of little fish.

We're only No. 2 in rent a cars. We'd be swallowed up if we didn't try harder.

There's no rest for us.

We're always emptying ashtrays. Making sure gas tanks are full before we rent our cars. Seeing that the batteries are full of life. Checking our windshield wipers.

And the cars we rent out can't be anything less than lively new super-torque Fords.

And since we're not the big fish, you won't feel like a sardine when you come to our counter.

We're not jammed with customers.

Avis is only No. 2 in rent a cars. So why go with us?

We try harder.

(When you're not the biggest, you have to.)

We just can't afford dirty ashtrays. Or half-empty gas tanks. Or worn wipers. Or unwashed cars. Or low tires. Or anything less than seat-adjusters that adjust. Heaters that heat. Defrosters that defrost.

Obviously, the thing we try hardest for is just to be nice. To start you out right with a new car, like a lively, super-torque Ford, and a pleasant smile. To let you know, say, where you can get a good, hot pastrami sandwich in Duluth.

Why?

Because we can't afford to take you for granted. Go with us next time.

The line at our counter is shorter.

Think small.

Our little car isn't so much of a novelty any more.

A couple of dozen college kids don't try to squeeze inside it.

The guy at the gas station doesn't ask where the gas goes.

Nobody even stares at our shape.

In fact, some people who drive our little flivver don't even think 32 miles to the gallon is going any great guns.

Or using five pints of oil instead of five quarts.

Or never needing anti-freeze.

Or racking up 40,000 miles on a set of tires.

That's because once you get used to some of our economies, you don't even think about them any more.

Except when you squeeze into a small parking spot. Or renew your small insur-ance. Or pay a small repair bill. Or trade in your old VW for a new one.

Think it over.

"You can <u>see</u> the lemon in Schweppes Bitter Lemon. That's because Schweppes uses whole, fresh lemons. Juice, pulp, peel, <u>everything</u>."

So says Commander Whitehead, President of Schweppes (USA) Ltd.

"Schweppes *invented* Bitter Lemon," he continues. "It was our first new product in one hundred years, and we did not stint."

Schweppes uses whole, fresh lemons in making Bitter Lemon. Juice, pulp, peel, everything. Thus its tart, grown-up taste.

"Schweppes Bitter Lemon is the first *adult* soft drink," declares the Schweppesman, "the only one you can order without feeling like a *sissy*."

There are at least two more uses for Schweppes Bitter Lemon. It is an unobtrusive way to sit out a round or two. It is also the most versatile new *mixer* since Schweppes Tonic itself.

No matter how you use Bitter Lemon, always turn the bottle upside down before you open it.

That way, everyone gets his fair share of lemon morsels.

Will you love Schweppes in December as you did in May?

ABOVE you see, not Nanook of the North and not the Abominable Snowman—but Commander Edward Whitehead, Ambassador from the House of Schweppes in London.

The Commander will tell you that this winter's most fashionable drink is Vodka-and-Tonic. (*All* the rage from coast to coast.) And that no capable barman would try to mix an authentic Vodka-and-Tonic without *Schweppes*.

In one hundred years, nobody has found a substitute for Schweppes bittersweet flavor. A flavor that makes every Tonic drink (Vodka-and-Tonic, Gin-and-Tonic, Rum-and-Tonic) taste so *curiously refreshing*.

And nobody has been able to copy Schwepp*ervescence* — those patrician little bubbles that last your whole drink through.

Make sure you get the *original* Schweppes when you ask for it. Tastes as good in December as it did in May!

Above *An essay in the art of image-building. For 18 years I used the face of my client Commander Whitehead as the symbol of his own product. It worked to beat the band on a peppercorn budget.*

Brand image

You now have to decide what 'image' you want for your brand. Image means *personality*. Products, like people, have personalities, and they can make or break them in the market place. The personality of a product is an amalgam of many things – its name, its packaging, its price, the style of its advertising, and, above all, the nature of the product itself.

Every advertisement should be thought of as a contribution to the brand image. It follows that your advertising should consistently project the *same* image, year after year. This is difficult to achieve, because there are always forces at work to change the advertising – like a new agency, or a new Marketing Director who wants to make his mark.

It pays to give most products an image of quality – *a First Class ticket*. This is particularly true of products whose brand-name is visible to your friends, like beer, cigarettes and automobiles: products you 'wear'. If your advertising looks cheap or shoddy, it will rub off on your product. Who wants to be seen using shoddy products?

Take whiskey. Why do some people chose Jack Daniel's, while others choose Grand Dad or Taylor? Have they tried all three and compared the taste? Don't make me laugh. The reality is that these three brands have different *images* which appeal to different kinds of people. It isn't the whiskey they choose, it's the image. The brand image is 90 per cent of what the distiller has to sell.

Researchers at the Department of Psychology at the University of California gave distilled water to students. They told some of them that it was distilled water, and asked them to describe its taste. Most said it

If you'd like to know more about Jack Daniel's Whiskey, drop us a line.

WOODSMEN DROP IN from all around Tennessee carrying truckloads of maple for Jack Daniel's.

It has to be hard, sugar maple taken from high ground. Our Jack Bateman (that's him saying hello to the driver) will split it and stack it and burn it to get charcoal. And nothing smooths out whiskey like this special charcoal does. Of course, none of these woodsmen work regular hours. So you never know when they'll drop in. But after a sip of Jack Daniel's, we believe, you'll know why they're always welcome.

CHARCOAL
MELLOWED
◊
DROP
◊
BY DROP

Tennessee Whiskey • 90 Proof • Distilled and Bottled by Jack Daniel Distillery
Lem Motlow, Prop., Inc., Route 1, Lynchburg (Pop. 361), Tennessee 37352
Placed in the National Register of Historic Places by the United States Government

Above *When you choose a brand of whiskey you are choosing an image. Jack Daniel's advertisements project an image of homespun honesty and thereby persuade you that Jack Daniel's is worth its premium price.*
Right *Leo Burnett's campaign for Marlboro projects an image which has made it the biggest-selling cigarette in the world. It has been running, almost without change, for 25 years.*

had no taste of any kind. They told the other students that the distilled water came out of the tap. Most of them said it tasted *horrible*. The mere mention of *tap* conjured up an image of chlorine.

Give people a taste of Old Crow, and *tell* them it's Old Crow. Then give them another taste of Old Crow, *but tell them it's Jack Daniel's*. Ask them which they prefer. They'll think the two drinks are quite different. *They are tasting images.*

I have always been hypnotized by Jack Daniel's. The label and the advertising convey an image of homespun honesty, and the high price makes me assume that Jack Daniel's must be superior.

Writing advertising for any kind of liquor is an extremely subtle art. I once tried using rational facts to *argue* the consumer into choosing a brand of whiskey. It didn't work. You don't catch Coca Cola advertising that Coke contains 50 per cent more cola berries.

Next time an apostle of hard-sell questions the importance of

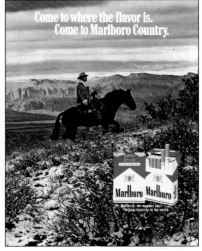

brand images, ask him how Marlboro climbed from obscurity to become the biggest-selling cigarette in the world. Leo Burnett's cowboy campaign, started 25 years ago and continued to this day, has given the brand an image which appeals to smokers all over the world.

What's the big idea?

You can do homework from now until doomsday, but you will never win fame and fortune unless you also invent *big ideas*. It takes a big idea to attract the attention of consumers and get them to buy your product. Unless your advertising contains a big idea, it will pass like a ship in the night.

I doubt if more than one campaign in a hundred contains a big idea. I am supposed to be one of the more fertile inventors of big ideas, but in my long career as a copywriter I have not had more than 20, if that. Big ideas come from the unconscious. This is true in art, in science and in advertising. But your unconscious has to be *well informed*, or your idea will be irrelevant. Stuff your conscious mind with information, then unhook your rational thought process. You can help this process by going for a long walk, or taking a hot bath, or drinking half a pint of claret. Suddenly, if the telephone line from your unconscious is open, a big idea wells up within you.

My partner Esty Stowell complained that the first commercial I wrote for Pepperidge Farm bread was sound enough, but lacking in imagery. That night I dreamed of two white horses pulling a baker's delivery van along a country lane at a smart trot. Today, 27 years later, that horse-drawn van is still driving up that lane in Pepperidge commercials.

When asked what was the best asset a man could have, Albert Lasker – the most astute of all advertising men – replied, 'Humility in the presence of a good idea.' It is horribly difficult to *recognize* a good idea. I shudder to think how many I have rejected. Research can't help you much, because it cannot predict the *cumulative* value of an idea, and no idea is big unless it will work for thirty years.

One of my partners came up with the idea of parading a herd of bulls through Merrill Lynch commercials under the slogan – 'Merrill Lynch is *bullish* on America.' I thought it was dopey, but fortunately it had been approved before I saw it. Those bulls are still parading, long after the account moved to another agency.

It will help you recognize a big idea if you ask yourself five questions:

1 Did it make me gasp when I first saw it?

2 Do I wish I had thought of it myself?

3 Is it unique?

4 Does it fit the strategy to perfection?

5 *Could it be used for 30 years?*

You can count on your fingers the number of advertising campaigns that run even for five years. These are the superstars, the campaigns that

Opposite *Sometimes, the best idea of all is to show the product – with utter simplicity. This takes courage, because you will be accused of not being 'creative.'*

Grethe Meyers nye stel "Rødtop" fås i 38 dele til både bord og køkken.

Sådan fornyer man en klassiker

designet af Grethe Meyer.

Det er tyve år siden Grethe Meyer lavede "Blåkant" for Den Kongelige Porcelainsfabrik. Og lige fra starten var vi klar over, at her stod vi overfor en klassiker på linie med Børge Mogensens møbler og PH's lamper.

Tiden har givet os ret. Grethe Meyers rene, gennemtænkte formgivning og diskrete dekorationskunst er blevet højt præmieret og højt elsket i mange lande.

Men kunst er fornyelse, og Grethe Meyer har netop fornyet "Blåkant's" tidløse former med en glad, rød kant og en lysere bundfarve. Ændringen er lille, men virkningen stor, og "Rødtop" er næsten lige så forskellig fra

"Blåkant" som sommer fra vinter. Hvad De foretrækker, ved vi ikke. Vi er bare glade og stolte over at kunne give Dem muligheden for at vælge.

DEN KONGELIGE

go right on producing results through boom and recession, against shifting competitive pressures, and changes of personnel. The Hathaway eyepatch first appeared in 1951 and is still going strong. Every Dove commercial since 1955 has promised that, 'Dove doesn't dry your skin the way soap can.' The American Express commercials, 'Do you know me?' have been running since 1975. And Leo Burnett's Marlboro campaign has been running for 25 years.

Make the product the hero

Whenever you can, make the product itself the hero of your advertising. If you think the product too dull, I have news for you: there are no dull products, only dull writers. I never assign a product to a writer unless I know that he is personally interested in it. Every time I have written a bad campaign, it has been because the product did not interest me.

A problem which confronts agencies is that so many products are no different from their competitors. Manufacturers have access to the same technology; marketing people use the same research procedures to

Below *To my chagrin, this campaign, which I thought enchanting, created scarcely a ripple. The dog was my briard Crème Brûlée. Judson Irish wrote the dialogue in the style of Alfred Jingle in* Pickwick Papers.

Right *Good ideas come from the unconscious. The author dreamed about an old baker driving his horse and wagon along a country lane on his way to deliver Pepperidge Farm bread. Twenty-five years later the horse and wagon are still in the commercials.*

determine consumer preferences for color, size, design, taste and so on. When faced with selling 'parity' products, all you can hope to do is explain their virtues more persuasively than your competitors, and to differentiate them by the style of your advertising. This is the 'added value' which advertising contributes, and I am not sufficiently puritanical to hate myself for it.

'The positively good'

My partner Joel Raphaelson has articulated a feeling which has been growing in my mind for some time:

> 'In the past, just about every advertiser has assumed that in order to sell his goods he has to convince consumers that his product is *superior* to his competitor's.
>
> 'This may not be necessary. It may be sufficient to convince consumers that your product is *positively good*. If the consumer feels certain that your product is good and feels uncertain about your competitor's, he will buy yours.
>
> 'If you and your competitors all make excellent products, don't try to imply that your product is *better*. Just say what's good about your product – *and do a clearer, more honest, more informative job of saying it.*
>
> 'If this theory is right, sales will swing to the marketer who does the best job of creating confidence that his product is *positively good*.'

This approach to advertising parity products does not insult the intelligence of consumers. Who can blame you for putting your best foot forward?

Repeat your winners

If you are lucky enough to write a good advertisement, repeat it until it stops selling. Scores of good advertisements have been discarded before they lost their potency.

Research shows that the readership of an advertisement does not decline when it is run several times in the same magazine. Readership

'You aren't advertising to a standing army; you are advertising to a moving parade.'

remains at the same level throughout at least four repetitions.

You aren't advertising to a standing army; you are advertising to a moving parade. The advertisement which sold a refrigerator to couples who got married last year will probably be just as successful with couples who get married this year. A good advertisement can be thought of as a radar sweep, constantly hunting new prospects as they come into the market. Get a good radar, and keep it sweeping.

Henry Ford once said to a copywriter on his account, 'Bill, that campaign of yours is dandy, but do we have to run it *forever?*' To which the copywriter replied, 'Mr Ford, the campaign has not yet appeared.' Ford had seen it too often at too many meetings. The best way to settle such arguments is to measure the selling effectiveness of your campaign at regular intervals, and to go on running it until the research shows that it has worn out.

Word of mouth

It sometimes happens that advertising campaigns enter the culture. Thus the musical theme in a Maxwell House coffee commercial became Number 7 on the hit parade. After Commander Whitehead started appearing in Schweppes advertising, he became a popular participant in talk shows on television. This kind of thing is manna from heaven, but nobody knows how to do it on purpose. At least, I don't.

Fifty years ago attempts were made in England to cultivate word-of-mouth advertising by spreading anecdotes like this one:

> 'An old farmer was walking down a road, bent double with rheumatism. Someone in a Rolls-Royce stopped to speak to him. Told him to take Beecham's Pills. Do you know who it was? *The King's Doctor!*'

Down with committees

Most campaigns are too complicated. They reflect a long list of objectives, and try to reconcile the divergent views of too many executives. By attempting to cover too many things, they achieve nothing.

Many commercials and many advertisements look like the minutes of a committee. In my experience, committees can criticize but they cannot create.

> 'Search the parks in all your cities
> You'll find no statues of committees.'

Agencies have a way of creating campaigns in committees. They call it 'team-work'. Who can argue with team-work?

The process of producing advertising campaigns moves at a snail's pace. Questions of strategy are argued by committees of the client's brand managers and the agency's account executives, who have a vested interest in prolonging the argument as much as possible; it is how they earn their living. The researchers take months to answer elementary questions. When the copywriters finally get down to work, they dawdle about in brain-storming sessions and other forms of wheel-spinning. If a copywriter averages an hour a week actually *writing*, he is exceptional.

Gestation

Rats
22 days

Rabbits
31 days

Skunks
62 days

Hyenas
110 days

Ad Agencies
117 days

Goats
151 days

Baboons
183 days

Elephants
365 days

Above *Advertising agencies have a genius for wheel-spinning. The average time it takes them to produce a campaign is 117 days – faster than goats but slower than hyenas.*

The average period of gestation is somewhere between that of hyenas (110 days) and goats (151 days). For example, storyboards for commercials are argued at level after level in the agency, and level after level in the client's organization. If they survive, they are then produced and tested. The average copywriter gets only three commercials a year on air.

Ambition

Few copywriters are ambitious. It does not occur to them that if they tried hard enough, they might double the client's sales, and make themselves famous. 'Raise your sights!' I exhort them. 'Blaze new trails! Hit the ball out of the park!! Compete with the immortals!!!'

Leo Burnett said it better, 'When you reach for the stars, you may not quite get one, but you won't come up with a handful of mud either.'

Pursuit of knowledge

I once asked Sir Hugh Rigby, Surgeon to King George V, 'What makes a great surgeon?' Sir Hugh replied, 'There isn't much to choose between surgeons in manual dexterity. What distinguishes the great surgeon is that he *knows* more than other surgeons.' It is the same with advertising agents. The good ones *know* more.

I asked an indifferent copywriter what books he had read about advertising. He told me that he had not read any; he preferred to rely on his own intuition. 'Suppose,' I asked, 'your gall-bladder has to be removed this evening. Will you choose a surgeon who has read some books on anatomy and knows where to find your gall-bladder, or a surgeon who relies on his intuition? Why should our clients be expected to bet millions of dollars on your intuition?'

This willful refusal to learn the rudiments of the craft is all too common. I cannot think of any other profession which gets by on such a small corpus of knowledge. Millions are spent on testing individual commercials and advertisements, but next to nothing is done to analyse the results of those tests in search of plus and minus factors. Advertising textbooks have nothing to say on the subject.

When he had been head of J. Walter Thompson for 45 years, the great Stanley Resor told me, 'Every year we spend hundreds of millions of dollars of our clients' money. At the end of it, what do we *know*? Nothing. So two years ago I asked four of our people to try and identify factors which usually work. They already have twelve.' I was too polite to tell him that I had ninety-six.

Advertising agencies waste their client's money repeating the same mistakes. I recently counted 49 advertisements set in reverse (white type on black background) in one issue of a magazine, long years after research demonstrated that reverse is *difficult to read*.

What is the reason for this failure to codify experience? Is it that advertising does not attract inquiring minds? Is it that any kind of scientific method is beyond the grasp of 'creative' people? Are they afraid that knowledge would impose some discipline on their work?

It has not always been so. When George Gallup was Research Director at Young & Rubicam in the thirties, he not only measured the readership of advertisements, *he accumulated the scores and analyzed them.* Certain techniques, he found, consistently out-performed others. A brilliant art director called Vaughn Flannery latched on to Gallup's discoveries and applied them. Within a few months, Young & Rubicam advertisements were being read by more people than any other agency's, to the incalculable benefit of their clients.

Mills Shepherd conducted similar research on the editorial content in *McCall's,* and came up with similar results. He found, for example, that photographs of finished dishes consistently attracted more readers than photographs of the raw ingredients. Recipes printed on recipe cards, were sure-fire with housewives.

Using the same research technique, Harold Sykes measured the readership of advertisements in newspapers. He reported that 'editorial' graphics were consistently high performers.

In 1947, Harold Rudolph, who had been Research Director in Stirling Getchel's agency, published a book on the subject.* One of his observations was that photographs with an element of 'story appeal'

Attention and Interest Factors in Advertising by H. Rudolph. Funk & Wagnall, 1947

If more copywriters were ambitious, they too would find fame and fortune. This is Touffou, the medieval castle where the author holes up when he is not visiting one of the Ogilvy & Mather offices.

were far above average in attracting attention. This led me to put an eye-patch on the model in my advertisements for Hathaway shirts.

Later, the advertising community turned its back on such research. Agencies which pioneered the search for knowledge now excel in violating the principles their predecessors had discovered.

Clients sometimes change agencies because one agency can buy circulation at a slightly lower cost than another. They don't realize that a copywriter who knows his factors – the triggers which make people read advertisements – can reach many times more readers than a copywriter who doesn't.

'A blind pig can sometimes find truffles, but it helps to know that they are found in oak forests.'

For 35 years I have continued on the course charted by Gallup, collecting factors the way other men collect pictures and postage stamps. If you choose to ignore these factors, good luck to you. A blind pig can sometimes find truffles, but it helps to know that they are found in oak forests.

It is remarkable how little the plus and minus factors have changed over the years. With very few exceptions, consumers continue to react to the same techniques in the same ways.

The lessons of direct response

For all their research, most advertisers never know for sure whether their advertisements sell. Too many other factors cloud the equation. But direct-response advertisers, who solicit orders by mail or telephone, know to a dollar how much each advertisement sells. So watch the kind of advertising they do. You will notice important differences between their techniques and the techniques of general advertisers. For example:

> General advertisers use *30-second* commercials. But the direct response fraternity have learned that it is more profitable to use *two-minute* commercials. Who, do you suppose, is more likely to be right?

> General advertisers broadcast their commercials in expensive *prime time*, when the audience is at its peak. But direct response advertisers have learned that they make more sales *late at night*. Who, do you suppose, is more likely to be right?

> In their magazine advertisements, general advertisers use *short* copy, but the direct response people invariably use *long* copy. Who, do you suppose, is more likely to be right?

I am convinced that if all advertisers were to follow the example of their direct response brethren, they would get more sales per dollar. Every copywriter should start his career by spending two years in direct response. One glance at any campaign tells me whether its author has ever had that experience.

Do I practice what I preach? Not always. I have created my share of fancy campaigns, but if you ask which of my advertisements has been the most successful, I will answer without hesitation that it was the first ad I wrote for industrial development in Puerto Rico. It won no awards for 'creativity', but it persuaded scores of manufacturers to start factories in that poverty-stricken island.

Sad to say, an agency which produced nothing but this kind of down-to-earth advertising would never win a reputation for 'creativity', and would wither on the vine.

What is a good advertisement? An advertisement which pleases you because of its style, or an advertisement which *sells* the most? They are seldom the same. Go through a magazine and pick out the advertisements you *like* best. You will probably pick those with beautiful illustrations, or clever copy. You forget to ask yourself whether your favorite advertisements would make you want to buy the product. Says Rosser Reeves, of the Ted Bates agency:

> 'I'm not saying that charming, witty and warm copy won't sell. I'm just saying that I've seen thousands of charming, witty campaigns that didn't. Let's say you are a manufacturer. Your advertising isn't working and your sales are going down. And everything depends on it. Your future depends on it, your family's future depends on it, other people's families depend on it. And you walk in this office and talk to me, and you sit in that chair. Now, what do you want out of me? Fine writing? Do you want masterpieces? Do you want glowing things that can be framed by copywriters? *Or do you want to see the goddamned sales curve stop moving down and start moving up?*'*

' If it doesn't sell, it isn't creative.'

The cult of 'creativity'

The Benton & Bowles agency holds that 'if it doesn't sell, it isn't creative.' Amen.

You won't find 'creativity' in the 12-volume Oxford Dictionary. Do you think it means *originality?* Says Reeves, 'Originality is the most dangerous word in advertising. Preoccupied with originality, copywriters pursue something as illusory as swamp fire, for which the Latin phrase is *ignis fatuus.*'

Mozart said, 'I have never made the slightest effort to compose anything original.'

I occasionally use the hideous word *creative* myself, for lack of a better. If you take the subject more seriously than I do, I suggest you read *The Creative Organization*, published by the University of Chicago Press. Meanwhile, I have to invent a Big Idea for a new advertising campaign, and I have to invent it before Tuesday. 'Creativity' strikes me as a high-falutin word for the work I have to do between now and Tuesday.

A few years ago, Harry McMahan drew attention to the kind of commercials which were winning the famous Clio awards for creativity:

> Agencies that won four of the Clios had lost the accounts.

> Another Clio winner was out of business.

Reality in Advertising, by R. Reeves. Alfred A. Knopf, Inc., 1961

Above *Rosser Reeves: 'Do you want fine writing? Do you want masterpieces? Or do you want to see the goddamned sales curve start moving up?'*

Right *This is my first advertisement and it embarrasses me to reproduce it. No headline, no promise, no information about the product. Certainly, nobody had ever shown a nude in an advertisement before, but, in this case, it was irrelevant to the product – a cooking stove.*

Another Clio winner had taken its budget out of TV.

Another Clio winner had given half his account to another agency.

Another refused to put his winning entry on the air.

Of 81 television classics picked by the Clio festival in previous years, 36 of the agencies involved had either lost the account or gone out of business.

What about sex?

The first advertisement I ever produced showed a naked woman. It was a mistake, not because it was sexy, but because it was irrelevant to the product – a cooking stove.

The test is *relevance*. To show bosoms in a detergent advertisement would not sell the detergent. Nor is there any excuse for the sexy girls you sometimes see draped across the hoods in automobile advertisements. On the other hand, there is a *functional* reason to show nudes in advertisements for beauty products.

Advertising *reflects* the mores of society, but does not *influence* them. Thus it is that you find more explicit sex in magazines and novels than in advertisements. The word *fuck* is commonplace in contemporary literature, but has yet to appear in advertisements.

There used to be an unwritten law against showing women in advertisements for cigarettes. It was not until long after people got used to seeing them smoke in public that this taboo was lifted. I was the first to show women in liquor advertisements – 30 years after they started drinking in public.

Not long ago, all Paris was agog over a series of posters which appeared on the hoardings. The first showed a nubile girl in a bikini, saying, 'On September 2, I will take off the top.' On September 2 a new poster appeared – she had taken off the top. This time she promised, 'On September 4, I will take off the *bottom*.' All Paris was asking if she would also keep this promise. She did.

Few Parisians were shocked. But I would not advise you to put up these posters in South Dakota.

In Pakistan, an Islamic authority recently complained that 'our women are being exploited and commercialized on television and in the newspapers. This goes against God's will and violates the tradition of *purdah* dictated in the Koran.' He proposed a ban on women appearing in advertisements. In Saudi Arabia it is illegal to use *photographs* of women in advertising, but OK to use *drawings*, provided you don't show

Below *In 1981 all Paris was agog over this series of posters. The first promised, 'On September 2, I take off the top.' The second promised, 'On September 4, I take off the bottom.' Would she keep that promise too? She did. (It was meant to prove that posters are a good medium for advertising.)*

Right *For a long time, the idea that women might drink liquor as well as men affronted American puritanism sufficiently to keep women out of liquor ads. I was the first to break this taboo.*

"Everyone knows we've been to Puerto Rico when we uncork the __rum__,"

say the Terrell Van Ingens of New Canaan, Conn.

"I always have liked rum," says Terry Van Ingen, "but we developed a new *enthusiasm* for it on our trip to Puerto Rico.

"Puerto Rican rum really tastes different. So *dry* and *clean*. Like Caribbean sunshine, Zella says. Makes a darn good *sour* —a *rum* sour.

"Now all our cohorts in Fairfield County are jumping on the band wagon—daiquiris, rum-on-the-rocks, rum-and-tonic. Rum is all the rage.

"Incidentally, Puerto Rico surprised us as much as the rum. Wonderful climate there. Grand place for a vacation."

◄ Mr. and Mrs. Terrell Van Ingen aboard the Puchi II in San Juan harbor. Photograph by Elliott Erwitt.

Commonwealth of Puerto Rico, Rum Promotion Division, 527 Madison Ave., New York 22, N. Y.

"Rum sours taste just as good in Connecticut as they do in the sunny Caribbean," say Terry and Zella Van Ingen.

bare arms or cleavage. When a commercial for a soft drink showed a little girl licking her lips because she liked the taste, it was banned as obscene.

While we are on the subject of taste, I deplore the current fashion of using clergymen, monks and angels as comic figures in advertising. It may amuse *you*, but it shocks a lot of people.

But I don't object to scatological humor in advertising. I had no qualms about presenting the Grand Prize in a Clio ceremony to a Japanese soap commercial which featured a small boy farting in a public bath.

The most *risqué* copy I have seen was for Paco Rabanne men's cologne. Sales went up 25 per cent, and the advertisement was voted the best to appear in magazines in 1981.

The Health Education Council in England uses advertising to encourage girls to get free contraceptives from Family Planning Clinics.

Above left and right *There is a functional reason to show nudes in these ads for beauty products. Nudes have become commonplace in European advertising and are beginning to appear in American advertisements, too.*

Hello?

You snore.

And you steal all the covers. What time did you leave?

Six-thirty. You looked like a toppled Greek statue lying there. Only some tourist had swiped your fig leaf. I was tempted to wake you up.

I miss you already.

You're going to miss something else. Have you looked in the bathroom yet?

Why?

I took your bottle of Paco Rabanne cologne.

What on earth are you going to do with it…give it to a secret lover you've got stashed away in San Francisco?

I'm going to take some and rub it on my body when I go to bed tonight. And then I'm going to remember every little thing about you…and last night.

Do you know what your voice is doing to me?

You aren't the only one with imagination. I've got to go; they're calling my flight. I'll be back Tuesday. Can I bring you anything?

My Paco Rabanne. And a fig leaf.

Paco Rabanne
A cologne for men
What is remembered is up to you

If you follow the advice I have given you, you will do your homework, avoid committees, learn from research, watch what the direct-response advertisers do, and stay away from *irrelevant* sex.

In later chapters I will uncork some of the things I have learned about producing *print* advertisements which make the cash register ring. After that, *television.*

Top *One of my partners wrote this* risqué *advertisement for men's cologne.*
Above *The Health Education Council in England ran this advertisement to encourage girls to get free contraceptives from Family Planning Clinics – 'whether you are married or not.'*

3 Jobs in advertising – and how to get them

Cosimo de Medici persuaded Benvenuto Cellini, the Florentine sculptor, to enter his service by writing him a letter which concluded, 'Come, I will choke you with gold.'

Advertising offers four different career paths:

1 You can join a television network, a radio station, a magazine or a newspaper and sell time or space to advertisers and their agencies.

2 You can join a retailer like Sears Roebuck, and work as a copywriter, art director or advertising manager.

3 You can join a manufacturing company like Procter & Gamble, and work as a brand manager.

4 You can join an advertising agency.

These are not watertight compartments. Copywriters trained at Sears Roebuck sometimes migrate to agencies. Brand managers escape from Procter & Gamble to join agencies. Time-buyers at agencies move to broadcasting networks.

I am competent to write only about jobs in *agencies*. I don't know any other trade which offers such *variety*. The atmosphere is extraordinarily stimulating. Agencies are psychological hothouses. You will never be bored.

All the big agencies are *international* and offer job opportunities in Europe, Asia and Latin America. If you are fluent in a foreign language, it helps.

At the start of your career in advertising, what you *learn* is more important than what you *earn*. Some agencies take great pains to train their people. As in teaching hospitals, their top people devote an enormous amount of time to teaching the interns. Agency employees in countries where advertising is relatively mature do not always welcome attempts to teach them. However wet behind the ears, they believe that they have nothing to learn. But in Asia and other developing areas, they welcome lecturers with open arms and hang on their every word. Not surprisingly, Asian standards of competence are rapidly improving. I now see campaigns in India, Thailand, Singapore, Hong Kong, Malaysia, and Indonesia which are better than many campaigns coming out of Europe and the United States. (See Chapter 17.)

Copywriters

Like all trades and professions, advertising has its establishment. You will find the names in the roster of 84 men and four women who have been elected to the Advertising Hall of Fame since its foundaticn 32 years ago. I regret to say that only 13 of them are copywriters.

Copywriters may not be the most visible people in agencies, but they are the most important. The hallmarks of a potentially successful copywriter include:

Obsessive curiosity about products, people and advertising.

A sense of humor.

A habit of hard work.

The ability to write interesting prose for printed media, and natural dialogue for television.

The ability to think *visually*. Television commercials depenc more on pictures than words.

The ambition to write better campaigns than anyone has ever written before.

'Most good copywriters', says William Maynard of the Bates agency, 'fall into two categories. Poets. And killers. Poets see an ad as an end. Killers as a means to an end.' If you are both killer *and* poet, you get rich.

Art directors

You cannot get a job as an art director unless you have had some training in film, layout, photography and typography. It helps to be endowed with good taste.

Since print went out of fashion, many art directors have turned themselves into television producers. Television, being a *visual* medium, is a natural outlet for their talents.

Art directors used to be the handmaidens of copywriters, but they have now gone up in the world. Indeed, some art directors have risen to become distinguished Creative Directors – notably Bob Gage at Doyle Dane Bernbach, Hal Riney at Ogilvy & Mather, and Keith Reinhard at Needham, Harper & Steers.

'Art directors used to be the handmaidens of copywriters, but they have now gone up in the world.'

Account executives

The chief role of account executives is to extract the best possible work from the other departments of the agency. They are in daily touch with clients.

If I wanted to become an account executive, I would first spend a couple of years at Procter & Gamble in brand management, followed by a year in a consumer research company, learning what makes people tick – particularly people who are less well educated than I am.

Some agencies now hire more women account executives than men. In the New York office of Ogilvy & Mather, 69 per cent of the account executives are women.

It used to be that account executives were better paid than the brand managers who were their opposite numbers on the client side, and were often responsible not only for the advertising, but for the total marketing plan. But those days are over. The clients now recruit at the same business schools, and pay higher salaries than agencies. As a result, the role of the account executive at many agencies has been reduced to one of co-ordination. On an airplane not long ago, I overheard the following conversation:

'What business are you in?'
'Engineer. You?'
'I'm an account executive in an ad agency.'
'You write the ads?'
'No, copywriters do that.'
'That must be a fun job.'
'It's not that easy. We do a lot of research.'
'You do the research?'
'No, we have research people for that.'
'Do you bring in the new clients?'
'That's not my job.'

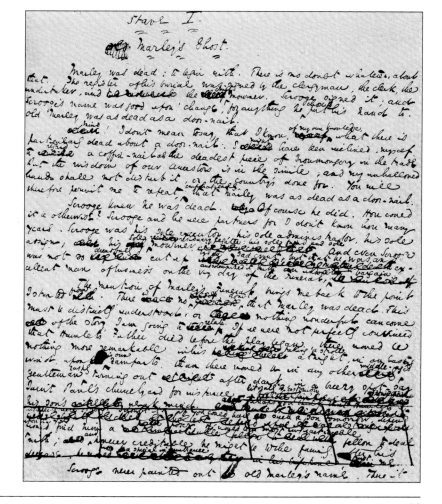

'Forgive me, but what *is* your job?'
'*Marketing.*'
'You do the marketing for the clients?'
'*No, they do it themselves.*'
'Are you in management?'
'*No, but I soon will be.*'

If this dismal dialogue does not put you off, and you still want to start your career as an account executive, I repeat the advice I offered in my *Confessions*. Set yourself to becoming the best-informed person in the agency on the account to which you are assigned. If, for example, it is a gasoline account, read books on oil geology and the production of petroleum products. Read the trade journals in the field. Spend Saturday mornings in service stations, talking to motorists. Visit your client's refineries and research laboratories. At the end of your first year, you will know more about the oil business than your boss, and be ready to succeed him.

Most of the work you do will be routine maintenance. Your golden opportunity will come when you rise to a great occasion. Some years ago, Lever Brothers asked their seven agencies to submit policy papers on the television medium, which was then quite new. The other agencies put in adequate papers of five or six pages, but a young man on my staff took the trouble to assemble every conceivable statistic and, after working day and night for three weeks, came up with an analysis which covered one hundred and seventy-seven pages. The following year he was elected to our board of directors.

Some young men and women are attracted by the travel and entertainment which attach to the work of an account executive. They soon find that lunching in expensive restaurants is no fun if you have to explain a declining share-of-market while eating the soufflé. Riding the circuit of test markets can be a nightmare if one of your children is in hospital.

Account executives can be divided into custodians and contributors. You can probably get by if you never function as more than a channel of communication between your client and your service departments, like a waiter who shuttles between the chefs in the kitchen and the customers in the dining room. No doubt you will perform this function with aplomb, but I hope you will contribute more than that. Like inventing big ideas for selling the product.

However hard you work, and however knowledgeable you become, you will be unable to represent your agency at the client's policy levels until you are at least 30 years old. One of my partners owes the rapidity of his ascent to the fact that he had the good fortune to have his hair turn white at twenty-seven.

You will never become a successful account executive unless you learn to make *good presentations*. Most of your clients will be corporations, and you must be able to sell campaigns to their committees. Your presentations must be well written, and well delivered.

Do not make the common mistake of regarding your clients as dopes. Make friends with them. Buy shares in their companies. But try not to become entangled in their politics. Emulate Talleyrand, who served France through seven regimes.

Always tell your client what you would do if you were in his shoes, but don't grudge him the prerogative of deciding what advertising to run. It is his product, his money, and ultimately his responsibility.

In your day-to-day dealings with clients and colleagues, fight for the kings, queens and bishops, but throw away the pawns. A habit of graceful surrender on trivial issues will make you difficult to resist when you stand and fight on a major issue.

Don't discuss your clients' business in public places. Keep their secrets under lock and key. A reputation for leaking can ruin you.

Learn to write lucid memoranda. The senior people to whom they are addressed have more homework than you do. The longer and more turgid your memos, the less likely they are to be read by executives who have the power to act on them. In 1941, Winston Churchill sent the following memo to the First Lord of the Admiralty:

> 'Pray state this day, on one side of a sheet of paper, how the Royal Navy is being adapted to meet the conditions of modern warfare.'

Researchers

To get a job in the Research Department of a good agency, you probably need a degree in statistics or psychology. You also need an analytical mind, and the ability to write readable reports.

You must also be able to work sympathetically with creative people, most of whom are stubbornly allergic to research. Above all you must be intellectually honest. A researcher who injects bias into his reports does awful damage.

Grateful as I am to the researchers who have helped me to produce effective advertising, I have nine bones to pick with them:

'Why does it take agency researchers three months to answer a few simple questions?'

1 They take three months when I only have three weeks. When Eisenhower was President, the White House called Dr. Gallup one evening at six o'clock. Eisenhower wanted to know the state of public opinion on an important issue of foreign policy. The report had to be on the President's desk at eight o'clock the next morning. Gallup sent for six of his henchmen and dictated three questions. Then each of the henchmen telephoned six interviewers in different parts of the country, and they interviewed ten people each. By midnight they had called in their results. Gallup tabulated them, wrote his report and dictated it to a White House stenographer. The report was on Eisenhower's desk two hours before it was due.

Nor is this merely an example of presidential clout. When Robert Kennedy lost the Oregon primary in 1968, his campaign manager had a research report on his desk eighteen hours after the polls closed, analysing the reasons for his defeat.

When I first went to run the Audience Research Institute for Dr. Gallup, it took our statisticians *two months* to deliver their reports. I bullied them into telescoping the work into *two days*, thereby making the reports of much greater value to the Hollywood executives who were our clients.

So why does it take agency researchers three months to answer a few simple questions? They are natural slowpokes, and too frightened of making mistakes.

2 They cannot agree among themselves on methodology. It recently took the Research Directors of the 21 biggest agencies two years to reach agreement on the *principles* which should govern copy-testing. Now they have started to debate *methodology*. Five years?

3 It is in research departments that you find the eggheads of the agency business. Too many of them are more interested in sociology and economics than advertising. They concentrate their attention on subjects which are only peripherally related to advertising.

4 They have little or no system for retrieving research which has already been conducted. Reports are read, sometimes acted on, and filed. Two years later the researcher, the account executive, the copywriter and the brand manager have moved to fresh pastures. Even if somebody remembers that the research was done, nobody can *find* it. So we re-invent the wheel, year after year.

'Advertising research is full of fads.'

5 Advertising research is full of fads. In the sixties we saw Eye Cameras, Latin Squares, Facturals, Randomized

Blocks, Greco-Latin Squares. Some of them were useful, but all went out of fashion.

6 Researchers use graphs which are incomprehensible to laymen. And their reports are too long. When he was an executive at Procter & Gamble, Ralph Glendinning refused to read any research report which was more than a quarter of an inch *thick*.

7 Researchers have a maddening way of refusing to undertake projects which they consider imperfect by their perfectionist standards, even when the project would produce actionable results. Said Winston Churchill, 'PERFECTIONISM is spelled PARALYSIS.'

8 Ninety-nine researchers out of a hundred content themselves with conducting surveys for which they are asked, but seldom take initiatives. Stop asking them questions, and they grind to a halt.

9 Worst of all, researchers use pretentious jargon – such as *attitudinal paradigms, judgmentally, demassification, reconceptualize, sub-optimal, symbiotic linkage, splinterization*. Come off it, professor.

Media

I have never worked in the media department of an agency, but observation of those who have been successful in this field leads me to think that they need an analytical mind, the ability to communicate numerical data in non-numerical formats, stability under pressure, and a taste for negotiation with the owners of media.

Chief Executive Officer

The most difficult job in an agency is Chief Executive Officer. He (or she) must be a good leader of frightened people. He must have financial acumen, administrative skill, thrust, and the courage to fire non-performers. He must be a good salesman, because he is responsible for bringing in new clients. He must be resilient in adversity. Above all, he must have the physical stamina to work 12 hours a day, dine out several times a week, and spend half his time in airplanes.*

A recent study reveals that the death rate from stress-related causes is 14 per cent higher among senior advertising executives than their counterparts in other white-collar occupations.

Creative Director

As a Creative Director myself, I dare to list the attributes needed for this back-breaking job. You must be:

1 A good psychologist.

2 Willing and able to set high standards.

*Last year my partner Michael Ball flew 300,000 miles and spent 131 nights in hotels.

3 An efficient administrator.

4 Capable of strategic thinking – 'positioning' and all that.

5 Research-minded.

6 Equally good at television and print.

7 Equally good at package goods and other kinds of accounts.

8 Well versed in graphics and typography.

9 A hard worker – and fast.

10 Slow to quarrel.

11 Prepared to share credit for good work, and accept blame for bad work.

12 A good presenter.

13 A good teacher and a good recruiter.

14 Full of infectious *joie de vivre*.

Notice that I put 'good psychologist' at the top of the list. Albert Lasker, who made the largest fortune in the history of the advertising business, once told a group of copywriters, 'You think managing copywriters is a snap? You have taken some hairs out of me. I had a breakdown that kept me five and one-half months. I couldn't talk for five minutes without starting to weep.'

Women in advertising
Feminists are doing dreadful things to the English language. I refuse to write spokesperson, chairperson, househusband or womanhole cover.

Like most boys of my generation, I started life believing that women belonged in the home, until I noticed how much happier my mother was when she went out to work. My first woman Vice-President was Reva Korda, a brilliant copywriter who later became head of the Creative Department. For all her brains and ability, even Reva encountered male copywriters and art directors who felt uncomfortable working under *any* woman. But there are now 52 women Vice-Presidents in the New York office of Ogilvy & Mather, and there appears to be no resentment of them among the male staff.

The *majority* of people now being recruited by advertising agencies in the United States for so-called 'professional' jobs are women.

Firing and hiring
Agencies used to fire people at the drop of a hat. Stirling Getchel's otherwise admirable agency had a turnover in staff of 137 per cent in one year. Another agency fired a copywriter because he dared to talk to the boss in the men's room. Today the boot is on the other foot. The people who work in agencies are lamentably nomadic. I recently hired a

'You might suppose that a business which depends entirely on the talent of its people would take recruiting seriously, but that is not yet the case.'

40-year-old copywriter who had already changed jobs eleven times.

You might suppose that a business which depends entirely on the talent of its people would take recruiting seriously, but that is not yet the case. In most agencies, the recruiting is still sloppy and haphazard. Even today, it is rare for any agency to ask an applicant's former employers what they think of him. I know two men who were hired and fired as Presidents of three agencies – without their references being checked.

Education for advertising

Eighty-seven American universities offer undergraduate courses in advertising, and some even give degrees in it. With a few conspicuous exceptions, the teachers lack the practical experience to be relevant. All of them are handicapped by the poor quality of the textbooks, and very few do research of their own. Most of their graduates get jobs with small agencies, the big agencies preferring to recruit people who have furnished their minds by studying history, languages, economics and so forth.

The fashion for recruiting at schools of business administration seems to have passed its peak. Give or take a few stars like the Baker Scholars at the Harvard Business School, their alumni are more remarkable for stodginess and arrogance than imagination.

Social status

When I was a door-to-door salesman for Aga cooking stoves in Scotland, I paid a cold call on an aristocrat. He threw me out. What right had I to invade his privacy? 'Sir,' I said, 'you are a Director of two companies which sell their products door-to-door. How dare you insult me for doing something which your own salesmen do every day?' His disdain for salesmen is mirrored in the snobbish attitude of the British establishment towards advertising. Not so in the United States.

Moonlighting

If you need more income than your agency is willing to pay you, make up the difference by moonlighting. I have been moonlighting for 30 years. The Curtis Publishing Company gave me two magnificent china lamps for writing an advertisement for *Holiday* magazine. They had been bullying their editors and I had reason to believe that they were about to fire Ted Patrick, the marvelous editor of *Holiday*. So I persuaded the heads of the 12 biggest agencies to join me in a testimonial to Ted, applauding him for his 'indifference to the heckling of publishers.' The Curtis people were too dumb to realize that this would make it impossible for them to fire Ted, and ran my advertisement.

The *Reader's Digest* gave $10,000 to the Scottish school which had educated me, in return for an advertisement I wrote for them.

Omega, the watch company, paid me $25,000 to spend four days at their headquarters in Switzerland, advising them how to improve their advertising. To my surprise, they got their money's worth. Even today, I am retained by the Campbell Soup Company as their consultant on marketing.

Ted Patrick, appointed Editor of Holiday in 1946, still going strong.

An open letter to Ted Patrick from 12 of Holiday's 3,263,000 readers

Dear Ted:

HOLIDAY is your baby. In eighteen years as Editor, you have produced 210 glorious issues. They get more glorious every year.

We applaud your belief that "an editor's only boss is the reader." We applaud your indifference to the pressures of advertisers and the heckling of publishers.

You deserve your success. Nobody else could have created a magazine which is equally distinguished for its graphics and its writing. Cartier-Bresson and Steinbeck, Arnold Newman and William Golding, Slim Aarons and Sean O'Faolain, John Lewis Stage and Laurens van der Post.

Month after month, year after year, you entertain us and you enthrall us. We happen to know that you also provide an atmosphere which sells goods.

You have pursued excellence, and you have achieved it.

You are a great editor.

Affectionately yours,

Right *Curtis Publishing paid me two antique china lamps for writing this advertisement in my spare time. They did not guess my real motive: to make it impossible for them to fire the editor of* Holiday *magazine. The signatories were the heads of the twelve biggest agencies –* Holiday's *customers.*

Opposite *In gratitude for my writing this advertisement,* Reader's Digest *gave $10,000 to the Scottish school where I was educated. Because it was to appear over my signature, I took great pains to write it well – well enough for Raymond Rubicam to call it 'a masterpiece.' If all clients insisted on their agencies signing their ads, they would get better ads.*

'Be happy while you're living'

'Chess', wrote Raymond Chandler, 'is about as elaborate a waste of human intelligence as you could find anywhere outside an advertising agency.' If advertising is a waste of intelligence, it isn't a very serious one. Not more than 100,000 men and women work in advertising agencies in the United States – less than 0.1 per cent of the working population. About 15,000 work in British agencies.

Most of the people I know in agencies strike me as well cast for their work and reasonably happy in it. Whenever I think that someone is wasting his talents in advertising, I tell him so. One of my partners is a superb naturalist, and secretly resented every day he spent in the agency. On my advice he retired – and went on to save endangered species of fauna from extinction. In the words of the Scottish proverb, 'Be happy while you're living, for you're a long time dead.'

A few advertising people regard advertising as an unworthy occupation. Thus the head of the agency in Paris that helped François Mitterrand become President of France called his autobiography: *Don't tell my mother I work in an advertising agency – she thinks I play the piano in a whorehouse.* Poor chap.

Confessions of a magazine reader

by DAVID OGILVY
Author of "Confessions of an Advertising Man"

I READ 34 magazines every month. I like them all, but the one I *admire* most is Reader's Digest.

The editors of The Digest are in possession of a remarkable technique: *they know how to present complicated subjects in a way that engages the reader.*

This gives The Digest's editors great influence in the world. They put their influence to admirable use.

They are on the side of the angels. They are crusaders, and they carry their crusades, in 14 languages, to 75 million souls a month.

They crusade against cigarettes, which kill people. They crusade against billboards, which make the world hideous. They crusade against boxing, which turns men into vegetables. They crusade against pornography.

They crusade for integration, for the inter-faith movement, for the Public Defender system, for human freedom in all its forms.

Good Pope John once told The Digest editors, "How comforting it will be for you, when you come to the close of your lives on earth, to be able to say to yourselves: *We have served the truth.*"

No log-rolling, no back-scratching

Ten years ago Reader's Digest first opened its columns to advertising. This worried me. I was afraid that The Digest editors would start pulling their punches in deference to advertisers and even give editorial support to advertisers—an obvious temptation to magazine editors. But this has not happened; The Digest has remained incorruptible. No log-rolling, no back-scratching.

The success of The Digest is deserved. It does not depend on prurience, voyeurism or cheap sensationalism. What The Digest editors offer their readers are *ideas, education* (practical and spiritual) and *self-improvement.*

The instinct of these editors is toward *clarity of expression.* The current issue,

as I write, includes articles on religion in schools, on the Congo, urban renewal, violence on television, Abraham Lincoln and safe driving. Each of these subjects is presented in a way which I can understand. If I did not read about them in The Digest, I wouldn't read about them anywhere. I wouldn't have time.

Some highbrows may look down their noses at The Digest, charging it with superficiality and over-simplification. There is a modicum of justice in this charge; you *can* learn more about the Congo if you read about it in *Foreign Affairs Quarterly,* and you *can* learn more about Abraham Lincoln in Carl Sandburg's books about him. But have you time?

Never boring

I seldom read a highbrow magazine without wishing that a Digest editor had worked his will upon it. I would then find it more *readable.* The Digest articles are never long-winded, never obscure, never boring.

I also admire the editors' *courage.* They have the guts to open their readers'

minds on delicate subjects. They grasp nettles. Like venereal disease, cancer, mental illness. They are not humorless prigs. Their sense of humor is uproarious. They make me *laugh.*

Editorial technique

Their *techniques* fascinate me. First, the way they present the contents on the cover—a tantalizing menu which invites you to the feast inside. (I have never understood why *all* magazines don't do this.)

Second, the ingenious way they write the titles on their articles. They pique your curiosity—and they promise to satisfy it. For example:

What Truckers Say About Your Driving
Professional drivers sound off on the
most common—and dangerous—faults
of the amateur.

How could anybody resist reading an article with a title like that?

I earn my living as a copywriter in an advertising agency. It is a matter of life and death for me to get people to read my advertisements. I have discovered that more than half the battle is to write headlines which grab people's attention and *force* them to read the copy. *I learned how to do this by studying headlines in* The Digest.

The Digest editors do not start their articles in the front of the magazine and carry them over in the back. They carry you through their magazine without this maddening interruption, and I bless them for it.

The battle for men's minds

You and I, gentle reader, live in the United States, and we think of The Reader's Digest as an *American* magazine. So it is—15 million Americans buy it every month. But it is also published in 20 other countries—10,500,000 copies a month. It is the most popular magazine in several countries abroad, including all of the Spanish-speaking countries.

The International editions of The Digest carry more or less the same articles as the U.S. editions. The editors have dis-

covered that subjects which are important to people in Iowa, California and New York are equally important to people in France, Tokyo and Rio.

Thus it comes about that Digest editors have a profound influence on people who are free to read what they want. *This magazine exports the best in American life.*

In my opinion, The Digest is doing as much as the United States Information Agency to win the battle for men's minds.

Credit where credit is due. I know nobody who deserves the gratitude of their fellow Americans more than DeWitt and Lila Acheson Wallace. The Digest is the lengthened shadow of these two great editors. Theirs are the names at the top of the masthead. It is the most formidable of all mastheads: no less than 208 men and women. Among them you will find some of the most distinguished journalists in the world. No other magazine is so richly endowed with professional competence.

Some magazines are dominated by the men who sell advertising space. In my experience, there has never been a good magazine which was not, like The Digest, dominated by its *editors.*

Long live The Reader's Digest!

David Ogilvy

"Reader's Digest asked me if I would comment on why I think so many people all over the world read it," Mr. Ogilvy says. "I agreed to try, because I regard The Digest as a major force for good in the world, and I wanted to say so. In return for my work The Digest will make a donation to Fettes, the Scottish school which gave me my education on a full scholarship."

'I have never felt any inclination to give up my job and become a clergyman.'

Those of us who study public opinion surveys are aware that the lay public thinks we admen are rascals. Dr. Gallup recently asked people to rate 24 professions for honesty. Top marks went to clergymen, bottom marks to trade-union leaders, car salesmen and advertising practitioners. The stereotype of the 'huckster' dies hard. But I don't think our poor image keeps many of us awake at night. I have never felt any inclination to give up my job and become a clergyman. I enjoy my work, and sometimes feel proud of its results.

How to apply for a job

Don't telephone – *write* to three or four agencies, and enclose your curriculum vitae. Be sure to *type* your letter, and take a lot of trouble with it. In their book *Writing that Works*,* my partners Kenneth Roman and Joel Raphaelson offer this golden advice:

1 Spell all names right

It's astonishing how often job applicants misspell the names of the agencies they want to work for. The message that gets through, right off the bat, is: 'This applicant can't be seriously interested in working here; he didn't even take the trouble to find out how to spell our name.'

2 Identify the sort of job you're applying for

State it clearly and at once. Say what led you to apply – a want ad, a recommendation from a friend, whatever. A letter applying for a job as a research analyst started in this mysterious way:

> Dear Ms. Smith:
> It's spring already – a time to think about planting seeds. Some seeds are small, like apple seeds. Others are bigger. Coconuts, for example. But big or little, a seed can grow and flourish if it's planted in proper soil.

The applicant would have done better to start like this:

> Dear Ms. Smith:
> I understand that you are looking for a research analyst.

Ms. Smith doesn't have time to play guessing games with her mail.

3 Be specific and factual

Once you've made clear what job you want, then touch on your chief qualifications. Avoid egotistical abstractions like: 'Ambition mixed with a striving for excellence is one of my strongest assets.'

4 Be personal, direct and natural

You are a human being writing to another human being. Neither of you is an institution. You should be businesslike and courteous, but never stiff and impersonal.

The more your letter sounds like *you*, the more it will stand apart from the letters of your competitors. But don't try to dazzle your reader with your sparkling personality. You wouldn't show off in an interview, so why show off in a letter? If you make each sentence sound the way you would *say* it across a desk, there will be plenty of personality in your letter.

Opposite *This is the first advertisement I wrote as the head of my own agency – at the age of 39.*

*Harper & Row, New York, 1981.

GUINNESS GUIDE TO OYSTERS

CAPE CODS : An oyster of superb flavor. Its chief enemy is the starfish, which wraps its arms about the oyster and forces the valves open with its feet. The battle lasts for hours, until the starfish is rewarded with a good meal, but alas, no Guinness.

NEW ORLEANS : This was Jean Lafitte's oyster, which is now used in Oysters Rockefeller. Valuable pearls are never found in *ostrea virginica*, the family to which East Coast oysters belong.

GREENPORT : These oysters have a salty flavor all their own. They were a smash hit with the whalers who shipped out of Greenport in olden days. Oysters contain iron, copper, iodine, calcium, magnesium, phosphorous, Vitamin A, thiamine, riboflavin and niacin. The Emperor Tiberius practically lived on oysters.

OYSTER BAY: Oyster Bays are mild and heavy-shelled. It is said that oysters yawn at night. Monkeys know this and arm themselves with small stones. They watch for an oyster to yawn and then pop the stone in between the shells. "Thus the oyster is exposed to the greed of the monkeys."

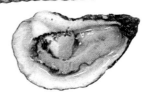

TANGIER : This is one of the sweetest and most succulent oysters. It comes from the Eastern Shore of Maryland. Pocahontas fed Tangiers to Captain John Smith, with famous results. Oysters go down best with Guinness, which has long been regarded as the perfect complement for all sea-food.

BLUEPOINTS : These delicious little oysters from Great South Bay somewhat resemble the famous English 'natives' of which Disraeli wrote: "I dined or rather supped at the Carlton . . . off oysters, Guinness and broiled bones, and got to bed at half past twelve. Thus ended the most remarkable day hitherto of my life."

LYNNHAVEN : These gigantic oysters were Diamond Jim Brady's favorites. More fishermen are employed catching oysters than any other sea food. The Damariscotta mound in Maine contains three million bushels of oyster shells, piled there by prehistoric Bradys.

DELAWARE BAY : This was William Penn's favorite oyster. Only 15% of oysters are eaten on the half-shell. The rest find their way into stews, or end their days in a blaze of glory as "Angels on Horseback." One oyster was distinctly heard to whistle.

CHINCOTEAGUES : Many epicures regard Chincoteagues as the supreme aristocrats of the oyster tribe, but some West Coast gourmets prefer the Olympia oyster, which is no bigger than your thumbnail. Both Chincoteagues and Olympias are at their best with Guinness.

ALL OYSTERS taste their best when washed down with drafts of Guinness—what Professor Saintsbury in "Notes On A Cellar-Book" called "that noble liquor—the comeliest of black malts." Most of the malt used in brewing Guinness comes from the fertile farms of Southern Ireland, and the yeast is descended from the yeast used by Guinness in Dublin one hundred and ninety years ago.

For a free reprint of this advertisement, suitable for framing, write Arthur Guinness Son & Co., Inc., 47-24 27th Street, Long Island City, New York.

Guinness® Stout brewed by Arthur Guinness Son & Co., Inc., Long Island City, N.Y. ©1951

5 Propose a specific next stop

Close your letter with a clear and precise statement of how you wish to proceed toward an interview. Avoid such mumblings as:

> 'Hoping to hear from you soon.'

> 'Thank you for your time and consideration.'

> 'I'm looking forward to the opportunity of discussing a position with you.'

All such conclusions place the burden of the next step on your busy prospective employer. Why make *him* work in *your* interest? Do the job yourself, like this:

> 'I'll call your office on Wednesday afternoon to see if you'd like me to come in for an interview.'

> 'I'm free for an interview every morning until 8:45, and Thursday after 2:30. I'll call your office on Wednesday afternoon to find out if you would like to get together at any of those times.'

At this stage a phone call makes things easy for the person at the other end. If you don't call him, he has to go to the trouble of calling or writing to you. The idea is to make it as simple as you possibly can for your prospective employer to set up an appointment at a time that's convenient to you.

*　　*　　*　　*　　*

'I am always surprised by the illiteracy of men and women who look for jobs in advertising.'

I am always surprised by the illiteracy of men and women who look for jobs in advertising. I am bombarded with applications like this recent lulu:

> 'My goal is to seek more challenging experiences to further develop my skills in marketing and advertising. I feel I have reached a plateau in my education. My objective is to obtain a top level management position utilizing extensive experiences in marketing communications areas as a viable contribution to corporate objectives. My creative background and expertise involves a wide range of areas in the development of objectives, strategies and marketing communications programs to meet these goals.'

*　　*　　*　　*　　*

If you will take my advice, don't get a job in advertising unless it interests you more than anything in the world.

There are many different kinds of jobs, calling for very different skills, all the way from art direction to statistics. All the jobs can be performed by women, in some cases better than by men.

The pay is good, but don't expect the gold that Cosimo de Medici promised Cellini. There are easier ways to get rich.

4

How to run an advertising agency

R unning an agency requires midnight oil, salesmanship of the highest order, a deep keel, guts, thrust, and a genius for sustaining the morale of men and women who work in a continuous state of anxiety.

It is popularly believed that advertising attracts neurotics who are naturally prone to anxiety. I don't believe this. What happens in agencies is enough to induce anxiety among the most phlegmatic people.

The *copywriter* lives with fear. Will he have a big idea before Tuesday morning? Will the client buy it? Will it get a high test score? Will it sell the product? I have never sat down to write an advertisement without thinking THIS TIME I AM GOING TO FAIL.

The *account executive* also has reasons for anxiety. He represents the agency to the client, and the client to the agency. When the agency goofs, the client holds *him* responsible. When the client is bloody-minded, the agency blames *him*.

The *head of the agency* also has his worries. Is such-and-such a client going to fire you? Is a valuable partner going to quit? Will you make a hash of the new business presentation on Thursday?

'When people aren't having any fun, they don't produce good advertising.'

Make it *fun* to work in your agency. When people aren't having any fun, they don't produce good advertising. Kill grimness with laughter. Encourage exuberance. Get rid of sad dogs who spread gloom.

What kind of paragons are the men and women who run successful agencies? My observation has been that they are enthusiasts. They are intellectually honest. They have the guts to face tough decisions. They are resilient in adversity. Most of them are natural charmers. They are not bullies. They encourage communications upwards, and are good listeners. Many of them drink too much, and read little except office paper, in which they drown.

With few exceptions, they are decent people, and worth knowing. It wasn't always so. When I first arrived in New York, some of the agencies were headed by bastards and phonies.

One of the most agreeable things about running an agency is that all your accounts are in different industries. In the morning you discuss the problems and opportunities of a client who makes soap. In the afternoon it is a bank, or an airline, or a manufacturer of medicines. But you pay a price for this variety. Every time you see a client, you have to be sufficiently briefed on his business to give relevant advice. When I was the chief executive of my agency, I always took home two briefcases, and spent four hours reading their contents. Not much fun for my wife. Next to homework, my worst enemy was the telephone. I was usually 25 return calls behind.

Agencies are breeding-grounds for sibling rivalry. Will Cadwallader get a corner office before Balfour? Why did you invite Pennypacker to lunch instead of Morgan? Why was Sidebottom made a Vice-President before Winterbottom? The agency I know best has two Chairmen, three Presidents, two Managing Directors, eight Executive Vice-Presidents, 67 Senior Vice-Presidents and 249 Vice-Presidents. You might suppose that nobody would take such nonsense seriously, but they do. Giving out the titles reminds me of Louis XIV: 'Every time I

This page *When you are appointed to head an office in the Ogilvy & Mather chain, I send you one of these Russian dolls. Inside the smallest you will find this message: 'If each of us hires people who are smaller than we are, we shall become a company of dwarfs, but if each of us hires people who are bigger than we are, Ogilvy & Mather will become a company of giants.'*

give someone a title, I make a hundred people angry and one person ungrateful.'

What can you do to keep sibling rivalry under control? You can be *fair*, and you can avoid playing favorites. Said Dr. William Menninger: 'The executive is inevitably a father figure. To be a good father, whether it is to his children or to his associates, requires that he be understanding, that he be considerate, and that he be human enough to be affectionate.' If Menninger had been into transactional analysis, he would have added that the best fathers are 'nurturing' rather than 'controlling.'

Laymen assume that if you work in an advertising agency, you produce advertisements. The fact is that 90 per cent of the staff *don't*. They do research, they prepare media plans, they buy space and time, they do things loosely described as 'marketing.' And about 60 per cent of them do clerical work.

In most agencies there are twice as many account executives as copywriters. If you were a dairy farmer, would you employ twice as many milkers as cows?

Friction between copywriters and account executives is endemic in all agencies. Copywriters traditionally regard account executives as brainless bullies. I know a few account executives who fit this stereotype, but most of them are sensitive and well educated. Account executives are apt to regard copywriters as irresponsible prima donnas. Some are.

Hiring

Success in running an agency depends on your ability to hire men and women of exceptional talent, to train them thoroughly, and to make the most of their talents. The most difficult people to find are those who have the capacity to become good copywriters. I have found that they always have well-furnished minds. They give evidence of exceptional curiosity about every subject under the sun. They have an above-average sense of humor. And they have a fanatical interest in the craft of advertising. I used to think that nobody could write good advertising before he was thirty. Then one day, on a visit to Frankfurt, I asked to meet the author of an exceptionally good campaign. She was eighteen.

I marvel at the ability of some copywriters to keep their creative juices flowing year after year. George Cecil wrote the American Telephone advertising for 40 years, and wrote it well. It is a tragedy of the advertising business that its best practitioners are always promoted into management. I was infinitely more useful to my clients when I wrote copy than when I was Chairman of the Board.

* * * * *

When someone is made the head of an office in the Ogilvy & Mather chain, I send him a Matrioshka doll from Gorky. If he has the curiosity to open it, and keep opening it until he comes to the inside of the smallest doll, he finds this message: *If each of us hires people who are smaller than we are, we shall become a company of* dwarfs. *But if each of us hires people who are bigger than we are, we shall become a company of* giants.

Even when you find someone who is better than you are, you

Wanted by Ogilvy & Mather International

Trumpeter Swans

In my experience, there are five kinds of Creative Director:

1. Sound on strategy, dull on execution.
2. Good managers who don't make waves...and don't produce brilliant campaigns either.
3. Duds.
4. The genius who is a lousy leader.
5. TRUMPETER SWANS who combine personal genius with inspiring leadership.

We have an opening for one of these rare birds in one of our offices overseas.

Write in inviolable secrecy to me, David Ogilvy, Touffou, 86300 Bonnes, France.

David Ogilvy

'I have always tried to hire what J.P. Morgan called "gentlemen with brains".'

won't always succeed in recruiting him. Among those I have failed to recruit are Helmut Krone, the great art director; Shirley Polykoff, of Clairol fame; and a young account executive called Bart Cummings who went on to become head of the Compton agency.

I have always tried to hire what J.P. Morgan called 'gentlemen with brains.' Did he mean gentlemen in the snobbish sense? I think so. The debt owed by the United States to Roosevelt, Dean Acheson, Averell Harriman, Robert Lovett, John J. McCloy, the Rockefeller brothers and many other aristocrats has not been sufficiently acknowledged. I have been particularly lucky with alumni of St Paul's and Harvard, notably my partners Esty Stowell and Jock Elliott. But I have also been lucky with gentlemen in the wider sense of the word.

Brains? It doesn't necessarily mean a high IQ. It means curiosity, common sense, wisdom, imagination and literacy. Why literacy? Because most communication between agencies and clients is in writing. I don't suggest that you have to be a poet, but you won't climb the ladder very high unless you can write lucid memoranda. I persuaded two of my partners to write a book on the subject. I commend it to you.*

Look for young men and women who can one day *lead* your agency. Is there any way of predicting the capacity to lead? The only way I know is to look at their college records. If they were leaders between the ages of 18 and 22, the odds are that they will emerge as leaders in middle life.

Make sure you have a Vice-President in charge of Revolution, to engender ferment among your more conventional colleagues.

Crown Princes

Spot the comers on your staff, and plan their careers. Royal Dutch Shell has found that the most reliable criteria for selecting what they call Crown Princes are these:

1   The power of analysis.

2   Imagination.

3   A sense of reality.

4   The 'helicopter quality'– the ability to look at facts and problems from an overall viewpoint.

John Loudon, the distinguished former head of Shell, believes that when it comes to picking people for senior jobs, *character* is more important than any of these qualities. Dare I confess that I have come to believe in *graphology* as an instrument for assessing character? It is regarded as fakery in the United States, but is widely used in French business. Before accepting my offer of marriage, my wife had my handwriting analysed by *two* graphologists. Their reports were consistent – and accurate.

Promote from within or hire from outside? 'Mr. Morgan *buys* his partners,' said Andrew Carnegie; 'I *grow* mine.' In the early days of Ogilvy & Mather, shortage of cash obliged me to pay peanut salaries. Pay peanuts, says Jimmy Goldsmith, and you get monkeys. I chose not to promote my monkeys, but to fill senior openings from outside, with stars like Esty Stowell, Jock Elliott and Andrew Kershaw. Even a mature agency with a pool of potential leaders does well to refresh its blood by occasionally hiring partners from outside.

Who not to hire

'Never hire your client's children.'

Never hire your friends. I have made this mistake three times, and had to fire all three. They are no longer my friends.

Never hire your client's children. If you have to fire them, you may lose the client. This is another mistake I have made.

Never hire your own children, or the children of your partners. However able they may be, ambitious people won't stay in outfits which practice nepotism. This is one mistake I did not make; my son is in the

Writing that Works, by Kenneth Roman and Joel Raphaelson, Harper & Row, 1981

real estate business, secure in the knowledge that he owes nothing of his success to his father.

Think twice before hiring people who have been successful in other fields. I have hired a magazine editor, a lawyer and an economist. None of them developed an interest in advertising.

And never hire your clients. The qualities which make someone a good client are not the qualities required for success in the agency business. I have made this mistake twice.

Office politicians

The hothouse atmosphere in agencies can cause outbreaks of psychological warfare to rival university faculties.* The politics became so vicious at Milton Biow's agency that he was forced to close down. I know of seven ways to squelch them:

1 Fire the worst of the politicians. You can identify them by how often they send you blind copies of their poison-pen memos to their rivals.

2 When somebody comes to your office and denounces his rival as an incompetent rascal, summon the rival and make the denouncer repeat what he has just told you.

3 Crusade against paper warfare. Make your people settle their fights face to face.

4 Start a luncheon club within the agency. It turns enemies into friends.

5 Discourage poaching.

6 Don't play favorites.

7 Don't play politics. If you practice the fiendish art of *divide et impera*, your agency will go up in smoke.

Discipline works

Insist that your people arrive on time, even if you have to pay them a bonus to do so. Insist that telephones are answered promptly. Be eternally vigilant about the security of your clients' secrets; indiscretion in elevators and restaurants, the premature use of outside typesetters, and the display of forthcoming advertisements on notice boards can do grave damage to your clients.

Sustain unremitting pressure on the professional standards of your staff. It is suicide to settle for second-rate performance. Above all, insist that due dates are kept, even if it means working all night and over the weekend. Hard work, says the Scottish proverb, never killed a man. People die of boredom and disease. There is nothing like an occasional all-night push to enliven morale – provided you are part of the push. Never leave the bridge in a storm.

*When Senator Benton left the Benton & Bowles agency and joined the University of Chicago, he found the politics much worse.

St Augustine had this to say about pressure:

'To be under pressure is inescapable. Pressure takes place
through all the world: war, siege, the worries of state. We all
know men who grumble under these pressures, and
complain. They are cowards. They lack splendor. But there
is another sort of man who is under the same pressure, but
does not complain. For it is the friction which polishes him.
It is pressure which refines and makes him noble.'

I have to admit that I have sometimes found the pressure unbearable;
my own fault for frittering away so much time on things which lead
nowhere. It is a good idea to start the year by writing down exactly what
you want to accomplish, and end the year by measuring how much you
have accomplished. McKinsey imposes this discipline on its partners
and pays them according to how many of the things on their lists they
accomplish.

Leadership

I have had unique opportunities for observing men who manage great
corporations – my clients. Most of them are good *problem-solvers* and
decision-makers, but few are outstanding *leaders.* Some of them, far from
inspiring their lieutenants, display a genius for castrating them.

Great leadership can have an electrifying effect on the
performance of any corporation. I have had the good fortune to work for
three inspiring leaders – Monsieur Pitard, who was my boss in the
kitchens of the Majestic Hotel in Paris; George Gallup; and Sir William
Stephenson of British Intelligence.

There has been a lot of research into leadership. It is the consensus
among the social scientists that success in leadership depends on the
circumstances. For example, a man who has been an outstanding
leader in an industrial company can be a flop when he goes to
Washington as Secretary of Commerce. And the kind of leadership
which works well in a new company seldom works well in a mature
company.

There appears to be no correlation between leadership and
academic achievement. I was relieved to learn this, because I have no
college degree. The motivation which makes a man a good student is
not the kind of motivation which makes him a good leader.

There is a tendency for corporations to reject executives who do
not fit their conventions. How many corporations would promote a
maverick like Charlie Kettering of General Motors? How many
advertising agencies would hire a 38-year-old man whose curriculum
vitae read: 'Unemployed farmer, former cook and university drop-out?'
(Me in the year I started Ogilvy & Mather.)

The best leaders are apt to be found among those executives who
have a strong component of unorthodoxy in their characters. Instead of
resisting innovation, they symbolize it – and companies cannot grow
without innovation.

Great leaders almost always exude *self-confidence.* They are never
petty. They are never buck-passers. They pick themselves up after

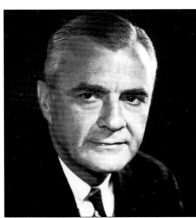

A 'visceral form of spiritual energy' characterized these great leaders. Top to bottom: Marvin Bower of McKinsey, Ted Moscoso of Puerto Rico, Henry Alexander of Morgan Guaranty.

defeat – the way Howard Clark of American Express picked himself up after the salad oil swindle. Under Howard's indomitable leadership, the price of American Express shares increased fourteen-fold.

Great leaders are always fanatically committed to their jobs. They do not suffer from the crippling need to be universally loved. They have the guts to make unpopular decisions – including the guts to fire non-performers. Gladstone once said that a great Prime Minister must be a good butcher.

I saw the head chef at the Hotel Majestic fire a pastry cook because the poor devil could not get his brioches to rise straight. This ruthlessness made all the other chefs feel that they were working in the best kitchen in the world.

Some men are good at leading the multitude – whether it be the labor force in their company, or the voting population in their country. But these same men are often miserable leaders of a small group.

Good leaders are *decisive*. They grasp nettles. Some of them are very odd characters. Lloyd George was sexually chaotic. General Grant, who won the Civil War, drank like a fish. On November 26, 1863, the *New York Herald* quoted Lincoln as saying: 'I wish some of you would tell me the brand of whiskey that Grant drinks. I would like to send a barrel of it to my other generals.'

Winston Churchill was another hardened drinker. He was capricious and petulant. He was grossly inconsiderate of his staff. He was a colossal egotist. Yet his Chief of Staff wrote of him:

'I shall always look back on the years I worked with him as
some of the most difficult and trying ones in my life. For all
that I thank God that I was given the opportunity of
working alongside of such a man, and of having my eyes
opened to the fact that occasionally such supermen exist on
this earth.'

I do not believe that *fear* is a tool used by good leaders. People do their best work in a happy atmosphere. Ferment and innovation depend on *joie de vivre*. I am indebted to Charlie Brower of BBDO for his amendment to the 13th chapter of St Paul's first Epistle to the Corinthians: 'A man who spendeth his life gathering gold for the United States Treasury and has no fun, is a sounding ass and a tinkling idiot.'

The great leaders I have known have been curiously *complicated* men. Howard Johnson, the former President of MIT, has described it as 'a visceral form of spiritual energy which provides the element of *mystery* in leadership.' I have seen this mysterious energy in Marvin Bower of McKinsey, Ted Moscoso of Puerto Rico, and Henry Alexander of Morgan Guaranty.

The most effective leader is the one who satisfies the psychological needs of his followers. For example, it is one thing to be a good leader of Americans, who are raised in a tradition of democracy and have a high need for independence. But the American brand of democratic leadership doesn't work so well in Europe, where executives have a psychological need for more *autocratic* leadership. That is one of many reasons why it is wise for American agencies to appoint locals to lead their foreign subsidiaries.

It does an agency no good when its leader never shares his leadership functions with his lieutenants. The more centers of leadership you create, the stronger your agency will become.

There is an art in being a good *follower*. On the night before a major battle, the first Duke of Marlborough was reconnoitering the terrain. He and his staff were on horseback. Marlborough dropped his glove. Cadogan, his chief of staff, dismounted, picked up the glove and handed it to Marlborough. The other officers thought this remarkably civil of Cadogan. Later that evening, Marlborough issued his final order: 'Cadogan, put a battery of guns where I dropped my glove.'

'I have already done so,' replied Cadogan. He had read Marlborough's mind, and anticipated his order. Cadogan was the kind of follower who makes leadership easy. I have known men whom *nobody* could lead.

Most of the great leaders I know have the ability to inspire people with their *speeches*. If you cannot write inspiring speeches yourself, use ghost-writers – but use *good* ones. Roosevelt used the poet Archibald MacLeish, the playwright Robert Sherwood and Judge Rosenmann. That is why he was more inspiring than any of the Presidents we have had since, with the exception of John F. Kennedy, who also used outstanding ghost-writers.

Very few chief executives are good on their feet. Whoever writes the speeches, the CEO delivers them atrociously. Competence, however, can be learned. All major politicians hire experts to teach them the art of delivery.*

The man who said the wisest things about leadership was Field Marshal Montgomery:

'The leader must have infectious optimism, and the determination to persevere in the face of difficulties. He must also radiate confidence, even when he himself is not too certain of the outcome.

'The final test of a leader is the feeling you have when you leave his presence after a conference. Have you a feeling of uplift and confidence?'

Alcoholics

It is reliably reported that seven out of every hundred executives in American business are alcoholics, and it is reasonable to assume that the proportion in your agency is at least as high. By alcoholic, I mean somebody whose drinking seriously interferes with his family life and his performance in the agency. He is on the way to losing his job, wrecking his marriage and dying of cirrhosis.

Your alcoholics may include some of your brightest stars. The problem is to *identify* them, protected as they always are by their secretaries and their colleagues. Invite the alcoholic's wife to join you in a surprise confrontation with her husband. Start by telling him that all present are devoted to him. Then say how worried you are about his drinking. His wife and his children are about to leave him, and you are

*Read *Speech Dynamics* by Dorothy Sarnoff, Doubleday, 1970

about to fire him – *unless he does what you ask*. A reservation has been made for him to enter a treatment center that very day.

Most alcoholics agree to go. It takes a week for the center to dry them out, and another four weeks to rehabilitate them. On returning home, they must go to daily meetings of Alcoholics Anonymous for at least a year.

This procedure works in about 60 per cent of cases. I have seen it salvage some valuable people of both sexes. If you would like further advice on the subject, consult the nearest chapter of Alcoholics Anonymous.

Written principles

Marvin Bower, who made McKinsey what it is today, believes that every company should have a written set of principles and purposes. So I drafted mine and sent them to Marvin for comment. On the first page I had listed seven purposes, starting with *Earn an increased profit every year.* Marvin gave me holy hell. He said that any service business which gave higher priority to profits than to serving its clients deserved to fail. So I relegated profit to seventh place on my list.

Do you think it childish to use a set of written principles to guide the management of an advertising agency? I can only tell you that mine have proved invaluable in keeping a complicated enterprise on course.

Profit and all that

I do not fancy myself as a financial wizard, but I have learned a thing or two from my partner Shelby Page, who has presided over the finances of Ogilvy & Mather since the first day. The average profit in agencies is less than 1 per cent after taxes. If you chisel on service, you can make more than that, but your clients will leave you. If your service is too generous, your clients will love you, but you will go broke.

'If your service is too generous, your clients will love you, but you will go broke.'

Size and profit are not the same thing. In 1981, Ogilvy & Mather made more profit than an agency which bills twice as much.

Agencies add new services the way universities add new courses. Nothing wrong with that if you also discontinue services which have outlived their relevance. To keep your boat moving through the water, keep scraping the barnacles off its bottom.

Seven of the twelve biggest agencies are public companies. Their share prices have increased 439 per cent during the last ten years, compared with 37 per cent for Standard & Poor's 500.

Many security analysts still believe that agencies are a poor investment. Not so Warren Buffett, one of the most successful investors in the world. He has taken substantial positions in three publicly held agencies, and is quoted as saying, 'The best business is a royalty on the growth of others, requiring very little capital itself . . . *such as the top international advertising agencies.'*

If you read the advertising columns in newspapers, you get the impression that the agency business is dangerously unstable. The reason is that the newspapers only report movements of accounts from one agency to another. Yet only 4 per cent of total US advertising changes agencies during a year.

The 25 biggest agencies in 1972 are, with only one exception, the 25 biggest today, 11 years later. Eight of the top ten are in their fifth or sixth generation of management. Only Ogilvy & Mather has its founder still on board.

How to get paid

You will have to choose between the traditional commission system and the newer system of fees.* The fee system has four advantages:

1   The advertiser pays for the services he wants – no more, no less.

2   Every fee account pays its own way. Unprofitable accounts do not ride on the coat-tails of profitable accounts, which is the case with the commission system.

3   Temporary cuts in clients' budgets do not oblige you to cut staff.

4   When you advise a client to increase his advertising, he does not suspect your motive.

I pioneered the fee system, but I no longer care how I get paid, provided I make a reasonable profit. In 1981, the average net profit of American agencies was 0.83 per cent of billing. Does that strike you as unreasonable?

When a client frets about the price of his agency's services, he ends up getting a low price and poor advertising.

What to do with your profits

First, you have to pay 52 per cent corporation tax. If you distribute what is left as dividends, your shareholders have to pay a further 40 per cent as income tax. When they *spend* their dividends, they have to pay sales tax. The Government has taken 73 cents out of every dollar you made as profit.

Some agencies have invested their profits in ventures outside their competence – an insurance company, a travel agency, a retail chain, a fish cannery, a motion picture company, even a small oil company. Not surprisingly, they all burned their fingers. (I resisted that temptation.)

The current fad is to invest part of your profit in buying other agencies. Beware! Agencies are seldom for sale unless they are in some kind of trouble. Perhaps you give their key people five-year contracts, because you think their clients would vamoose if they retired. But their ways are not your ways and the friction can be abominable.

Are there more sensible ways of investing your profits? I know of three:

1   You can open branch offices in other cities or other countries. This has the advantage that you don't inherit

*A commission is paid to the agency by the medium – print, television, radio – in which the agency has bought space on behalf of its client. Under this arrangement, the agency finances services to its clients out of commissions, rather than charge fees direct to the client.

other people's mistakes, and you preserve you own ethos, pure and undefiled. The disadvantage is that your start-up costs cannot be capitalized, so they reduce your earnings per share.

2   You can buy the building which houses your office. Young & Rubicam did this in New York two years ago.

3   You can build a reserve against a rainy day. On Wall Street they regard this as lunacy, but when times get hard, the lunatics may survive longer than their more adventurous competitors.

'Agencies are seldom for sale unless they are in some kind of trouble.'

A new gimmick is to acquire agencies and leave them to their own devices, even allowing them to compete with you in new business contests. One of the giant agencies has become little more than a holding company for a miscellaneous collection of independently operated subsidiaries.

Fortunes

The agency man who made the largest fortune was Albert Lasker of Lord & Thomas (now Foote, Cone & Belding), followed by Ted Bates, Jim Mathes, Ray Mithune and Cliff Fitzgerald. I estimate an average of about $20,000,000 each.

Some people have made fortunes out of selling their agencies to Interpublic, including David Williams, Tom Adams, Al Seaman and Hagen Bayles; my guess is that they averaged about $6,000,000 each. The admirable Bill Marsteller probably made more than that when he sold his agency to Young & Rubicam, as did the senior partners in Esty when they sold to Bates, and the senior partners in Compton when they sold to Saatchi & Saatchi.

Ed Ney, the head of Young & Rubicam, is the only present-day head of an agency who has built a large nest egg without selling out or going public. However big the egg, Ney is worth every penny.

Five tips

1   Never allow two people to do a job which one could do. George Washington observed, 'Whenever one person is found adequate to the discharge of a duty by close application thereto, it is worse executed by two persons, and scarcely done at all if three or more are employed therein.'

2   Never summon people to your office; it frightens them. Instead, go to see them in *their* offices, unannounced. A boss who never wanders about his agency becomes an invisible hermit.

3   If you want to get action, communicate *verbally*. If you want the voting to go your way at meetings, go to the meeting. Remember the French saying: 'He who is absent is always wrong.'

4   It is bad manners to use products which compete with your clients' products. When I got the Sears Roebuck account, I started buying all my clothes at Sears. This bugged my wife, but the following year a convention of clothing manufacturers voted me the best-dressed man in America. I would not dream of using any travelers checks except American Express, or drinking any coffee but Maxwell House, or washing with any soap except Dove. As the number of brands advertised by Ogilvy & Mather now exceeds two thousand, my personal inventory is getting complicated.

5 Never allow yourself the luxury of writing letters of complaint. After my first transatlantic voyage I wrote to my travel agency complaining that the service on the *Queen Mary* was slovenly and the decoration vulgar. Three months later we were on the point of getting the Cunard account when they happened to see my letter. It took them twenty years to forgive me and give us their account.

Right *When I got the Rolls-Royce account, I followed my rule of using the client's product. Other Rolls-Royce owners have included Rudyard Kipling, Henry Ford I, Ernest Hemingway, Woodrow Wilson, Charlie Chaplin, Baden Powell and Lenin. Mine lasted 22 years.*

5 How to get clients

Above *A big account walks in. (From* White Collar Zoo *by Clare Barnes Jr.)*

Here I go, boasting again. There are better copywriters than I am, and scores of better administrators, but I doubt if many people have matched my record as a new business collector.

In my *Confessions*, I told how I started by making a list of the clients I most wanted – General Foods, Lever Brothers, Bristol Myers, Campbell Soup Company and Shell. It took time, but in due course I got them all, plus American Express, Sears Roebuck, IBM, Morgan Guaranty, Merrill Lynch and a few others, including three governments. While some of these clients have since defected, their total billings with Ogilvy & Mather add up to more than three billion dollars – so far.

My policy has always been that of J.P. Morgan – 'only first-class business, and that in a first-class way' – but at first I had to take anything I could get, to pay the rent. A patent hairbrush, a tortoise, an English motorbike.

But I also had the good fortune to get four small accounts which gave me a chance to produce the kind of sophisticated advertising which attracts attention to an agency: Guinness, Hathaway shirts, Schweppes and Rolls-Royce.

The easiest way to get new clients is to *do good advertising*. During one period of seven years, we never failed to win an account for which we competed, and all I did was to show the campaigns we had created. Sometimes, I did not even have to do that. One afternoon, a man walked into my office without an appointment and gave me the IBM account; he knew our work.

This unparalleled run of success gave me a swelled head. When Dr. Anton Rupert told me that he had it in mind to market Rothmans cigarettes in the United States and asked me to do the advertising, I declined with such hubris that he said, 'Mr. Ogilvy, I hope to meet you again – when you are on your way *down*.' We did not meet again for 25 years, when we were both on the Executive Committee of the World Wildlife Fund. He is a great man.

In recent years, manufacturers have complicated the process of selecting agencies beyond reason. They start by sending long questionnaires to a dozen or more agencies. Idiotic questions like: 'How many persons are employed in your print production department?' To

Opposite *To get clients, do good advertising.*

58

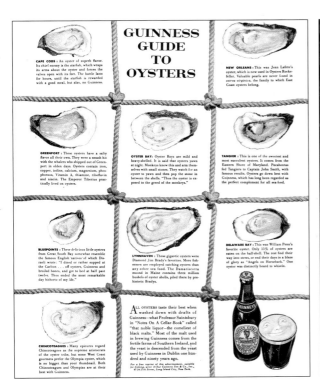

GUINNESS GUIDE TO OYSTERS

CAPE CODS : An oyster of superb flavor. Its chief enemy is the starfish, which wraps its arms about the oyster and forces the valves open with its feet. The battle lasts for hours, until the starfish is rewarded with a good meal, but alas, no Guinness.

NEW ORLEANS : This was Jean Lafitte's oyster, which is now used in Oysters Rockefeller. Valuable pearls are never found in *ostrea virginica*, the family to which East Coast oysters belong.

GREENPORT : These oysters have a salty flavor all their own. They were a smash hit with the whalers who shipped out of Greenport in olden days. Oysters contain iron, copper, iodine, calcium, magnesium, phosphorous, Vitamin A, thiamine, riboflavin and niacin. The Emperor Tiberius practically lived on oysters.

OYSTER BAY : Oyster Bays are mild and heavy-shelled. It is said that oysters yawn at night. Monkeys know this and arm themselves with small stones. They watch for an oyster to yawn and then pop the stone in between the shells. "Thus the oyster is exposed to the greed of the monkeys."

TANGIER : This is one of the sweetest and most succulent oysters. It comes from the Eastern Shore of Maryland. Pocahontas fed Tangiers to Captain John Smith, with famous results. Oysters go down best with Guinness, which has long been regarded as the perfect complement for all sea-food.

BLUEPOINTS : These delicious little oysters from Great South Bay somewhat resemble the famous English 'natives' of which Disraeli wrote: "I dined or rather supped at the Carlton . . . off oysters, Guinness and broiled bones, and got to bed at half past twelve. Thus ended the most remarkable day hitherto of my life."

LYNNHAVEN : These gigantic oysters were Diamond Jim Brady's favorites. More fishermen are employed catching oysters than any other sea food. The Damariscotta mound in Maine contains three million bushels of oyster shells, piled there by prehistoric Bradys.

DELAWARE BAY : This was William Penn's favorite oyster. Only 15% of oysters are eaten on the half-shell. The rest find their way into stews, or end their days in a blaze of glory as "Angels on Horseback." One oyster was distinctly heard to whistle.

CHINCOTEAGUES : Many epicures regard Chincoteagues as the supreme aristocrats of the oyster tribe, but some West Coast gourmets prefer the Olympia oyster, which is no bigger than your thumbnail. Both Chincoteagues and Olympias are at their best with Guinness.

ALL OYSTERS taste their best when washed down with drafts of Guinness—what Professor Saintsbury in "Notes On A Cellar-Book" called "that noble liquor—the comeliest of black malts." Most of the malt used in brewing Guinness comes from the fertile farms of Southern Ireland, and the yeast is descended from the yeast used by Guinness in Dublin one hundred and ninety years ago.

For a free reprint of this advertisement, suitable for framing, write Arthur Guinness Son & Co., Inc., 47-34 27th Street, Long Island City, New York.

The man in the Hathaway shirt

AMERICAN MEN are beginning to realize that it is ridiculous to buy good suits and then spoil the effect by wearing an ordinary, mass-produced shirt. Hence the growing popularity of HATHAWAY shirts, which are in a class by themselves.

HATHAWAY shirts *wear* infinitely longer—a matter of years. They make you look younger and more distinguished, because of the subtle way HATHAWAY cut collars. The whole shirt is tailored more *generously*, and is therefore more *comfortable*. The tails are longer, and stay in your trousers. The buttons are mother-of-pearl. Even the stitching has an ante-bellum elegance about it.

Above all, HATHAWAY make their shirts of remarkable *fabrics*, collected from the four corners of the earth—Viyella, and Aertex, from England, woolen taffeta from Scotland, Sea Island cotton from the West Indies, hand-woven madras from India, broadcloth from Manchester, batiste from Paris, hand-blocked silks from England, exclusive cottons from the best weavers in America. You will get a great deal of quiet satisfaction out of wearing shirts which are in such impeccable taste.

HATHAWAY shirts are made by a small company of dedicated craftsmen in the little town of Waterville, Maine. They have been at it, man and boy, for one hundred and twenty years.

At better stores everywhere, or write C. F. HATHAWAY, Waterville, Maine, for the name of your nearest store. In New York, telephone OX 7-5566. Prices from $5.95 to $20.00.

The man from Schweppes is here

MEET Commander Edward Whitehead, Schweppesman Extraordinary from London, England, where the house of Schweppes has been a great institution since 1794.

Commander Whitehead has come to these United States to make sure that every drop of Schweppes Quinine Water bottled here has the original flavor which has long made Schweppes...

The only mixer for an authentic Gin and Tonic.

He imports the original Schweppes elixir, and the secret of Schweppes antique carbonation is locked in his brief case. "Schweppervescence," says the Commander, "lasts the whole drink through."

It took Schweppes almost a hundred years to bring the flavor of their Quinine Water to its present bittersweet perfection. But it will take correspondingly seconds to mix it with ice and gin in a highball glass. Then, gentle reader, you will bless the day you read these words.

P.S. If your favorite store or bar doesn't yet have Schweppes, drop a card to me and we'll make the proper arrangements. Address Schweppes, 30 East 60th Street, New York City.

THE ROLLS-ROYCE SILVER CLOUD II — $13,995 P.O.E.

Should every corporation buy its president a Rolls-Royce?

There is much to be said for it. It is a prudent investment. It enhances the public image of the company. And rank is entitled to its rewards.

A GREAT MANY of the Rolls-Royce and Bentley cars sold in England are sold to companies for the use of their top executives. "Take a Rolls-Royce or Bentley into partnership," is a saying well observed by British businessmen.

What makes the Rolls-Royce the best executive car in the world? Consider these facts:

Longest guarantee

The Rolls-Royce chassis is guaranteed for *three years*—the longest warranty by far of any motor car.

A good part of the cost can often be written off in five years or less. The car will then be in the infancy of its usefulness. You can sell it for a good price or drive it for many more years.

The Rolls-Royce obviates the extravagant practice of trading in cars frequently for later models. This costs you money each time a change is made. With the money that is wasted in a few such transactions, the company could have bought a Rolls-Royce.

No "planned obsolescence"

The owner of a Rolls-Royce is not threatened by annual style changes. Only an expert can tell whether it was bought yesterday or five years ago. The Rolls-Royce people do not practice a cynical and self-serving policy of "planned obsolescence."

Maintenance is minimal. With Rolls-Royce dealers throughout the country, service is no problem.

Your president will live longer

Send the Rolls-Royce to fetch your president from his home every morning; he will reach the office in better shape. During the day, emancipate him from waiting for taxis on street corners, or take a nap. Do these things, and your president will be a *better* president. He will also live longer.

A safe car

On bad roads, or in heavy traffic, the Rolls-Royce can be handled like a sports car. It will not normally be so driven. But such driving shows the great ability of the vehicle to cope with critical circumstances.

The brakes have no equal in the world. There are *three independent linkages*. Should one fail (an unlikely event), the others will keep the car under control. "We would never produce a car that would outperform its brakes," says a Rolls-Royce engineer.

Free from exhibitionism

An executive's car, like his office, is undoubtedly influences public opinion toward his company. The Rolls-Royce implies taste, conservatism and a regard for quality. Of all luxury cars, it is the least exhibitionistic.

A source of contentment

There is satisfaction in owning such an exquisite piece of machinery. To handle a Rolls-Royce, to look at it, even to smell its leather, are pleasures which the executive of a successful company should not be denied.

Those presidents who feel diffident about driving a Rolls-Royce can be provided with a Bentley. It is exactly the same car, except for the radiator. It costs $300 less.

If you would like to try driving a Rolls-Royce or Bentley, write or telephone to one of the dealers listed on page 00, or to Rolls-Royce, Inc., 30 Rockefeller Plaza, New York 20, CIrcle 5-1144.

Two other models for executive use:

Long wheelbase Silver Cloud II with division, $19,185 P.O.E.

Phantom V, 7-passenger limousine, $25,895 P.O.E.

which I answered, 'I haven't the foggiest idea. I haven't been in the department for seven years. Why do you think it matters?'

If you are more polite and give enough right answers, you get on the short list, and a delegation comes to inspect you. They want to know what commission you will charge. I answer, 'If you are going to choose your agency on the basis of price, you are looking through the wrong end of the telescope. What you should worry about is not the price you pay for your agency's services, but the selling power of your advertising.'

The selectors show scant interest in the campaigns you have produced for other manufacturers. They want to know what you could do for *them*, so they invite you to analyse their problems and make finished commercials. They then have your commercials tested. If you get a higher score than your competitors, you win the account.

Some agencies now spend as much as $500,000 on new business presentations. They figure that if they win and keep the account for 20 years, they may come out ahead. Agencies which don't have the money to make such bets are at a disadvantage.

This long and expensive process does not necessarily result in the selection of the best agency. The agency which would create the best advertising over a period of years may not have the luck to come up with the best campaign in the few weeks allotted to the contest. In the next chapter I will suggest a better way to go about choosing an agency.

The meeting

At the meeting when you make your presentation, don't sit the client's team on one side of the table and your team opposite, like adversaries. Mix everybody up.

Rehearse before the meeting, but never speak from a prepared text; it locks you into a position which may become irrelevant during the meeting.

Above all, *listen*. The more you get the prospective client to talk, the easier it will be to decide whether you really want his account. A former head of Magnavox treated me to a two-hour lecture on advertising, about which he knew nothing. I gave him a cup of tea and showed him out.

Tell your prospective client what your weak points are, before he notices them. This will make you more credible when you boast about your strong points.

Don't get bogged down in case histories or research numbers. They put prospects to sleep. No manufacturer ever hired an agency because it increased market-share for somebody else.

The day after a new business presentation, send the prospect a three-page letter summarizing the reasons why he should pick your agency. This will help him make the right decision.

If you are too feeble to get accounts under your own steam, you can *buy* them – by buying agencies. But this practice has a way of backfiring. Adolph Toigo used it to quintuple the billings of Lennen & Newell, but he was unable to weld his acquisitions into a cohesive body. The result was a quarrelsome confederation which ended in bankruptcy.

Credit risks

Watch out for credit risks. Your profit margin is too slim to survive a prospective client's bankruptcy. When in doubt, I always ask the head of the incumbent agency.

Never pay a commission to an outsider who offers to introduce new business. No client who chooses his agency on the basis of such an introduction is worth having; and there is usually dirty work at the crossroads. Six weeks after I started my agency, I was so desperate for business that I offered a young man of my acquaintance 10 per cent of our stock if he brought in a vacuum-cleaner account which he had in his pocket. If he had accepted my offer, his stock in Ogilvy & Mather would now be worth $19,000,000. A lucky escape.

Some years later, when I was older and wiser, Ben Sonnenberg, the public-relations operator, asked me what percentage of our stock I would give him if he steered the Greyhound Bus account to us. When I said zero, he thought I was mad.

'Avoid clients whose ethos is incompatible with yours.'

Avoid clients whose ethos is incompatible with yours. I refused Charles Revson of Revlon and Lew Rosenstiel of Schenley.

Beware of ventures which spend little or nothing today but might *become* major advertisers, if all goes well. Servicing such non-accounts can be expensive, and few of them make it. Yes, there are exceptions. I once made the mistake of turning down a small company which made office machinery, because I had never heard of it. The name was Xerox.

*   *   *   *   *

The differences between agencies are less than they like to believe. Most of them can show that they have produced advertising that increased sales for some of their clients. Most have competent media departments and research departments. Thanks to inflation, almost all of them have grown in billings. So what's the difference between them?

Very often the decisive difference in new business contests is the personality of the head of the agency. Many clients went to Foote, Cone & Belding because they were impressed by Fax Cone's style. Conversely, many failures to win accounts are caused by the fact that the prospective client finds the head of the agency obnoxious. My personality has lost some contests and won others.

*   *   *   *   *

Aside: I have resigned accounts five times as often as I have been fired, and always for the same reason: the client's behavior was eroding the morale of the people working on his account. Erosion of morale does unacceptable damage to an agency.

Getting multinational accounts

If you get an account which also advertises in overseas markets, you stand a good chance of getting it around the world. I call this the *domino* system of new business acquisition. J. Walter Thompson, McCann-Erickam and Young & Rubicam built their overseas networks to meet the needs of such multinationals as General Motors, Coca Cola, Esso and General Foods. When I got the Shell account in the United States, Max Burns, the then President of Shell, asked me if I would also like to have the account in Canada. 'Yes,' said I, 'but I don't have an office in Canada.' 'Get one,' said Max, and that is how I started the network which was to spread to 40 countries.

In these cases your competition will be the local agencies in the countries concerned. They have a habit of wrapping themselves in their national flag and appealing to their governments for protection against us foreign invaders. They accuse us of imposing an alien culture, particularly in countries which have little culture of their own, and in some cases their appeals have been heard. The Canadian Government employs only Canadian agencies. In Nigeria, the foreign agencies have been expelled.

The fact is that almost all the overseas offices of American agencies are managed by nationals who would not know *how* to project American culture, even if they were foolish enough to try.

*   *   *   *   *

The old way to start a new agency was to defect from the agency which employed you and take some clients with you. Thus Ted Bates started his agency with accounts he had handled at Benton & Bowles. But this gambit has since been hampered by a legal decision. A man called Jones had a thriving agency, but he was an alcoholic and was always falling asleep during presentations. His associates begged him to retire. When the situation became intolerable, they crossed the street and set up their own agency – with some of Jones's clients. He sued them for conspiracy and won; they had to pay such heavy damages that they were forced to close their agency.

In 1981 an agency in New Zealand took successful action against its former Managing Director and Creative Director who had walked

Multinational accounts have propelled agencies into the international market. Shell was responsible for my building a worldwide network of agencies. This Shell ad is from Ogilvy & Mather's Frankfurt office.

Die meisten merken erst beim Sicherheitstraining, wie nötig sie es hatten.

Wer meint, daß er sein Motorrad sicher im Griff hat, wird sich hier ganz schön wundern. Spätestens auf der Kippe, wenn ihm der Motor „absäuft" oder in der Kiesgrube das Hinterrad „wegschmiert". Doch durch so ein Training lernen Sie, Ihr Motorrad auch in kritischen Situationen zu beherrschen. Und mit Übungen, wie Notbremsung, Schräglage und Ausweichen ins Gelände, wird die Fahrsicherheit trainiert. Für einen Motorradfahrer kann so etwas einmal lebenswichtig sein.

Wo Sie ein Sicherheitstraining machen können und weitere Tips, wie Sie sicher Motorrad fahren, finden Sie im neuen Shell Ratgeber Nr. 21 „Motorradfahren". Und bei Fragen, wie das Motorrad richtig gepflegt wird oder welches Öl Sie brauchen, hilft man Ihnen gerne an den Shell Stationen.

Shell. Wir helfen Ihnen weiter.

Joachim Horstmann von der Shell Station Sachsendamm 68-70 in Berlin. Wie an jeder Shell Station bekommen Sie dort Shell Quadro TX, das neue Spezialöl für alle 4-Takt-Motorräder.

Den neuen Shell Ratgeber Nr. 21 „Motorradfahren" erhalten Sie jetzt gratis an jeder Shell Station. Oder vom Shell Ratgeber-Service, Nordkanalstraße 49 in 2000 Hamburg 1, Telefon 040/24 41 51.

out with 17 members of the staff and nine accounts. Gentle reader, you have been warned.

With any luck, you will get accounts which *grow*. When I got American Express in 1962, the advertising budget was $1,000,000. It is now $70,000,000.

When you are head of an agency, you know that your staff looks to you to bring in new business, more than anything else. If you fail to do so over an extended period, you sense that you are losing their confidence, and are tempted to grab any account you can get. Don't. Above all, don't join the melancholy procession of agencies which always accompanies a dying brand on its way to the cemetery. When Pan American fell on hard times, they moved their account from J. Walter Thompson, who had done an exceptionally good job for 29 years, to Carl Ally. Seven years later, when they continued to decline, they moved to N. W. Ayer. Three years later, they moved to Doyle Dane Bernbach. Six months later they moved to Wells, Rich, Greene. But this kind of instability is rare. The American Telephone Company, General Motors and Exxon have employed the same agencies for more than 70 years; DuPont, General Electric, Procter & Gamble and Scott Paper have employed the same agencies for more than 50 years.

It is important to know how your agency is regarded in the marketing community. Don't trust your own ears; you will only hear *favorable* opinions. It is safer, if you can afford it, to have a research organization conduct an impartial survey. When they report weak spots in your reputation, you can probably correct them, but it will take longer than you expect. Opinion always lags behind reality.

If you aspire to building a portfolio of accounts in a wide variety of industries, you must be able to produce different *kinds* of advertising. An agency which can only play the package-goods tune disqualifies itself from corporate accounts. An agency which always produces *emotional* advertising is unlikely to be hired by a manufacturer of power tools. The broader your range, the broader the spectrum of accounts you will get.

It follows that you should recruit people with a wide range of talents. An agency should be like an orchestra, able to play anything from Palestrina to Jean-Michel Jarre with equal virtuosity.

Big agencies vs. small

It is very difficult for small agencies to get big accounts. They cannot afford the range of specialized departments which big accounts require – regional offices, research, sales promotion, direct mail, public relations, and so on. They cannot deploy enough bodies to match the bodies at the client end. And the risk of losing a big client scares them out of that independence of judgment which should be one of any agency's principal values to its clients.

The other side of the coin is that the bigger an agency grows, the more bureaucratic it becomes. Personal leadership gives way to hierarchy. The head of the agency no longer recognizes his staff in the elevators. I found working at Ogilvy & Mather more agreeable when it was small, but as I aspired to handling big accounts, I had no choice but to build a big agency.

However, there will always be more small accounts than big ones, so small agencies are not an endangered species. Within the limits of their resources, they can often out-perform the big ones. Creativity is not a function of size. Small can be beautiful.

Physician, heal thyself

It puzzles me why so few agencies advertise themselves. Perhaps it is because the partners cannot agree on what to say. Some want to improve their agency's reputation for 'creativity.' Some want to impress prospective clients with their agency's marketing skills. Some want new business leads in a hurry. Make up your mind which you want – before you start writing house ads.

Direct mail is probably the most efficient medium for your house campaign. If you can scrape up the money, use space advertising as well, but don't start it unless you mean to do it *consistently.* Young & Rubicam advertised in every issue of *Fortune* for 40 years.

Right *Advertising agencies seldom take their own medicine, but Young & Rubicam advertised in every issue of* Fortune *for 40 years. This was the fifth ad in the series and the best ever run for an agency. Raymond Rubicam wrote it and Vaughn Flannery was the art director.*

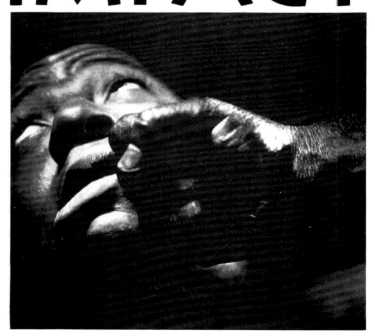

IMPACT

ACCORDING TO WEBSTER: The single instantaneous striking of a body in motion against another body.

ACCORDING TO YOUNG & RUBICAM: That quality in an advertisement which strikes suddenly against the reader's indifference and enlivens his mind to receive a sales message.

YOUNG & RUBICAM, INCORPORATED · ADVERTISING

NEW YORK · CHICAGO · DETROIT · SAN FRANCISCO · HOLLYWOOD · MONTREAL · TORONTO · MEXICO CITY · LONDON

Left alone, copywriters write house ads to impress other copywriters, and art directors make layouts to impress other art directors. But trendy layouts and fancy copy don't impress prospective clients who have come up through finance, production or sales. Writing house ads is a job for copywriters who can think like top-level businessmen. They should also be endowed with *patience*; it took me 22 years to get my first house ads approved by my partners.

The purpose of my ads was to project the agency as *knowing more about advertising*. You may argue that this strategy was ill-advised, knowledge being no guarantee of 'creativity.' But at least it was unique, because no other agency could have run such advertisements – they lacked the required knowledge. My ads not only *promised* useful information, they *provided* it. And they worked – in many countries.

But watch out: your *clients* will read your house advertisements. If you boast about your genius for brilliant ideas, you run the risk that they will ask you why you don't give *them* brilliant ideas.

Below *With these house ads, Ogilvy & Mather tell potential clients about the agency's wide-ranging expertise.*

6 Open letter to a client in search of an agency

Sir or Madam,

If you have decided to hire a new agency, permit me to suggest a simple way to go about it.

Don't delegate the selection to a committee of pettyfoggers. They usually get it wrong. Do it yourself.

Start by leafing through some magazines. Tear out the advertisements you *envy*, and find out which agencies did them.

Watch television for three evenings, make a list of the commercials you envy, and find out which agencies did them.

You now have a list of agencies. Find out which are working for your competitors, and thus unavailable to you.

By this time you have a short list. Meet the head of each agency and his Creative Director. Make sure the chemistry between you and them is good. Happy marriages fructify, unhappy ones don't.

But don't ask to meet the working-level people who would be assigned to your account. You might find them congenial, but have no way of judging their *talent*. Or you might find them repulsive – some of the most talented people are. A prospective client once passed up an opportunity to hire Ogilvy & Mather because the very able copywriter to whom I introduced him had long hair.

Ask to see each agency's six best print ads and six best television commercials. *Pick the agency whose campaigns interest you the most.*

Ask what the agency charges. If it is 15 per cent, insist on paying 16 per cent. The extra one per cent won't kill you, but it will double the agency's normal profit, and you will get better service. Whatever you

FOR THE PEOPLE OF CANADA
ON THE CENTENARY OF CANADA'S NATIONHOOD
FROM THE PEOPLE OF
THE UNITED STATES OF AMERICA

"THE GREAT RING OF CANADA," a gift from the people of the United States to the people of Canada, was unveiled at Montreal on May 25, 1967, by the President of the United States.

It symbolizes Canada: ten Provinces, two Territories together forming one great Nation.

Designed by Donald Pollard in collaboration with Alexander Seidel, the piece stands 40 inches high—28 inches in diameter.

The great ring is formed of twelve emerald-cut crystal plaques. They are engraved with the coats of arms and official flowers of the ten Provinces and two Territories of Canada.

The smaller ring of clear, cut crystal holds four plaques engraved with the Arms of Canada and the formal Maple Leaf of the Canadian flag. Around the smaller ring itself is Canada's motto: "A MARI USQUE AD MARE"—*from sea to sea*, taken from Psalm 72:8.

The rhodium-plated steel base is inscribed with the dedication: "for the people of Canada on the centenary of Canada's nationhood from the people of the United States of America." Designed and made by Steuben Glass.

STEUBEN GLASS

Don't keep a dog and bark yourself.
When Arthur Houghton asked me to do the advertising for Steuben Glass he said, 'We make the best glass. Your job is to make the best advertising.' An admirable division of labor.

'Any fool can write a bad advertisement, but it takes a genius to keep his hands off a good one.'

do, don't *haggle* over the agency's compensation. I know a big corporation which insists that its agencies negotiate terms of business with its Purchasing Department, as though they were selling office furniture. Would they do this with lawyers and accountants?

Insist on a five-year contract. This will delight the agency – and protect you from being resigned if one of your competitors ever tries to seduce them with a bigger budget.

* * * * *

Now you have your agency, *are you going to get the best out of them?* Clients get the advertising they deserve. I know some who are a malediction, and others who are an inspiration.

Don't keep a dog and bark yourself. Any fool can write a bad advertisement, but it takes a genius to keep his hands off a good one. I had just finished showing a new campaign to Charlie Kelstadt, the Chairman of Sears Roebuck, when his Comptroller came into the room, started to read my copy – and took a fountain-pen out of his pocket. 'Put that pen back in your pocket,' snapped Kelstadt.

Once a year give your agency a formal report on its performance. This will serve as an early warning of trouble which, if ignored, could end badly for all concerned.

One of the biggest corporations in the world allows five levels to chew up its advertising. Each level has the power to veto, but only the Chief Executive Officer has the power of final approval. Don't strain your agency's output through more than *two* levels.

Even the best copywriters are preternaturally thin-skinned. When

This ad was one of a series for Puerto Rico. The campaign was initiated by my most inspiring client, Ted Moscoso of the Puerto Rico Government.

you have to reject their work, do it gently, and praise them to the skies when they perform well. They are the geese who can lay golden eggs. Inspire them to keep laying. The most inspiring client I have ever had was Ted Moscoso, the economic head of the Government of Puerto Rico. The day he hired us, he said to me, 'Before we start advertising, we have to decide what we want Puerto Rico to become. A bridge between Latin America and the United States? An oasis of old Spanish culture? A modern industrial park?' We talked all night. On later occasions, whenever I made a suggestion which appealed to his imagination – such as starting a music festival in San Juan – Moscoso would make a note in his pocket diary; action always followed. Governor

Renaissance
—as seen by

THE HIGH SCHOOL GIRL in the foreg of our photograph is fifteen. When sh born, Puerto Rico was a "stricken land."

We wish you could be here to talk Puerto Rican girl today.

She might start by telling you about day things. The good food her mother b the new supermarket. The new house he ily lives in. Her father's job in one of Rico's new factories

Then, as she warmed up, she would pro have something to say about her lessons a teachers. How they teach her two langu Spanish *and* English. How they take museums and art exhibitions and concer

And she would surely want to tell you the interesting television programs that s her classmates watch on Channel Six, mirable new station in San Juan. Channe

© 1960 – Commonwealth of P

◀ Between classes at the Central High School in San Ju cially proud of having built its own historical museun Puerto Rican basketball championship. Photograph

Muñoz Marín, who was Ted's chief, would have made a good President of the United States. When their party was finally defeated, the new Republican governor moved the advertising to an agency which had handled his campaign in the election. I have never wept so bitterly.

Conflicts

There is a convention that agencies should not serve more than one client in any category. When we do the advertising for *Blogg's* Shoe Polish, we are not supposed to take on *Mogg's* Shoe Polish. Some clients are fiercely jealous when their agencies violate this convention, to the point of firing them.

It sounds simple, but it is a minefield. Suppose the agency has a shoe polish account, and another of its clients decides to go into the shoe polish business. What do we do?

Suppose we have a shoe polish account in our Vienna office, and our Kuala Lumpur office is offered another shoe polish. What do we do?

Some clients extend the definition of conflict to include any product which might *indirectly* reduce their sales. Suppose we have a shoe polish account and are offered a sandal account – *wooden* sandals, which don't require polish. What do we do?

Such conflicts as these *bedevil* agencies. Says Marvin Bower of McKinsey:

> 'If a company rests its policy of not letting its agencies serve competitors on the need for security of information, it does not have a very solid base. As a matter of realism, the interests of competing clients would not be harmed by an almost complete exchange of information among the people serving the two competing companies. Of course, no responsible personal service firm would do that – and indeed they go to great lengths to avoid even inadvertent exchanges. Nevertheless, as one who has been a repository of confidential information over many years, I am convinced that the history, makeup, ways of doing business, attitudes of people, operating philosophy and procedures of even directly competing companies are ordinarily so different that information could be exchanged between them with no harm to either.'

If I were you, I would think twice about firing my agency when it committed bigamy; another agency might not give you such good advertising. *Amour propre* can be an expensive luxury.

David Ogilvy

P.S. If your account is too small to interest a good agency, find an experienced copywriter who has retired and pay him to do your advertising. He will enjoy getting back into harness, and welcome the money.

7 Wanted: a renaissance in print advertising

'God is in the details'

Agency people find making television commercials far more exciting than making advertisements for newspapers and magazines. If their own talents are modest, the film producers can make them look good. In winter, they enjoy going on location at glamorous resorts, while their print colleagues are left behind in cold solitude.

The other day I read a *cri de cœur* from a senior executive in a food company:

> 'TV is so devouring a medium that you need to comb the agencies to find the old sweat who knows how to put together half-way decent print advertisements for food. The others invent food advertising all over again, without knowing which way is up.
>
> The silly thing is that there are just about infallible formulae for constructing advertisements which grab a woman's attention and don't let go of it until the message has been fully planted. Once these formulae are understood, even junior brand managers can assemble the makings of a hard-working food advertisement, while the bright ones will have women tearing out your ads and shoving them into kitchen drawers in a way you wouldn't believe.
>
> Try telling this to agencies. They've never heard of the fundamentals of food advertising. Mention formulae to them and their frail creative souls shrivel.'

The shortage of print know-how presents a serious problem to cigarette manufacturers and others who are not *allowed* to use television. It also presents a golden opportunity for copywriters and art directors who take the trouble to acquire the know-how.

In this chapter I will uncork what I have learned about print advertising. But I cannot do so without repeating some of the things – still valid – I have written elsewhere. I never cease to be struck by the consistency of consumer reactions to different kinds of headline, illustration, layout and copy – year after year, country after country.

The principal sources of my information are the factor analyses which I commission from Gallup and Robinson, the Starch Readership Service, the results of direct response tests, and my own observation.

Headlines

On the average, five times as many people read the headlines as read the body copy. It follows that unless your headline sells your product, you have wasted 90 per cent of your money.

The headlines which work best are those which promise the reader a benefit – like a whiter wash, more miles per gallon, freedom from pimples, fewer cavities. Riffle through a magazine and count the number of ads whose headlines promise a benefit of any kind.

Headlines which contain *news* are sure-fire. The news can be the announcement of a new product, an improvement in an old product, or a new way to use an old product – like serving Campbell's Soup on the rocks. On the average, ads with news are recalled by 22 per cent more people than ads without news.

If you are lucky enough to have some news to tell, don't bury it in your body copy, which nine out of ten people will not read. State it loud and clear in your headline. And don't scorn tried-and-true words like *amazing, introducing, now, suddenly.*

Ads with news are recalled by 22 per cent more people than ads without news. It does not have to be the announcement of a new product. It can be a new way of using an old product, as in this advertisement.

Soup on the rocks.

Cool off with Campbell's Beef Broth. Take it straight from the can and onto the ice. Try it with a dash of Worcestershire or lemon garnish. You can even add your own thing. It's a great way to cool off after a hot day on land or sea. As a matter of fact, don't even wait for a real hot day; start pouring now. Cheers!

M'm! M'm! Good!

Darling, I'm having the most extraordinary experience...

I'm head over heels in DOVE!

No, darling—DOVE. D—like in *delicious*.

I told you, sweet. I'm in the tub. Taking a bath. A DOVE bath—my very first.

And what a positively gorgeous time I'm having! It's just as if I'd never *really* bathed before!

No, dear, it isn't a *soap*. Soap was never like this! So *wickedly creamy*. That man on TV said that DOVE is one-quarter cleansing cream—that it *creams* my skin while I bathe—and now I really *believe* him.

Why, DOVE even *smells* creamy. Such a lovely, lush, *expensive* smell!

Remember "The Great Ziegfeld," dear? How Anna Held bathed in milk? And Cleopatra—one hundred mares or something *milked* every day for her bath?

Well, darling, I'm all over *cream*. Just imagine, cream tip to toe. Arms. Legs. *All* of me!

And *clean*! Simply *smothered* in suds. Oodles of suds! Oceans of. I don't know what I ever did to *deserve* DOVE!

And you know how soap leaves your skin so *dry*? That nasty stretched feeling? Well, DOVE makes me feel all velvet and silk, all *soft and smooth*. Just the most pampered, most spoiled, *girliest* girl in the world.

Darling, I'm *purring*.

And did I tell you DOVE is sort of *me*-shaped? That it's curved to fit my hand, so it doesn't keep slithering away in the tub? Soap is soap, but a bath with DOVE is *heaven!*

And just think, darling—tomorrow night, I can *do it again.*

NOTE TO EAVESDROPPERS

You can buy the remarkable new bath and toilet bar called DOVE today. DOVE is a completely new formula. DOVE makes rich lather in hardest water. DOVE leaves *no* bathtub ring. Lever Brothers guarantee that DOVE is better for *your face, your hands, all of you,* than regular toilet soap. If you don't agree, we'll return every penny you paid.

DOVE creams your skin while you bathe

'Headlines of ten words sell more merchandise than short headlines.'

Headlines that offer the reader *helpful information*, like HOW TO WIN FRIENDS AND INFLUENCE PEOPLE, attract above-average readership.

I advise you to include the brand name in your headline. If you don't, 80 per cent of readers (who don't read your body copy) will never know what product you are advertising.

If you are advertising a kind of product which is only bought by a small group of people, put a word in your headline which will flag them down, like *asthma, bedwetters, women over thirty-five*.

Left I used the word 'darling' in the headline for this ad because a psychologist had tested hundreds of words for their emotional impact and 'darling' had come out top. I was not aware that it is dangerous to use a telephone when you are taking a bath.

Starch reports that headlines with more than ten words get less readership than short headlines. On the other hand, a study of retail advertisements found that headlines of ten words sell more merchandise than short headlines. Conclusion: if you *need* a long headline, go ahead and write one, and if you want a short headline, that's all right too. The

FOR MINNEAPOLIS:
2 BELOW ZERO!

Weather bureau predicts sharp temperature drop tonight. Help your car start promptly in the morning by filling up tonight with Super Shell's winter blend. Its nine-ingredient formula is primed with an extra dose of quick-firing Butane —to help your car give top performance in coldest weather.

SHELL

Above When you advertise in local newspapers, you get better results if you include the name of each city in your headline. People are mostly interested in what is happening where they live.

Right On the average, long headlines sell more merchandise than short ones. This one-word headline is the exception that proves the rule.

Lemon.

This Volkswagen missed the boat.

The chrome strip on the glove compartment is blemished and must be replaced. Chances are you wouldn't have noticed it; Inspector Kurt Kroner did.

There are 3,389 men at our Wolfsburg factory with only one job: to inspect Volkswagens at each stage of production. (3000 Volkswagens are produced daily; there are more inspectors than cars.)

Every shock absorber is tested (spot checking won't do), every windshield is scanned. VWs have been rejected for surface scratches barely visible to the eye.

Final inspection is really something! VW inspectors run each car off the line onto the Funktionsprüfstand (car test stand), tote up 189 check points, gun ahead to the automatic brake stand, and say "no" to one VW out of fifty.

This preoccupation with detail means the VW lasts longer and requires less maintenance, by and large, than other cars. (It also means a used VW depreciates less than any other car.)

We pluck the lemons; you get the plums.

Shop at Sears and save

(their profit is less than 5%)

Sears, Roebuck always charges lower prices than others
charge for equal quality. Read how this enlightened
policy is made possible by unique know-how in buying,
combined with a modest margin of profit.

Above *Specifics are more credible and more memorable than generalities. That is why I specified that Sears' profit is less than 5 per cent.*

Opposite *On average, helpful information is read by 75 per cent more people than copy which deals only with the product. This ad told how Rinso gets out stains. It was read and remembered by more people than any detergent ad that had ever been researched, but it should never have run because it was 'off strategy' – it did not deliver the agreed selling promise that 'Rinso Washes Whiter.' The photograph shows different kinds of stains. The blood was my own; I am the only copywriter who has literally bled for his client.*

famous headline *Lemon* contributed a lot to the success of Volkswagen in the United States.

Specifics work better than generalities. When research reported that the average shopper thought Sears Roebuck made a profit of 37 per cent on sales, I headlined an advertisement *Sears makes a profit of 5 per cent*. This specific was more persuasive than saying that Sears' profit was 'less than you might suppose' or something equally vague.

When you put your headline in *quotes*, you increase recall by an average of 28 per cent.

When you advertise in local newspapers, you get better results if you include the name of each city in your headline. People are most interested in what is happening *where they live*.

A psychologist flashed hundreds of words on a screen and used an electric gadget to measure emotional reactions. High marks went to *darling*. So I used it in a headline for Dove.

Some copywriters write *tricky* headlines – double meanings, puns and other obscurities. This is counter-productive. In the average newspaper your headline has to compete with 350 others. Readers travel fast through this jungle. Your headline should *telegraph* what you want to say.

Some headlines are 'blind.' They don't say what the product is, or what it will do for you. They are about 20 per cent below average in recall.

Since headlines, more than anything else, decide the success or failure of an advertisement, the silliest thing of all is to run an ad without any headline at all – 'a headless wonder.'

If you would like more guidance on writing headlines, I commend you to John Caples' book *Tested Advertising Methods* (Prentice-Hall).

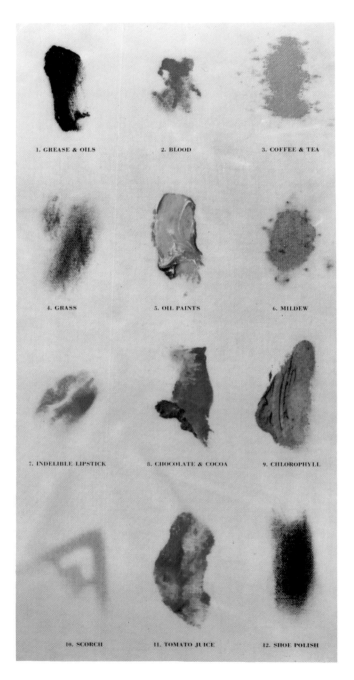

1. GREASE & OILS   2. BLOOD   3. COFFEE & TEA

4. GRASS   5. OIL PAINTS   6. MILDEW

7. INDELIBLE LIPSTICK   8. CHOCOLATE & COCOA   9. CHLOROPHYLL

10. SCORCH   11. TOMATO JUICE   12. SHOE POLISH

How to take out
STAINS

USE RINSO AND FOLLOW THESE EASY DIRECTIONS

If you have ever used Rinso in your washer, you've probably noticed that it gets clothes exceptionally *white*. This is due to the SOLIUM in Rinso.

What many women *don't* know is that Rinso also works like a charm on most common *stains* — if you know how to go about it. Here are some simple, tested hints from the scientists at Lever Brothers Company. Be *sure* fabric is colorfast and washable before following these directions.

1. GREASE & OIL. Use warm Rinso suds. Put plenty of Rinso on stained part, rub between hands.

2. BLOOD. Soak in cold water until stains turn light brown, then wash in warm Rinso suds.

3. COFFEE & TEA. To remove fresh stains, pour boiling water on stain from 2- or 3-foot height, then wash in warm Rinso suds. If any stain remains, dry in sun or use bleach. Do not bleach silk or wool.

4. GRASS. Use hot water and Rinso, rubbing well. If stains remain, use bleach. Once again, do not bleach silk or wool.

5. OIL PAINT, VARNISH, ENAMEL. Remove fresh stains from washable materials by washing with plenty of Rinso suds. If stain has dried, soften it first by rubbing in Spry, lard or vaseline.

6. MILDEW. Rinso suds will remove very fresh mildew stains from washable materials. Drying in sun helps bleach spots. If stain remains, use bleach except on silk or wool.

7. INDELIBLE LIPSTICK. Work vaseline or lard into stain. Then sponge with cleaning fluid. Remove any ring which may remain by laundering in Rinso suds. On rayon and colored materials, use 1 part alcohol to 2 parts water. Then launder with Rinso.

8. CHOCOLATE & COCOA. First scrape off excess with dull knife, then launder in warm Rinso suds.

9. CHLOROPHYLL. Wash with warm Rinso suds. If stain remains, use bleach except on silk or wool.

10. SCORCH. Use Rinso suds to remove slight stains from washable materials. Dry in the sun a day or two.

11. TOMATO JUICE, CATSUP. Sponge thoroughly with cold water, then work glycerine into stain, let stand half hour. Then wash in Rinso suds.

12. SHOE POLISH. Sponge thoroughly with plenty of Rinso suds.

SAVE 20%

You usually pay about 20% less for Rinso than for detergents because it now costs Lever Brothers less to make Rinso. This saving goes to you. Rinso is guaranteed, of course. To obtain free reprints of this page, write Lever Brothers Company, P.O. Box 44, New York 46, N.Y.

My favorite headlines

For lanolin as a cure for baldness: *Have you ever seen a bald-headed sheep?*

For a pile remedy: *Send us your dollar and we'll cure your piles, or keep your dollar and keep your piles.*

Illustrations

A picture, they say, can be worth a thousand words. The cowboy photographs for Marlboro, and Elliott Erwitt's photographs in the ads for Puerto Rico and France are examples.

Here are 15 ways to make your illustrations work for their living:

1 The *subject* of your illustration is all important. If you don't have a remarkable *idea* for it, not even a great photographer can save you.

2 The kind of photographs which work hardest are those which arouse the reader's curiosity. He glances at the photograph and says to himself, 'What goes on here?' Then he reads your copy to find out. Harold Rudolph called this magic element 'Story Appeal,' and demonstrated that the more of it you inject into your photographs, the more people look at your advertisements.

The final concert at last year's Festival Casals in San Juan. Photograph by Elliott Erwitt.

Tribute to the man who wasn't there — a poignant moment   **at last year's Festival Casals in Puerto Rico** · · · · · ·

PABLO CASALS was ill. His place in center-stage was empty. And somehow you couldn't forget it.

The festival ended the way that it should. The final performance was given by the absent Casals. It was his recording of an old Catalan ballad—*the Song of the Birds*. The ovation was thunderous.

Casals has said, "Each day I am reborn. Each day I must begin again." Such is the simple courage that has restored the Master to his music. Once again he is ready to take his place among a distinguished group of musicians—for the *second* Festival Casals in San Juan.

This 1958 festival will run from April 22 through May 8. The program will feature works by Mozart, Beethoven and Brahms. Principal performers will include Victoria de los Angeles, Mieczyslaw Horszowski, Eugene Istomin, Jesús María Sanromá, Alexander Schneider, Rudolf Serkin, Isaac Stern, Walter Trampler—and the Budapest String Quartet.

Who can doubt that this year's festival will be even more brilliant than the last?

The great man himself will be there.

For details, write Festival Casals, P. O. Box 2672, San Juan, Puerto Rico, or to 666 Fifth Avenue, New York. Announcement by the Commonwealth of Puerto Rico, 666 Fifth Avenue, New York 19.

Above and right *As ex-chef, (above) I assumed that housewives would find the Rinso photograph (right) as interesting as I did. They didn't.*

WHEN IT'S GOT TO BE REALLY <u>WHITE</u>—USE RINSO WITH SOLIUM

Rinso gets out more dirt than detergents and you usually pay about 20% less.

A chef's hat is his badge of office. If it isn't dazzling white, he doesn't rate. Some proud housewives we know feel the same way about their sheets, pillowcases, and the rest of their wash. They are the gals who use Rinso soap instead of chemical detergents. They want *their* wash to come out dazzling white, bless them.

Those chemical detergents are pretty good. We make them ourselves. But we also make soap, Rinso soap, and we can assure you that when it comes to doing your family wash, Rinso does a better job on grime and dirt. Yes, indeed.

You may have noticed that your sheets and pillow-cases actually look whiter after they have been washed in Rinso than when you first bought them. This is actually true. It's due to the SOLIUM in Rinso, and you can see the difference even before your wash is dry.

Our scientists can also prove that Rinso *gets out more dirt* than detergents. But, to be honest, you can't always detect this superiority with the naked eye—except when your wash is very dirty indeed. Then you will be able to see for yourself that Rinso does a better job.

You can safely wash almost any fabric in Rinso—not only your cottons, as you'd expect, but wool, nylon, rayon, orlon, linen and silk. Even your baby's diapers. And, as every alert young housewife has discovered, the mild, gentle *soap* in Rinso is kinder to your hands than harsh detergents. Last but not least, Rinso costs you less—you usually pay about 20% less for Rinso than for most detergents. Why? Because it now costs us less to make Rinso—and we *pass this saving on to you!*

It all adds up to this: for your family wash, Rinso with SOLIUM is far and away your "best buy." A great boon, and a great bargain. Rinso is unconditionally guaranteed to please you, or your money back plus postage if you return the guarantee panel from any Rinso package to Lever Brothers Company, 390 Park Avenue, New York 22, N.Y.

3 When you don't have a story to tell, it is often a good thing to make your *package* the subject of your illustration.

4 It pays to illustrate the *end-result* of using your product. Before-and-after photographs seem to fascinate readers. In a study of 70 campaigns whose sales results were known, Gallup did not find a single before-and-after campaign that did not increase sales.

5 When I arrived on Madison Avenue, most advertisements were illustrated with *drawings*. Then it was found that photographs attracted more readers, were more believable, and better remembered. When I took over the 'Come to Britain' advertising, I substituted photographs for the drawings which the previous agency had used. Readership tripled, and so did tourism to Britain. Direct-response advertisers find that photographs pull

Exclusivement chez les dépositaires officiels Rochas.

Un nouveau parfum est né

Above *When you don't have a story to tell in your photograph, make your product the subject of your illustration. This photograph was taken by Irving Penn, for Philippe Saalburg of FCB-Impact in Paris.*

more coupons than drawings, and department stores find that they sell more merchandise. However, photographs reproduce so badly in some newspapers that you can get a more lifelike picture by using a line drawing. I found that scratch-board drawings sold more Thom McCan shoes than photographs.

6 The use of characters known to people who see your television commercials boosts the recall of your print advertisements.

7 Keep your illustrations as *simple* as possible, with the focus of interest on one person. Crowd scenes don't pull.

8 Don't show human faces enlarged bigger than life size. They seem to repel readers.

9 Historical subjects bore the majority of readers.

10 Do not assume that subjects which interest *you* will necessarily interest consumers. Being a former chef, I assumed that *everyone* found chefs interesting – until I used them in an advertisement. I got miserable readership among the housewives who were the target audience. A friend at Campbell's Soup told me that he too had observed that housewives were turned off by chefs.

Above *Before-and-After photographs fascinate readers, as in this advertisement from the Milan office of Ogilvy & Mather. The plant on the left has not been treated with Baysol, while the plant on the right has.*

Right *The eyepatch injects the magic element of 'story appeal.' The model was Baron Wrangell, who had a habit of swaying in front of the camera, so that we had to strap him to an iron pipe.*

Hathaway revives the <u>striped</u> tartan

"I HAD not known that tartans were ever made in *stripes*, until I visited Drummond Castle, and there saw striped tartans dating back to the 18th century."

So wrote the head of Hathaway from Scotland early this year.

Fired by his discovery, he immediately bicycled over to the town of Auchterarder, there to closet himself with James White, the great Scottish weaver.

Out of that conference came a striped tartan in the great tradition. Woven into a magnificent new kind of *winter tattan*—lightweight but cozy. Just the ticket for any man who likes a comfortable shirt for cold weather but doesn't like wool.

It comes in no less than fifty-two striped tartans and other designs. Each shirt is identified by the famous **H** for Hathaway at the gusset on the tail. For store names, write C. F. Hathaway, Waterville, Maine. In New York, call OX 7-5566.

AMAZING PHOTOGRAPH

When our photographer arrived to take this picture, he found Baron Wrangell playing bridge. At that very minute, the Baron had been dealt thirteen spades — an event so rare that it happens only once in 635,013,559,596 hands.

11 My brother Francis once asked a Cockney editor of the *Daily Mirror* (London) what kind of photographs most interested his readers. He answered, 'Babies with an 'eart-throb, animals with an 'eart-throb, and what you might call sex.' This is still true today.

12 When I worked for Dr. Gallup, I noticed that moviegoers were more interested in actors of their own sex than actors of the opposite sex. People want to see movie stars with whom they can *identify*. The same force is at work in advertisements. When you use a photograph of a woman, men ignore your advertisement.

13 Advertisements in four colors cost 50 per cent more than black-and-white, but, on the average, they are 100 per cent more *memorable*. A good bargain.

14 I cannot resist the temptation to quote a verse which gives valuable advice on illustration:

> When the client moans and sighs,
> Make his logo twice the size.
> If he still should prove refractory
> Show a picture of his factory.
> Only in the gravest cases
> Should you show the clients' faces.

15 When you advertise products for use in cooking, you attract more readers if you show a photograph of the finished dish than the ingredients.

Warning

My former partner Douglas Haines has recently demonstrated that the illustrations in advertisements are often *misunderstood*. In a pilot study, he came across a woman who thought that the photograph of a luxurious hotel foyer in a cigarette advertisement was a hospital ward for cancer patients.

Body copy

'Nobody reads body copy.' True or false? It depends on two things. First, on how many people are interested in the kind of product you are advertising: a lot of women will read copy about food products, but few will read copy about cigars. Second, on how many people have been enticed into your ad by your illustration and headline.

The *average* readership of the body copy in magazine ads is about 5 per cent. That does not sound like a lot until you remember that 5 per cent of readers of the *Reader's Digest* adds up to 1,500,000 men and women.

Do not, however, address your readers as though they were gathered together in a stadium. When people read your copy, they are *alone*. Pretend you are writing each of them a letter on behalf of your client. One human being to another, second person *singular*.

Queen Victoria complained that Gladstone talked to her as if he were addressing a public meeting. She preferred Disraeli, who talked to her like a human being. When you write copy, follow Disraeli's example.

It isn't as easy as you may think. Aldous Huxley, who was once a copywriter, said, 'It is easier to write ten passably effective sonnets than one effective advertisement.'

You cannot *bore* people into buying your product. You can only *interest* them in buying it.

It pays to write short sentences and short paragraphs, and to avoid difficult words. I once wrote that Dove made soap 'obsolete,' only to discover that the majority of housewives did not know what the word meant. I had to change it to 'old-fashioned.' When I used the word *ineffable* in copy for Hathaway, a reporter telephoned to ask me what it meant. I hadn't the faintest idea. Nowadays I keep a dictionary beside my telephone.

'You cannot *bore* people into buying your product.'

Above *Note the* editorial layout, *and the* story form – *both* plus *factors. This advertisement promised 'If it ever fails to work, we'll fix it free.' Every morning hundreds of old and battered Zippos arrived in the mail. They were returned the same day, in perfect working order – and no charge.*

Above right *John Caples' famous direct-mail advertisement for the U.S. School of Music deployed story-appeal at its most effective.*

When copywriters argue with me about some esoteric word they want to use, I say to them, 'Get on a bus. Go to Iowa. Stay on a farm for a week and talk to the farmer. Come back to New York by train and talk to your fellow passengers in the day-coach. If you *still* want to use the word, go ahead.'

Copy should be written in the language people use in everyday conversation, as in this anonymous verse:

> Carnation Milk is the best in the land,
> Here I sit with a can in my hand.
> No tits to pull, no hay to pitch,
> Just punch a hole in the son-of-a-bitch.

Don't write *essays*. Tell your reader what your product will do for him or her, and tell it with specifics.

Write your copy in the form of a *story*, as in the advertisement which carried the headline, 'The amazing story of a Zippo that worked after being taken from the belly of a fish.' One of the most famous advertisements ever written was by John Caples for International Correspondence School, under the headline 'They Laughed When I Sat Down at the Piano – But When I Started to Play . . . '.

I advise you to avoid *analogies*. Gallup has found that they are widely misunderstood. If you are writing copy for a face cream and say, 'Just as plants require moisture, so too does your skin,' readers don't complete the equation. If you show a Rembrandt and say, 'Just as this Rembrandt portrait is a masterpiece, so too is our product,' readers think you are selling the Rembrandt.

Stay away from superlatives like 'Our product is the best in the world.' Gallup calls this *Brag and Boast*. It convinces nobody.

If you include a *testimonial* in your copy, you make it more credible. Readers find the endorsements of fellow consumers more persuasive than the puffery of anonymous copywriters. Says James Webb Young, one of the best copywriters in history, 'Every type of advertiser has the same problem: to be *believed*. The mail-order man knows nothing so potent for this purpose as the testimonial, yet the general advertiser seldom uses it.'

Sometimes you can cast your entire advertisement in the form of a testimonial. My first ad for Austin cars took the form of a letter from an 'anonymous diplomat' who was sending his son to Groton with money he had saved driving an Austin. A combination of snobbery and

Below *Beautiful but dumb. This ad from Switzerland would have interested more housewives if it had shown a finished dish instead of the raw ingredients. It would have been better read if it had been given a headline. And it would have been more persuasive if the copy had contained some specifics instead of vague generalities.*

Opposite right *You can cast an entire advertisement in the form of a testimonial, as in this one for Austin cars. When the headmaster of Groton discovered that the 'anonymous diplomat' was the author of this book, I found it expedient to send my son to another school.*

Vous savez ce qui est bon et appréciez des menus variés, de haute qualité. Mais vous n'aimez pas passer des heures dans votre cuisine. Avez-vous déjà goûté les fameuses spécialités aux pâtes Hero prêtes à être dégustées? Nous les avons créées pour vous avec des ingrédients choisis, selon d'authentiques recettes italiennes. Les voici toutes les cinq! En boîtes, elles sont particulièrement avantageuses pour les familles; en sachets-fraîcheur, elles sont pratiques pour les «petits ménages». A vous de choisir Ou – mieux encore – goûtez-les toutes les cinq!

Buon appetito!

Hero
plaisir de la table

A-40 Somerset 4-door DeLuxe Sedan $1795, f.o.b. coastal port of entry. *A-40 Somerset DeLuxe Convertible $1945, f.o.b. coastal port of entry.*

"I am sending my son to Groton with money I have saved driving Austins"

Private Letter from Anonymous Diplomat

RECENTLY we got this letter from a man who used to ornament the Diplomatic Corps. He writes:

"Soon after I left the Embassy I bought an AUSTIN. We don't have a chauffeur nowadays—my wife has taken over that job. She drives me to and from the station every day. She drives the children to school. She does the shopping. She drives over to Greenwich Hospital, and to Garden Club meetings. And so on and so forth.

"A dozen times I have heard her say: 'I simply couldn't cope with all this chauffeuring if I still had to lug around that heavy old juggernaut we used to own.'

"My own enthusiasm for AUSTIN is based on more material considerations. In a word, the car has *saved me a fortune*. At a dinner party last night I heard myself saying: 'I am going to send my son to Groton with the money I have saved owning an AUSTIN!'"

Fantastic Economy

Gentle reader, you may think that our friend the diplomat is exaggerating about the economies of an AUSTIN. He isn't. Work it out for yourself, in the light of these facts:

1. You can now buy the new 4-door AUSTIN Somerset DeLuxe Sedan for only $1795, including $250 worth of extras. This is a great bargain.

2. Gasoline costs more than 60 cents a gallon in England, so we have had to develop a car which will deliver maximum mileage. The new AUSTIN gives you 35 miles per gallon—somewhat less if you drive furiously.

3. It takes ten gallons to fill our tank, and then you can drive 350 miles—from New York to Richmond, Virginia—without refueling.

4. Your AUSTIN has an exceptionally low rate of depreciation, for two reasons: First, we in England build cars to *last*. Second, the demand for used AUSTINS is far greater than the supply, so their trade-in value is one of the highest for any quality car.

5. *The savings are endless. All in all, an AUSTIN cuts your operating costs up to 50 per cent, as near as we can figure it.*

Can You Get Service?

Prospective customers often ask us how they can get service and spare parts for an imported car.

In our case the answer is simple: We now have more than a thousand dealers from coast to coast, in the United States and Canada.

So service and spare parts are no longer any problem with AUSTIN. Our cars aren't that rare any more. As a matter of fact, we now have more than 85,000 AUSTINS on the road over here.

Cruises at 65 M. P. H.

The new AUSTIN handles like a sports car. It has a precision-built 4-cylinder engine with over-head valves, and an exceptionally high compression ratio—7.2 to 1.

It accelerates from a standing start to 50 m. p. h. in 19.8 seconds, and cruises at 65 m. p. h.

Because it has four forward speeds and superb traction, you can take it over impossible country. Through deep mud and snow. Across fields. Up mountains.

The AUSTIN is an unusually *safe* car to drive. It hugs the road like a hedgehog. It doesn't roll on curves. It's a very *stable* car, beautifully sprung. Well mannered.

At 30 m.p.h. you can stop in thirty-two feet. Superb brakes.

If you have children, take comfort from the fact that the AUSTIN has special safety locks on the rear doors. And these doors can take it! They're not "tinny." The AUSTIN is built with much thicker steel than ordinary domestic cars.

Big Enough for Giants

At first sight the AUSTIN looks smaller than conventional American cars. But when you open the door and get in, you will be surprised to find how roomy and luxurious it is.

There is no waste over-hang. Every inch of space is used *inside* the car. Room for four six-foot grownups in comfort.

Another major advantage: You can always find a place to park your AUSTIN. This is something which commuters — and their chauffeur-wives—never stop talking about.

$250 Worth of Extras Included in the AUSTIN Price

The price of our new 4-door DeLuxe AUSTIN is $1795. This includes more than $250 worth of special equipment, for which you would normally expect to pay extra. Here are some of these "free" extras:

1. Foam-rubber cushions and real leather upholstery—you don't need seat covers.

2. A revolutionary new jacking system which operates from inside the car.

3. A first-class heater and twin defrosters.

4. Electric windshield wipers for extra safety . . . no chance of failure on hills.

5. A *twelve*-volt battery, strong enough to start a truck.

6. Illuminated arms which stick out when you are going to turn, and then go back in automatically.

GOING ABROAD?

If you're planning a trip abroad you can order your new AUSTIN here, at the regular U. S. price, for delivery in England. We'll ship your AUSTIN back to the U. S. without charge on your return. Other delivery plans for Paris, Rome or Düsseldorf.

An ex-safecracker confesses that he never cracked a Chubb safe

Up until a few years ago I never did an honest day's work in my life. It was too easy to make lots of money by breaking into offices and shops and pinching whatever was in the safe. But I'm going straight now. Seen the light you might say.

In my time I must have knocked over scores of safes. The kinds I'd learned to take apart. Once I knew what made a particular safe tick, I would go round looking for those safes, find one, break in and crack it.

I tried to crack Chubb safes. Believe me I tried.

Understand this—some safes are easier to beat than others. It's all a matter of degree of difficulty. I've had to use drills and torches to open some safes. Others I've only had to use a few well-aimed blows from a sledge hammer. Some have demanded a more scientific approach — pouring acid through the locks and stuff like that. I've tried the whole lot on Chubb safes. Spent up to 12 nerve-wracking hours mucking around trying one thing after another. But to no avail. I always left empty handed — except for a few blisters. But they don't count.

Hollywood has given people a false idea about safes

In the movies you see blokes

'I never heard Chubb ever and that's saying something'

sandpaper their fingers, listen a bit with a stethoscope and before you know it, they've got the combination and the safe is open.

The result is that most people figure there's no point in paying a lot of money for a good safe, if some dude can just walk in and tickle it open. But they're wrong. A good modern safe can't be opened that way.

A cheap safe can be opened with a crowbar or a hammer.

A better safe requires acid, drill or torch. But against a Chubb safe — well, nothing ever worked for me. Those people who bought Chubb safes knew what they were getting — real security. They weren't fooled by Hollywood, not one bit. That's why I never got my hands on their valuables.

Some advice from an old pro

If you've got something of value to protect, talk to Chubb. They'll fix you up. They make safes and security alarm systems that make it virtually impossible for blokes like me to get our hands on your valuables.

Since I've been going straight I've a bit of money and you'll never guess where it is. Right. It's in a Chubb safe.

For Chubb protection, peace of mind and a very safe investment, act now. Fill in the coupon and send it to Chubb.

© Chubb

This story is based on various techniques used to illegally open safes.

Above *Testimonials from experts can be extremely effective. This advertisement by Ogilvy & Mather appeared in Singapore.*

economy. Unfortunately, a *Time* editor guessed that I was the anonymous diplomat, and asked the headmaster of Groton to comment. I had to send my son to another school.

Testimonials from celebrities get high recall scores, but I have stopped using them because readers remember the celebrity and forget the product. What's more, they assume that the celebrity has been *bought,* which is usually the case. On the other hand, testimonials from *experts* can be persuasive – like having an ex-burglar testify that he had never been able to crack a Chubb safe.

Most copywriters believe that markdowns and special offers are boring, but consumers don't think so. They are above average in recall.

Always try to include the *price* of your products. You may see a necklace in a jeweler's window, but you don't consider *buying* it because the price is not shown and you are too shy to go in and ask. It is the same way with advertisements. When the price of the product is left out, people have a way of turning the page. When Ellerton Jetté retired as head of Hathaway and became a picture dealer, he violated tradition in the art trade by showing the price of the pictures in his advertisements. Unfortunately it is seldom possible for manufacturers to do this in their advertisements, because they cannot dictate prices to retailers. This reduces the selling power of their ads. I don't think it matters with package goods, but it matters a lot with products which cost real money, like cars and refrigerators.

Below *This two-page advertisement for the World Wildlife Fund appeared in the* New York Times. *It contains 3,232 words.*

Opposite *This advertisement contains 6,540 words – the most anybody has ever used in a single page. When it appeared in the* New York Times, *it pulled 10,000 responses to an offer of a booklet buried near the end. It was written by the late Louis Engel of Merrill Lynch.*

I believe that all copy should be *signed by the agency.* This is never done in the United States, on the ground that manufacturers buy space to advertise their products, not their agencies. Short-sighted. My experience suggests that when agencies sign their ads, they produce better ones. When *Reader's Digest* asked me to write an advertisement for their magazine (see page 41), they specified that I *had* to sign it. Golly, did I work hard on that ad. Everyone was going to know who wrote it.

It is now the convention for agencies in Germany and France to sign their ads. The FCB-Impact agency in Paris even gives its copywriters a by-line. Jolly good.

Short copy or long?

All my experience says that for a great many products, long copy sells more than short. I have failed only twice with long copy, once for a popular-priced cigar and once for a premium-priced whiskey. Here are nine examples which were successful:

1 The late Louis Engel wrote an advertisement of 6,450 words for Merill Lynch. One insertion in the *New York Times* pulled 10,000 responses – without a coupon.

What everybody ought to know . . .
About This Stock And Bond Business

Some plain talk about a simple business that often sounds complicated.

WHY WE ARE PUBLISHING THIS INFORMATION

A little while ago we were talking with the editor of a big national magazine, a well-informed man. He said that he had never done business with a broker because he was afraid he wouldn't understand the "lingo they talk."

Since we are brokers, you can imagine that was something of a shock . . . made us think.

The financial business *does* use a lot of specialized words, but there really isn't anything complicated or mysterious about what those words *mean*. Because we've used them so long and so frequently, we've just assumed that everybody understood them.

That has been our mistake. And a big mistake. For if people don't understand what stocks and bonds are, they aren't likely to invest their money in them.

"So what?" you ask. Well, here's "what".

If people do not invest their funds in securities, American business and American government will not have the capital they need for growth – for new products, new plants, new jobs. That capital can come from just one place: People. Not just a few people with great fortunes – there aren't many of them any more–but from millions of people.

Or look at it from the social point of view. People who don't understand investments are easy prey for a wide variety of "get-rich-quick" artists.

Or look at it from the purely personal point of view. A lot of people might like to invest their surplus savings where they could earn a fair return on them. But if they are unfamiliar with securities, they aren't likely to invest their money in them.

For all these reasons, it is important that people should know as much as they can about this stock and bond business.

But where do you start?

Well, it would seem that a good place to start would be with the "lingo" that our friend the editor complained about. And we might as well go back to the most common words in the business. You may find a lot of this explanation pretty elementary. But the next fellow may not be wholly clear about the exact difference between a stock and a bond. So we'll start right there, in the belief that you'll be obliging enough to skip what you already know.

MERRILL LYNCH,
PIERCE, FENNER & BEANE

What Are Stocks?

The stock of a company represents the ownership of that company. If you own a share of stock in a company – let's call it the Typical Manufacturing Company – you own a piece of that company – a part of its plant, its production, a part of everything in that company. If the Typical Company has 1,000 shares of stock and you own 10 shares, you own one hundredth of the company, or 1% of it.

Some companies have only a few shares of stock and a few owners, while others – the big corporations like U. S. Steel and General Motors – have millions of shares of stock and hundreds of thousands of stockholders or owners.

Why Should Anybody Buy Stocks?

For the same reason that he might go into any other business for himself. To make money.

If you own 1% of the Typical Company, you own 1% of whatever it earns. Normally, some of those earnings or profits will be paid out to you and the other stockholders as dividends – so much on each share. The rest of the earnings will be put back into the business to do more work, make more earnings, more dividends.

How Big Are Dividends?

That depends on the company and how much it earns. Some companies pay out a substantial portion of their earnings as dividends. Other companies, particularly those that are expanding, may plow a greater proportion of earnings back into the business. Some companies pay no dividends. Of all the companies whose stocks are bought and sold on the New York Stock Exchange, about 90% are paying dividends. (That was the record last year.) The average dividend paid by these companies is a little better than 5% of what the stocks are selling at. Thus, if you bought one share of stock in each you could figure on making 5% on your money in a year. Some pay more. Some pay less.

Most companies try to pay dividends regularly. (The Pennsylvania Railroad has paid a dividend every year for more than a century.)

A company's board of directors decides what dividends will be paid and when. These directors are your representatives. You and the other stockholders elect them, each for a definite term. Ordinarily, you get one vote for every share of stock you own. The directors are the real heads of a company. The president and other officers are responsible to the directors for their management of the company.

What Do Stocks Cost?

The price of a stock, like the price of food or clothing, depends on how much other buyers are willing to pay for it, how cheaply those who own it are willing to sell. When a company first offers or "floats" its stock so that it can raise the money it needs to begin business, a specific price is set on that stock. But once the stock is traded in the market, its price is *not fixed or pegged by anybody or any agency*. It is determined by free and open bidding – by supply and demand.

That's why stock prices rise and fall constantly – sometimes rapidly. Some people who buy Typical Company stock do so not because they want to get the dividends that are paid on it but because they think the price of Typical stock will rise and that they will be able to sell it later at a profit. This is risky business for anyone who cannot afford to lose money, because the price of Typical stock may drop. Nobody ever knows for sure what's going to happen to the price of any stock.

What Are Preferred Stocks?

In addition to its common stock, some companies also have preferred stock, usually offered at $100 a share. This stock generally bears a set dividend rate, say of $4. Holders of preferred stock get those dividends before common stockholders get anything – that's one reason why it is called "preferred"–but if the company has a good year, preferred stockholders don't, as a rule, get anything more than the specified $4 dividend per share.

The stock is also called "preferred" because if the company is liquidated, holders of such stock get a first claim on whatever assets may be left after creditors' claims are satisfied. (Assets are property, such as plants or goods, that can be converted into money.)

Although preferred stocks differ widely in the *exact* terms of the preferred treatment which they provide owners, they always offer *some* preferences. Hence, the prices of preferred stock usually do not fluctuate as much as the prices of common stock over a given period.

Although preferred stockholders, like common stockholders, are part owners of the company, they often have no voice in management, no vote in electing directors.

What Are Bonds?

Bonds are a kind of promissory note. People who buy a company's bonds lend their money to that company, and the company agrees to pay them back at a set date, known as the maturity date. For the use of the money, the company generally agrees to pay a set rate of interest of, say, 3% per year. Bonds are usually backed by a mortgage on the company's property or by the general credit of the company.

Unlike stockholders, bondholders are *not* part owners of the company. They are *creditors* of the company.

Of course, as creditors their claims must be satisfied if the company goes broke, before stockholders – the owners – can divide so much as a dime's worth of the company's assets – if any.

Because bonds have this prior claim, they are regarded as the safest kind of security. That's why they appeal to conservative investors–widows, retired people, anyone who is willing to take a smaller return on his money, provided it's a surer one.

In times of economic uncertainty, bonds are always comparatively more attractive than stocks. Their prices do not fluctuate as much as stock prices, because they bear a fixed rate of interest and the element of risk is not as immediate a factor in the price.

Of course, the price of any bond is apt to be depressed, especially if there is any suspicion that the company is having a hard time.

In addition to corporate bonds, there are state, city, and government bonds. On state and city bonds, the revenue from taxes is frequently pledged as security for repayment. Back of U. S. Government bonds – the highest-grade investment there is – lies the integrity of the nation. Just that and nothing more, because nothing else is needed and nothing could add greater security. The integrity of the country is the standard of investment values.

State and city bonds are attractive to many investors, because the federal government does not tax the income from these bonds, as it does the income from company stocks and bonds or most U. S. Government bonds.

Bonds are usually issued in $1,000 units (sometimes $500), but as a matter of tradition they are usually quoted as though the price were a percentage of the face value. Thus, if a corporate bond is said to sell at 98½, it actually sells at $985.

Government bonds are quoted in 1/32nds. Thus a quote of 100.16 means 100 16/32 or in actual dollars, $1,005.

What Are Common Stocks Worth?

That depends on what people are willing to pay for them. And what they are willing to pay for a particular stock is largely determined by one factor – earnings. That includes what the company *has* earned (its past record), what it *is* earning (its present state of health), and what it *might* earn (its prospects for the future).

So you see it's not just a matter of figures. It's a matter of facts . . . knowledge . . . judgment. How aggressive is the company? How good is its management? How popular are its products? What part of earnings will have to be paid out as preferred stock dividends or bond interest? After all, these must be paid first, and what is available for common stockholders depends on how much is left.

Then you have to look outside the company and consider the whole industry in which it operates. Is its future bright? (The buggy industry once offered many good investments.) And what about competitors? Are they in better shape than your company? Might they take the market away from Typical Manufacturing?

Finally, you have to consider general business factors. For instance, will rising costs of labor and raw materials pinch your company?

These are just some of the questions to which the intelligent investor wants answers so that he can form a reliable opinion of what his stock is likely to be worth – *tomorrow*.

Investment values constantly change. That's why this firm has always urged stockholders to "Investigate – then Invest", and to keep on investigating afterwards.

Why Do Stock Prices Change?

At any given time, you may not agree with the price at which a particular stock is selling. You may think it is too high or too low.

There is a simple reason for that: What a stock is "worth" is a matter of personal opinion. But what it actually sells at is the sum total of a lot of individual judgments about it. The *price* of a security is nothing more than the collective expression of all the opinions of all the people who are buying or selling it.

If a number of people conclude at about the same time that a particular stock is overpriced, they may decide to sell it, and the price will probably fall. Or they may think it is selling at bargain prices and decide to buy it. Their combined orders may cause the price to rise.

That's why stock prices sometimes fluctuate sharply. Instead of changing by an eighth or a quarter of a point – which means an eighth or a quarter of a dollar – the price may change by several dollars, either up or down, in a short time.

Whenever there is a sharp price movement in either direction, it may pick up momentum and continue for a little while. That's because such a price movement is likely to attract other buyers or sellers.

For instance, if the price of Typical Manufacturing were suddenly to advance from $25 to $27 a share, others might notice the advance and quickly conclude that it was a good buy. So they might decide to buy it too, and that would lift the price still higher, perhaps to $28 or $29. At that point, some of those who originally bought Typical stock at, say, $25 might decide to take their profit of $3 or $4 a share and sell out. Then the price might start down again.

What Are Bull and Bear Markets?

Sometimes a great many people will decide more or less at the same time, perhaps just on the basis of the general business outlook, that it is a good idea to buy stocks–all kinds of stocks. Such general buying action raises the average price of all stocks. If the price rise is big enough and lasts long enough, we have what is called a bull market.

A bear market is just the opposite. The average price of all stocks drops because of widespread selling. To be bullish or bearish simply means to believe that stocks are going up or down.

Incidentally, it is a simple business to keep track of whether the market as a whole is moving up or down, because almost every major newspaper in the country publishes daily the average price of some group of key stocks and reports whether that average is moving up or down. The Dow Jones Averages are the best known of these indexes.

When Should You Buy or Sell Stocks?

Deciding when to buy or sell is often just as important as deciding what to buy or sell. This matter of timing is particularly important to the speculator.

But first, what is a speculator? And what useful purpose does he serve?

A speculator is a man who buys securities, expecting the price to rise so that he will make a profit on his purchase, usually in a short period of time. Or he may sell securities expecting the price to drop. The important point is that he doesn't buy securities as investments – for the sake of the dividends that they pay.

The speculator performs a valuable service in the stock market because he is willing to take risks – and risk, the risk of a sudden price change, is an inevitable part of any free market, whether it be a market for securities or foodstuffs or any other commodity.

Suppose you own stock in Typical Manufacturing, and suppose you want to sell that stock because you think the earnings outlook is bad. You might not be able to sell at anything like a fair price if it were not for a speculator and his willingness to assume the risk that you want to dispose of.

But no one should speculate unless he can afford to take risks. We've said that repeatedly in public advertisements and in counseling our customers. Nevertheless we are realistic enough to recognize the fact that there's enough desire for gain in even the most conservative investor so that he naturally wants to buy as low as he can and sell as high as he can. He doesn't want to lose an unnecessary dollar by an ill-timed purchase or sale. That's why we are always urging stockholders to make close and continuous study of the markets, for it is only through such study that one can reduce the risks in deciding *when* to buy or sell.

That point is especially important with respect to the *sale* of stock. If you own a stock which has risen to such a high price that you wouldn't consider buying it, it is only good sense that you at least consider selling it.

Too many people make the mistake of buying stocks, then putting them away and forgetting about them. That's bad business. If you want to invest successfully, you've got to pay attention to your securities and be always alert to new investment opportunities. What may have been a good buy last year or even last month may not be a good buy next year or next month.

Like everything else in this world, "securities are perishable."

How Are Stocks Traded?

There are thousands of different stocks and bonds – they are both called securities–but the ones that are bought and sold most frequently are those that are traded on the floor of the New York Stock Exchange. The securities of more than 1,100 major companies are "listed" on that Exchange, which means that they have been accepted for trading there.

All buying and selling on the Exchange is done between the hours of 10 A.M. and 3 P.M., New York time, Monday through Friday, and 10 A.M. to noon on Saturdays except in the summer.

What is the New York Stock Exchange? Physically, it is a large area, about two-thirds the size of a football field, in the Stock Exchange building at the corner of Wall and Broad Streets in New York City. Functionally, it is an organization consisting of 1,375 members who have bought memberships (commonly called "seats") on the Exchange.

Many of these members represent brokerage firms whose primary business is carrying out the orders of other people, the public generally, for the purchase or sale of securities. They are paid commissions for executing these orders for their customers. To provide service for investors throughout the country, these firms maintain many branch offices. All told, there are 609 member firms of the Stock Exchange that operate 936 branch offices in 370 cities. *This* firm alone has 98 offices in 96 cities.

What Is the Stock Exchange?

The Exchange is a voluntary association, as it has been since it was established 157 years ago, and it functions as an open auction market.

Before the Exchange agrees to list the securities of any company, it must be assured that the company is a substantial concern, that its securities are legally issued, that those securities are widely owned, and that the company agrees to issue regularly adequate public statements of its financial health.

Only member brokers can execute orders to buy or sell listed securities on the Exchange. If you give an order to someone who is not part of a New York Stock Exchange broker's organization, he turns that order over to a member broker. In such circumstance, you may be charged a small commission or service fee over and above the commission to the member broker.

What About Unlisted Stocks?

The New York Stock Exchange or "Big Board" is the biggest formal market for stocks and bonds, but there are thousands of security issues which aren't traded on that Exchange. Many are traded on the 24 other exchanges, such as the New York Curb Exchange, the Chicago Stock Exchange, or the Los Angeles Stock Exchange.

Still other stocks and bonds aren't listed on any exchange. These securities are called unlisted or off board securities; they are traded in what is popularly called the over-the-counter market. Government and municipal bonds are mainly traded in that market. So are the stocks of most banks and insurance companies, as well as the securities of many big corporations such as Time, Inc., Texas Eastern Transmission Corp., and the Weyerhaeuser Timber Co. By and large, however, unlisted securities are those of small companies that are apt to be better known locally than nationally.

They are bought and sold not only by many brokers who are members of the New York Stock Exchange but also by thousands of local security dealers.

Suppose a man in New York owns some stock in an Ohio machinery company and he wants to sell it. He doesn't know what it's worth because there is no regular market for that stock, and its price may not be published in the newspaper, as New York Stock Exchange prices are in many papers.

He goes to his broker, and the broker may ask for a price quotation by phone or wire from other brokers or security dealers who trade entirely in unlisted securities. He may find that the best bid for the stock is $23, while the lowest that anybody else is willing to sell it for is $25. If the stock is traded very frequently, the difference between bid and offer prices may be less. If it is almost unknown, the broker may have a hard time finding a market at any price. In this transaction, the broker acts as an agent and is paid a commission. However, in many over-the-counter transactions, the broker or dealer will buy the security himself, or he will sell such a security out of the supply of such stocks that he owns. In such trades, the dealer acts as a principal instead of as an agent, and the customer and the dealer agree on what is a fair *net price*, which includes a return to the dealer in place of a commission. In the end, the dealer may gain or lose on such transactions.

Merrill Lynch handles over-the-counter transactions either as a principal or an agent *as the customer chooses*. If a transaction is handled on a *commission* basis, it is the policy of this firm to charge commission rates that are even lower than those that now prevail on New York Stock Exchange transactions. If we handle such transactions on a *net* basis, we believe our price will be as low (if you're buying) or as high (if you're selling) as any you are likely to find. Further, we will trade only those stocks on a *net price* basis whose quality has been approved by our Research Division.

Who May Buy Stocks and Bonds?

Anybody – or perhaps we should say any honest and responsible citizen. For their own protection, brokers have to be sure about the responsibility of their customers because they accept oral orders to buy or sell. You'll find it a relatively simple matter to establish your reliability with a broker and to open an account.

Many potential investors haven't bought stocks and bonds simply because they don't know how to go about it. Some may have hesitated simply because they don't know a broker. They may even have thought of him as a somewhat unapproachable individual. He isn't. You can walk into any brokerage office in America without leave.

Finally, a lot of people probably have the idea that brokers only do business with people who invest thousands or tens of thousands of dollars at a time. Well, in our 98 offices we're proud to do business with people who talk in hundreds of dollars as well as people who deal in four and five figures. Last year, we found that 41% of our customers had incomes of less than $5,000 a year. At the other end of the scale were some who counted their income in hundreds of thousands. So you see, regardless of how big a customer you are, you'll always be welcome in any Merrill Lynch office.

But not everybody should buy stocks and bonds. We have consistently said that nobody should invest in the stock market unless he has savings sufficient to meet an emergency. And he should have insurance to protect his family. Then if he has surplus funds, he can probably invest them in stocks or bonds to his advantage.

You can tell your broker just as little or as much as you want to about your money problems, but whatever you tell him will be held in strict confidence.

Frankly, we hope you will want to tell us enough so that we can help you work out an investment program that will best fit your needs.

Does that mean that we will tell you how to invest your money? This is a point we want to make absolutely clear, for it involves a fundamental Merrill Lynch principle. Certainly, we'll try to help you if you want us to – if you *ask* for our advice and counsel. But we will not give you *unasked* advice; we will not foist our opinions or our recommendations upon you. What you buy or sell is your own business. We don't want to be accused of trying to make up your mind for you.

This firm spends about a million dollars a year in preparing and distributing to investors factual information about securities.

We'll give you all the facts and figures we have on any stock or bond you are interested in. There'll be no charge for them. We *want* you to have them – before you buy and *after* you buy. If you ask us, we'll even tell you how we think those facts and figures add up in terms of your own investment needs.

But in the end, the *decision is yours*. That's what we mean when we say

"Investigate . . . then Invest."

How to Buy and Sell Securities

How Do You Do Business with a Broker?

Here is what actually happens when a customer – let's call him Kenneth Smith – comes into our office, at 70 Pine Street to place an order for a hundred shares of Typical Manufacturing Company.

Mr. Smith goes directly to the desk of the man who regularly handles his business. (We'll call him John Ross.) Ross is registered with the New York Stock Exchange, which means that he is qualified as a man of good character and has passed an examination on the operation of the securities business. He is an employee of ours, with the title in our firm of "account executive." He's a man who thoroughly knows his business.

Smith might ask Ross for information about Typical Manufacturing from our Securities Research Division, and discuss the findings with him. But in this instance Smith has already checked on the company and knows that he wants to buy 100 shares of common stock. So he gets right down to business.

"What's Typical selling at now?" he asks.

If Typical Manufacturing were one of the major companies, Smith wouldn't have to ask, for he could look at the big electric quotation board which automatically shows the price at which the last previous sale was made. It also shows the high and low prices for the day and the closing price on the preceding day. The quote board in our 70 Pine Street office provides that information on 209 leading stocks, but Typical isn't among them.

"Sorry, I don't know the quote", says Ross, "but I'll let you know in a minute". Ross knows he can get that quote by a quick phone call, and the account executives in any of our 96 out-of-town offices can give equally good service by using the leased teletype wires that connect direct to our New York headquarters.

While Smith waits, he looks at the Trans Lux screen on which the ticker tape is projected to see if any sales of Typical are being reported right then. When a stock is sold on the Exchange floor, that transaction is reported on the tape. The price is shown and the number of shares involved in the sale. Because there are so many transactions, it is necessary to use a kind of shorthand, and the various stocks are referred to by initials or combinations of letters, such as C for Chrysler Corporation, CP for Canadian Pacific, and CGW for Chicago Great Western.

"Typical is quoted at 25 bid, 25¼ asked", says Ross in a minute or so. By that he means that $25 a share is the highest price that anyone is then willing to pay for it and that $25.25 is the lowest at which anyone is willing to sell it.

"Shall I place your order at the market?" he asks. A *market order* is one for immediate execution at the best price that prevails when the order reaches the floor of the Exchange, regardless of how the price may have changed – up or down a fraction of a point, sometimes more – in the interval between the time the order is placed and the time it can be filled.

Smith agrees. His order is immediately phoned over to one of our booths on the floor of the Exchange. There one of our floor brokers goes to the trading post at which Typical is bought or sold. There are 18 such posts on the floor of the Exchange, and at each of them a certain number of stocks are regularly traded.

At the trading post, our broker asks what the market is. Other brokers with orders to buy or sell Typical Manufacturing make their bids or offers in an audible voice. Secret transactions are not permitted on the Exchange floor.

Our broker immediately fills Smith's order at the lowest price at which the stock is offered, and Ross is advised by phone that the order has been filled.

The whole operation may have taken only two or three minutes. Smith may still be in the office. If he is, Ross will tell him that the purchase has been completed. If he is gone, Ross will telephone him.

As a matter of fact, most of our customers are apt to place their orders and handle all their business on the phone. Others do it wholly by mail. *It isn't necessary for a customer to come into the office at all to place an order.*

A customer can, if he wants, set the price that he is willing to pay. This is called a *limit order*. Smith might tell us, for instance, to buy Typical only if it could be bought at 24½. Further, he might say that any such order is good for a day, a week, a month, or indefinitely. Then if Typical is offered at 24½ within the time that Smith has set, his order to buy is executed, unless there are other similar orders on file that have precedence. Of course, the price of Typical might move right on up to 26 or 27. In such case, Smith would have lost his chance to buy at 25 or thereabouts. That's why any decision to buy that turns exclusively on the probable gain of a fraction of a point is apt not to be a good decision for most investors.

Limit orders can also be used in reverse – in selling stock. Thus, if Smith *owned* Typical, he might tell us to sell his stock for him, if we could, at 26.

How Big Does an Order Have to Be?

One hundred shares – a "round lot" – is the usual unit of trading on the New York Stock Exchange. But that doesn't mean that a customer can only buy or sell a hundred shares at a time. Many people want to buy only 5 or 10 or 25 shares at a time. These are called odd lots.

Suppose Smith wanted to buy only 10 shares of Typical. When we get that order we would fill it through an odd-lot dealer whose business it is to buy or sell in less than 100-share units. Such odd-lot dealers do business only with other brokers on the Stock Exchange floor, not with the public.

For rendering their service they charge one-eighth of a point or 12½c for every share of stock that they buy or sell to fill odd-lot orders for the customers of other brokers.

Apart from that extra eighth, odd-lot dealers don't charge any more for the stock that they sell than the price prevailing in the general market. On a 10-share order for Typical, Smith would pay that price which prevailed on the *next round-lot sale* after our broker gives Smith's order to the odd-lot dealer. Suppose the next sale was at 25. Smith would pay 25 per share, plus ⅛ for the odd-lot dealer, or 25⅛. If Smith were selling the stock, he would sell at 25, less ⅛ for the odd-lot dealer, or 24⅞.

What Does It Cost to Buy or Sell Stocks?

All transactions on the Stock Exchange are handled by member firms at reasonable commissions. The rates vary with the size of the order, being a little less proportionally on big orders than on small ones. At the present time, however, commissions on stock transactions average only 0.85 of 1%. On bonds the average commission is even less.

New York State and the federal government also levy transfer taxes on security sales or transfers, but these involve only a few pennies a share.

When Smith gets our bill the next day, it will state exactly what he bought, what price was paid, what commission is due, what postage or a tax, if any, is incurred, and what total amount is due. We do not make any charge for special services, such as research or information or carrying an inactive account or safe-keeping of securities, etc.

After Smith pays his bill – probably by check – he can obtain his stock certificate which shows that so many shares of Typical Manufacturing Co. have been registered in his name and that he is entitled to all rights, privileges, and dividends due stockholders in that company. But Smith, like an increasing number of our customers, may find it more convenient to leave the certificate in safe-keeping with us. That way he has protection against losing the certificate, and it is right here whenever the time comes that he wants to sell the stock. He will thus be relieved of the responsibility of personally delivering it at such time.

"WHAT'S THIS? . . . WHAT'S THAT?"

This isn't the *complete* story of how to buy stocks and bonds, of course. That would take volumes.

All we have tried to do here is set down answers to some of the most common questions that are asked us. And we have excluded a lot of things many people are curious about but that bear little relation to a program of prudent investment for *most* people.

For instance, there's "short selling", which simply means reversing the normal procedure – selling a stock first in the belief that it is overpriced, then buying it back at what you hope is a lower price.

Or maybe you'd like to know about buying "on margin", which means buying partly on credit.

In the main, these procedures are not important to the investor. But we'll be glad to tell you anything more you want to know.

Other market terms such as "rights", "ex-dividend", "stock splits", "debentures", "noncumulative preferred", "stop orders", and dozens of others we've had to omit simply for lack of space, but an understanding of them isn't likely to be important to most investors, except in occasional cases.

Again, for lack of space, we have not defined a whole host of financial terms that you are likely to encounter when you begin investigating various companies.

These terms are defined in a booklet, "How to Invest", which we have just published. A basic guidebook for all security owners, this new publication develops in greater detail the story of how this stock and bond business works. It reviews the basic principles of sound investing, such as the analysis of market trends, the diversification of holdings, and the management of a portfolio. We will be glad to send you a copy.

Copies of this advertisement in pamphlet form are available on request.
No charge, no obligation. Just write or phone . . .

MERRILL LYNCH, PIERCE, FENNER & BEANE

Underwriters and Distributors of Investment Securities
Brokers in Securities and Commodities

10 Post Office Square
BOSTON 9

Telephone: HUbbard 2-5700

Viyella robe by State o' Maine; breakfast-set by Wedgwood.

See The Conquering Hero Comes—in a Viyella® Robe!

Sound the trumpets, beat the drums, see the conquering hero comes—dressed to the nines in a Viyella robe, and armed with Sunday breakfast for his deserving bride. The superb thing about a Viyella bathrobe is that you can *wash* it. If it shrinks, we replace. Lamby-soft Viyella (rhymes with hi-fella) wears for *years*. A customer who bought a Viyella shirt eleven years ago tells us that he has had it washed and cleaned more than sixty times. "The colors are just as bright and distinct as when it was new . . . the only casualty throughout the years has been the loss of two buttons." Viyella robes (like the one our hero is wearing) come in authentic tartans, tattersalls, checks, stripes and plain colors. They weigh only 21 ounces and can be packed in your brief case next time you travel. $28.50 at fine stores everywhere. For the name of your nearest retailer write William Hollins & Company, Inc., 347 Madison Avenue, New York 17, New York. MU 4-7330.

Left and below *For some years I used this layout in all my magazine advertisements. It gives a large photograph, a headline up to nine words, and 240 words of copy. Recommended when your illustration is to carry the main load of selling.*

Below right *This is my second perfect layout. It gives a wide, shallow photograph, a headline up to 20 words, a subhead up to 28 words, four or five cross-heads and 600 words of body copy. Recommended when your copy is more important than your illustration.*

2 Claude Hopkins wrote an advertisement for Schlitz beer with five pages of solid text. In a few months, Schlitz moved from fifth in sales to first.

3 I wrote 700 words for Good Luck margarine. Sales responded.

4 My first ad for Puerto Rico contained 600 words (signed by Beardsley Ruml but written by me). Fourteen thousand readers sent in the coupon, and scores of them built factories in Puerto Rico.

5 A series of newspaper ads for Shell carried 800 words. Twenty-six per cent of men read more than half of them, and Shell's share of the market reversed a seven-year decline.

6 My partner Francis X. Houghton wrote an advertisement for US Trust which contained 4,750 words. It was a success.

7 In advertisements for Ogilvy & Mather, I used 2,500 words. They brought in a lot of new business.

8 In an advertisement for the World Wildlife Fund, I used 3,232 words.

9 In a series for Morgan Guaranty, I used 800 words. They did the bank a lot of good.

The ship you see is the *Carinthia*, Cunard Steam-Ship Company Limited

Unloading Schweppes elixir on Pier 92

ABOVE YOU SEE Commander Edward Whitehead, President of Schweppes U.S.A., welcoming still another cargo of Schweppes elixir to America.

The Commander imports this precious essence from England, to make sure that every drop of Schweppes Tonic bottled in America has the original flavor. The *curiously refreshing* flavor that has made Schweppes famous all over the world as the authentic Gin-and-Tonic mixer.

Says Commander Whitehead: "It took the House of Schweppes more than a century to bring Schweppes Tonic to its bittersweet perfection. And to develop Schweppervescence, the patrician little bubbles that always last *your whole drink through.*"

But it will take you only seconds to mix Gin or Vodka with Schweppes and enjoy the delicious results.

P.S. Add this new drink to your Schweppertory: a jigger of Dry Vermouth over ice and Schweppes Tonic. Tastes almost like champagne!

Street scene in Paris. You can fly there on KLM and see 5 other cities at no extra fare.

What you should know about KLM and the careful, <u>reliable</u> Dutch before your next flight to Paris, Rome, Amsterdam or 34 other cities in Europe

KLM Royal Dutch Airlines have had more years of experience than any other airline. Founded in 1919, KLM is literally the world's <u>first</u> airline. Read 15 other reasons why so many experienced travelers believe that the dependable, punctual Dutch have made KLM the most <u>reliable</u> of all airlines.

1. KLM flies an average of 133,000 miles *every* day. The equivalent of five times around the world. Or about halfway to the moon.

2. KLM's total route network is 168,000 miles. KLM can fly you to *37 cities in Europe* alone.

3. KLM was the first European airline to be authorized by the U.S. Federal Aviation Agency to overhaul planes for U.S. airlines without further inspection.

4. Every KLM Royal 8 Jet has no less than *seven* navigational systems.

Three pilots

5. All KLM jets flying across the Atlantic carry *three* pilots, one flight engineer and radar which lets the captain see the weather 150 miles ahead.

6. Some groups who have *chartered* KLM planes in recent years are the New York City Ballet, Vienna State Opera, Boston Symphony Orchestra, New York Philharmonic Orchestra, and the entire cast of "My Fair Lady."

7. Every KLM stewardess *must* speak Dutch, English, French and German. Some actually speak 7 or 8 languages.

8. A KLM stewardess walks *8 miles* on a trip to Europe. A delighted passenger from New York recently wrote to KLM: "The friendly, courteous and solicitous attention of your hostesses was all that anyone could hope for."

9. A typical first-class menu on a KLM jet reads like this: Caviar Frais sur Socle, Cocktail de Homard, Pamplemousse au Sherry, Crème de Volaille, Tournedos Maître d'Hôtel, Côtelettes d'Agneau, Biscuit Glacé, Fromages Divers, Fruits de Saison.

10. The cabin of a KLM Royal 8 Jet gets a fresh supply of air every three minutes. It is air-conditioned on the ground as well as in the air.

11. KLM loves babies. Every KLM plane carries a "baby box" with ointments, oils, powder and baby soap.

12. At Amsterdam Airport you can buy cameras, watches, perfumes and 150 brands of liquor at a fraction of the U.S. prices. Even tax-free European cars—at savings up to $3,000. What you save may pay for your entire trip.

13. Not all airlines offer you a choice of jet *and* propeller flights. KLM does. The advantage: round-trip economy class fares cost *$36 less* on a DC-7C.

Paris—$53 down

14. You can fly to Paris for only $53 down (round-trip jet economy class fare), and take two years to pay the balance with KLM's pay-later plan.

15. Ask your travel agent to explain the full possibilities of stopovers on your next KLM trip. Example: Your ticket to Paris will also take you to Brussels, Amsterdam, London, Manchester and Glasgow—*at no extra fare.*

For information, see your travel agent, call KLM or mail coupon.

KLM Royal Dutch Airlines
609 Fifth Ave., New York 17. Tel: PLaza 9-3600
Please send comprehensive color portfolio, "Europe in the palm of your hand."

Name _____

Address _____

City _____ Zone ___ State ___

(Name of your travel agent)

I could give you countless other examples of long copy which has made the cash register ring, notably for Mercedes cars. Not only in the United States, but all over the world.

I believe, without any research to support me, that advertisements with long copy convey the impression that you have *something important to say*, whether people read the copy or not.

After studying the results of advertising for retailers, Dr. Charles Edwards concluded that 'the more facts you tell, the more you sell.' An advertisement's chance for success invariably increases as the number of pertinent merchandise facts included in the advertisement increases.

Direct-response advertisers *know* that short copy doesn't sell. In split-run tests, long copy invariably outsells short copy.

But I must warn you that if you want your long copy to be *read*, you had better write it well. In particular, your first paragraph should be a grabber. You won't hold many readers if you begin with a mushy statement of the obvious like this one in an ad for a vacation resort: 'Going on vacation is a pleasure to which everyone looks forward.'

A Harvard professor used to begin his series of lectures with a sentence that took his students by the throat: 'Cesare Borgia murdered his brother-in-law for the love of his sister, who was the mistress of their father – the Pope.'

How to become a good copywriter

It is no bad thing to learn the craft of advertising by copying your elders and betters. Helmut Krone, one of the most innovative of art directors, has said: 'I asked one of our writers recently what was more important, doing your own thing or making the ad as good as it can be. The answer was, "Doing my own thing". I disagree violently with that. I'd like to propose a new idea for our age: until you've got a better answer, you *copy*. I copied Bob Gage for 5 years, I even copied the leading between his lines of type. And Bob originally copied Paul Rand, and Rand first copied a German typographer named Tschichold.'

I, too, started by copying. Working in a London agency, I used to copy the best American ads. Later, I began to do my own thing.

Layouts

Advertising suffers from sporadic epidemics of Artdirectoritis. Those afflicted with this disease speak in hushed voices of 'cool grey bands of type,' as if the copy in advertisements was a mere *design* element. They extol the importance of 'movement,' 'balance' and other mysterious principles of design. I tell them KISS – an acronym for Keep It Simple, Stupid.

In the early days of Ogilvy & Mather I used the same, simple layout for all our advertisements in magazines. (See 86 and 87.) Later, when a competitor accused me of foisting a house-style on all our clients, I invented a second layout which allowed space for more copy. I challenge you to invent a better layout than these.

Readers look first at the illustration, then at the headline, then at the copy. So put these elements in that order – illustration at the top, headline under the illustration, copy under the headline. This follows the normal order of scanning, which is from top to bottom. If you put the headline *above* the illustration, you are asking people to scan in an order which does not fit their habit.

On the average, headlines *below* the illustration are read by 10 per cent more people than headlines *above* the illustration. You may not think the difference worth writing about, but consider the fact that 10 per cent of, say, 20,000,000 readers is *two million*. Not to be sneezed at. Yet in 59 per cent of magazine advertisements the headlines are *above*.

Some dopes even put their headline at the bottom, under the copy!

More people read the captions under illustrations than read the body copy, so never use an illustration without putting a caption under it. Your caption should include the brand name and the promise.

Advertising people have an unconscious belief that advertise-

When you have to communicate a lot of different sales points, use 'call-outs'. They are above average in recall tests.

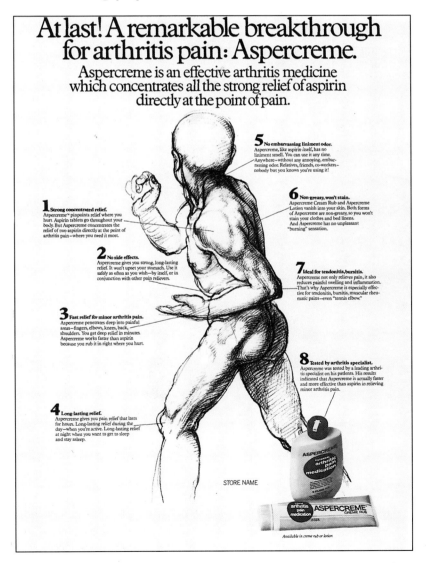

ments have to *look* like advertisements. They have inherited graphic conventions which telegraph to the reader, 'This is only an advertisement. *Skip it.*'

There is no law which says that advertisements have to look like advertisements. If you make them look like editorial pages, you will attract more readers. Roughly six times as many people read the average article as the average advertisement. Very few advertisements are read by more than one reader in twenty. I conclude that editors communicate better than admen.

Look at the news magazines which have been successful in attracting readers: *Time* and *Newsweek* in the United States, *L'Express* and *Le Point* in France, *Der Spiegel* in Germany, *L'Espresso* in Italy, *Cambio 16* in Spain. They all use the same graphics:

○ Copy has priority over illustration.

○ The copy is set in *serif* type.

○ Three columns of type, 35 to 45 characters wide.

○ Every photograph has a caption.

○ The copy starts with drop-initials.

○ The type is set black on white.

Below left *Pierre Lemonnier and Philippe Saalburg at the FCB-IMPACT agency in Paris pinched my 'editorial' layouts and improved them. Their ads don't look like ads.*

Below right *All news magazines use the same format. Copy has priority over illustration. Three columns of type, set in serif faces. Captions under photographs. But the advertisements in these magazines do not follow any of these conventions, so very few people read them. Next time you construct an ad, pretend you are an editor; you will get more readership.*

Un foie gras qui a valu à Prédault le Prix de la gastronomie au Salon international de l'alimentation, Paris 1976.

Le foie gras frais entier au naturel
de Paul Prédault

Now look at the advertisements in the same magazines. You will see that:

○ Illustrations are given priority over copy.

○ The copy is often set in *sanserif*, which is hard to read; we are accustomed to serifs in books, magazines and newspapers.

○ The copy is often set in one column of 120 characters or more – too wide to be readable.

○ Few of the photographs have captions, because the art directors are not aware that four times as many people read captions as read body copy.

○ There are very few drop-initials, because the art directors are not aware that they increase readership.

○ The copy is frequently set in reverse – white on black. I have even seen *coupons* in reverse; you cannot fill them out unless you have white ink in the house.

If you pretend you are an editor, you will get better results. When the magazine insists that you slug your ads with the word *advertisement*, set it

Below *Only use two-page spreads when you have a long product and need to show it horizontally, as with this hammer. If you swear off the self-indulgence of spreads, you will be able to buy twice as many ads, thereby doubling your reach or your frequency.*

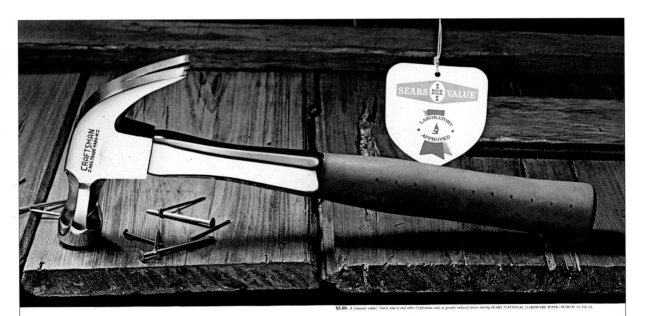

$5.00. *A fantastic value! You'll find it and other Craftsman tools at greatly reduced prices during SEARS NATIONAL HARDWARE WEEK—MARCH 14 TO 23.*

A new hammer free if this Sears Four-Star Value ever breaks

This hammer is a Sears, Roebuck and Co. Four-Star Value. It is unconditionally guaranteed to give satisfaction or Sears will replace. This is just one reason the hammer is a Sears Four-Star Value. Read 8 other reasons.

THERE are over 200,000 items in the Sears Catalog. Each is an excellent value or it wouldn't be there. But one out of every 1,400 of these items is a *fantastic* value. It is called a Sears Four-Star Value. This means it has been picked by a jury of 21 hyper-critical Sears merchants, to represent the *141 most amazing values* at Sears.

The jury picked the hammer in the picture to be a Four-Star Value. The verdict was based upon this evidence:

1. Like a golf club, baseball bat, or tennis racket, this Sears hammer was designed with the correct feel, weight, and *balance* to give it maximum striking force at impact.

2. This is the only hammer made with reinforced claws. Thirty men together could not apply enough pressure to break them.

3. A "V"-shaped nail slot in the edge of the left claw lets you pull out nails in tight corners where ordinary hammers are useless.

4. The striking face is machined and crowned to hit the nail *squarely*. It is beveled to minimize chipping.

5. The steel head was drop-forged for enormous strength. A jet aircraft's landing gear is drop-forged for the same reason.

6. The Sears laboratory reports the tubular steel handle of this hammer withstood forces that *broke* all other handles tested.

7. A patented hickory plug assembly is inside the steel handle. This assembly absorbs shock and locks the head to the handle.

8. The neoprene grip is permanently bonded to the handle. It is resistant to oil and grease, and will not conduct electricity.

The Sears hammer costs $5.00. If you buy it, you will never have to buy another one unless you lose it. It is one of the most outstanding values you can find – at Sears or anywhere else in the world. And remember, you can always charge it at Sears.

When you are at Sears during Sears National Hardware Week (March 14 to March 23) look for the Four-Star Value seal. It's the fastest way to *shop at Sears and save.*

in italic caps, in reverse. Then nobody can read it.

The FCB-Impact agency in Paris consistently produces better magazine advertisements than any other agency, *and none of them look like advertisements*. Hats off to Pierre Lemonnier, the copywriter who is Impact, and Philippe Saalburg who was his art director for many years. They pinched my techniques and improved them.

If you abandon the conventional graphics of advertisements and adopt editorial graphics, your campaigns will become islands of good taste in an ocean of vulgarity.

*　*　*　*　*

Layouts are often pinned up on bulletin boards at meetings and approved at a distance of 15 feet, as if they were posters. This leads to setting headlines in 72-point, which is impossible to read at the normal distance of 20 inches.

Are two-page spreads worth the cost? They cost twice as much as single

Right *Editorial graphics also work well in newspapers. I made this launch ad for Guinness look like the front page of a newspaper.*

Opposite left *This looks like an editorial page in the French newspaper* Le Monde. *Actually it is an advertisement on behalf of French sheep farmers who opposed the importation of duty-free mutton from England.*

Opposite right *This front-page format is particularly appropriate for the announcement of a new product.*

Opposite below *A superb example of FCB-Impact's editorial style, this time for Mumm champagne.*

Alain Chapel,
paysan de la grande cuisine

S I JE CONTINUE à recevoir des photographes, je n'aurai plus le temps de faire la cuisine...»

Allons bon, cela commence mal. Chapel aurait-il, lui aussi, des coquetteries de vedette?..

Un silence : nous doutons un instant. Mais non... Voici que Chapel reprend : « A 35 ans, j'ai voulu faire du sensationnel. Aujourd'hui, je veux simplement être simple. »

Simplement être simple : il n'en dira pas plus ce premier soir...

Racines

Au matin, sous les arcades du jardin, un Cordon Rouge 75 relance les confidences. Nemo, le grand labrador noir, est venu là, en témoin. Le saule, complètement échevelé, disperse ses feuilles jusque sur la nappe. « Le vent des Dombes, explique Chapel... »

Il parle des Dombes, son pays. De Mionnay, qu'il ne quitte guère. De David, son fils nouveau-né, dont les premiers cris à la vie l'empêchent - mais cela le ravit - de dormir les quelques heures qu'il ne consacre pas à son restaurant. Ce sont là ses racines. Nous devinons qu'elles sont trop profondes pour lui donner envie de céder aux appels du pied de l'étranger. Paysan de la grande cuisine, Chapel n'a pas une âme de fugueur.

Une gelée de pigeonneau et des petites fanes de persil frites font bifurquer la conversation. La nouvelle cuisine aujourd'hui ? A force de vouloir se renouveler, la voilà tombée dans la manie de la recherche pour la recherche : Chapel sait que sa vérité à lui est ailleurs.

Un Cordon Rouge pour les « instants fériés »

Le champagne, pour Alain Chapel, c'est d'abord le vin de la fête. Mais la fête, ce peut être aussi bien un instin à 11 heures, qu'à cœur de la nuit. Ce peut être la présence de la femme que l'on aime, ou l'arrivée d'un ami, ou simplement le plaisir d'avoir couru la campagne avec Nemo, le labrador.

Pour ces « instants fériés », Chapel débouche un Cordon Rouge de Mumm. En bon bourguignon, il apprécie que le Cordon Rouge soit d'abord un grand vin, dont chaque millésime raconte les humeurs de la vigne...

Ailleurs, tout près : dans la « sincérité » des produits, rien de plus. « Le produit seul est la vedette », répète Chapel dans son livre*. Sans doute. Ajoutons tout de même, puisqu'il ne lui dit pas, que toute vedette a besoin d'un metteur en scène. Dans ses cuisines-coulisses, Chapel sait comment faire jouer juste les ombles chevaliers, les poulardes de Bresse et les petits légumes nouveaux...

Demandez à la terre

Et où trouve-t-on, aujourd'hui, les poulardes et les petits légumes ? Ici, tout près... Détaillant les bulles du Cordon Rouge, Chapel affirme que la terre, autour de Mionnay, n'a pas changé. Elle peut encore tout faire pousser. Il faut simplement savoir le faire : il cultive pour Mionnay des légumes si jeunes et frais qu'on en mange les fanes. Avec lui et quelques autres - de Marinette la fermière à Pierre Ramonet, vigneron-seigneur de Chassagne-Montrachet - Chapel a sa confrérie de jardiniers, partageant la même foi.

Cela ne l'empêche pas d'être là, tôt le matin, l'œil vert aux aguets. Car à Mionnay, la vérité ne sort pas seulement de l'assiette : elle s'exprime dans chaque détail. Jusqu'aux pivoines et lupins des champs qui viennent fleurir les tables.

Les hôtes de Chapel comprennent le langage des fleurs, cela est sûr : de janvier à décembre, sa maison ne désemplit pas.

Hélène DELPUECH

« La cuisine, c'est beaucoup plus que des recettes », éditions Robert Laffont.

Restaurant A. Chapel, à Mionnay (Ain).
Michelin
Gault et Millau
Kléber

pages, but seldom get twice the readership, or pull twice as many coupons.

Occasionally there is a functional reason for using a double-spread, as when your product is a long one and has to be shown horizontally. But nine times out of ten, double-spreads are no more than self-indulgence by an art director who wants his advertisements to look big and juicy. If you swear off double-spreads, you will be able to run twice as many advertisements for the same money, thereby doubling your reach or your frequency.*

Posters

For better or worse, posters are still with us, so I had better tell you what little is known about designing them to maximum effect. There has been little or no research on the subject.

It pays to make your poster what Savignac called a 'visual

Below One in a series of posters that appeared in England during the thirties. They made Guinness part of the warp and woof of English life, and have never been excelled – anywhere.

* This is one of my over-simplifications. Starch finds that *on the average*, two-page spreads achieve only 28 per cent higher rating than single pages, but Edwin Bird Wilson has drawn attention to the fact that two-page spreads for *financial* advertisers achieve an average of 150 per cent more readership than single pages. The readership of ads for *low-interest* products benefits more from big spaces than ads for *high-interest* products.

scandal.' But don't overdo the scandal or you will stop the traffic and cause fatal accidents.

Your poster should deliver your selling promise not only in words, but also pictorially. Use the largest possible type. Make your brand name visible at a long distance. Use strong, pure colors. Never use more than three elements in your design.

If you know more than that, please tell me.

Subway cards

If it falls to you to produce advertisements for the subway, it may help to know that the average rider in the New York subway will be exposed to your advertisement for 21 minutes, which is long enough to read quite a long message. Only 15 per cent of passengers carry anything to read. The other 85 per cent have nothing to do but read your copy.

Trademarks are an anachronism

In olden days, before people could read, manufacturers used trademarks to identify their brands. If you saw a *tiger* on a bottle of beer, you knew it was Tiger beer.

Many companies, unaware that consumers are no longer

Below *It pays to make your poster a 'visual scandal', as in this British example for FCO Univas.*

It also sticks handles to teapots. ARALDITE

Right *Don't make the mistake of designing subway cards to look like billboards – all display and only five or six words. In New York subways, the average rider is exposed to your card for twenty-one minutes and 85 per cent carry nothing else to read. That is why I wrote 76 words for this card.*

How to pay bills quickly, easily

If you still pay bills with <u>cash</u>, you waste hours running around town and standing in line. And you run the risk of losing large sums or meeting a thief. Be smart—open a Special Checking Account at <u>Chase</u>, and pay your bills by <u>mail</u>. A check is permanent proof of payment. You can start your <u>Chase</u> account today. No minimum balance required. No deposit charges.

The CHASE National Bank
(MEMBER FEDERAL DEPOSIT INSURANCE CORP.)

illiterate, still use graphic symbols to identify their brands, and insist on them being displayed in their advertisements. They add to the gadgetry which clutters up layouts, and proclaim 'this is only an advertisement'. *Readership of the advertisement is reduced.*

One of my clients was persuaded that his company's symbol was too old-fashioned and paid a fancy firm $75,000 to design a new one. At the unveiling I whispered to one of the Vice-Presidents, 'A tyro in our art department could have designed a better symbol for $75.' 'No doubt,' he replied, 'but we would have argued it to death.'

Typography – 'the eye is a creature of habit'
Good typography *helps* people read your copy, while bad typography prevents them doing so.

Advertising agencies usually set their headlines in capital letters. This is a mistake. Professor Tinker of Stanford has established that capitals retard reading. They have no ascenders or descenders to help you recognize *words*, and tend to be read *letter by letter.*

The eye is a creature of habit. People are accustomed to reading books, magazines and newspapers in *lower case*. Look how difficult it is to read the all-caps headline in the ABN advertisement opposite.

Another way to make headlines hard to read is to superimpose them on your illustration.

Another mistake is to put a period at the end of headlines. Periods are also called full stops, because they stop the reader dead in his tracks. You will find no full stops at the end of headlines in newspapers.

Yet another common mistake is to set copy in a measure which is too wide or too narrow to be legible. People are accustomed to reading newspapers which are set about 40 characters wide.

Which typefaces are easiest to read? Those which people are *accustomed* to reading, like the Century family, Caslon, Baskerville and Jenson. The more outlandish the typeface, the harder it is to read. The drama belongs in what you say, not in the typeface.

Sanserif faces like this are particularly difficult to read. Says John Updike, 'Serifs exist for a purpose. They help the eye pick up the shape of the letter. Piquant in little amounts, sanserif in page-size sheets repels readership as wax paper repels water; it has a sleazy, cloudy look.'

Some art directors use copy as the raw material for designing queer shapes, thus making it illegible.

In a recent issue of a magazine I found 47 advertisements with the copy set in *reverse* – white type on a black background. It is almost impossible to read.

If you have to set *very long* copy, there are some typographical devices which increase its readership:

1 A subhead of two lines, between your headline and your body copy, heightens the reader's appetite for the feast to come.

2 If you start your body copy with a drop-initial, you increase readership by an average of 13 per cent.

3 Limit your opening paragraph to a maximum of 11 words.

4 After two or three inches of copy, insert a cross-head, and thereafter throughout. Cross-heads keep the reader

Right *Capital letters are extremely difficult to read. I tried to read this advertisement but gave up.*

DOWN TO EARTH

TO KNOW YOUR BANK, KNOW YOUR MAN ı DOWN TO EARTH, DOWN TO BUSINESS ı WE'VE BEEN KNOWN FOR CENTURIES ı CONSISTENT, SOBER, KNOWLEDGEABLE ı VERY DUTCH ı PATIENTLY BUILDING A NETWORK ı OVER 200 FOREIGN BRANCHES, 42 COUNTRIES, 5 CONTINENTS ı AT HOME IN ALL FINANCIAL CENTRES ı ADAPTABLE ı MOVING IN TO STAY ı THE DUTCH BANKER ı OUR TOTAL ASSETS ARE NOW OVER $ 45,000,000,000 ı AND GROWING ı MEET US IN YOUR OWN LANGUAGE ı WHEREVER YOU ARE ı
ABN Bank THE DUTCH BANKER

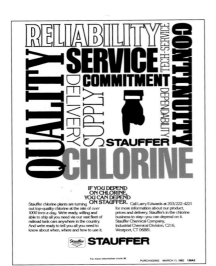

The search for a sweeter cantaloupe

How 10 years of crossbreeding at Burpee produced <u>Ambrosia</u>, the sweetest, juiciest cantaloupe this side of heaven

"This is it!" Burpee vegetable breeder Ted Torrey said, after his first mouth-watering bite of a new hybrid cantaloupe he had developed at Burpee's Foodhook Farm. After the second bite, he put down his spoon and sighed, "A food for the gods."

And so when we named our new hybrid cantaloupe we borrowed from mythology and called it *Ambrosia*—literally a food for the gods. What a treat and surprise you are in for the first time you open and taste one of these extraordinary melons.

Ambrosia is like no other cantaloupe we've ever seen or tasted before. Unbelievably juicy and sweet—each bite dripping with a rare haunting flavor words can't even begin to describe. And the delicious flesh is so smooth and tender you can eat it right down to the thin rind. Although it doesn't grow much larger than 6 inches, the melons average a jumbo 4½ to 5 pounds, because the flesh is so thick and the seed cavities so extremely small.

How Burpee develops superior hybrids for the home gardener

To create a new plant variety, Burpee horticulturists often spend years crosspollinating hundreds of varieties with hundreds of other varieties to find the one superior combination. *Ambrosia* is a perfect example of how new and better hybrids are continually being developed at Burpee's breeding farms.

Over 15 years ago Ted Torrey began his search for a new variety of cantaloupe. One that not only had a lighter, sweeter flavor, and more weight in proportion to its size, but also the increased growing vigor, stamina, and disease resistance of a hybrid for the home gardener.

It took him more than 10 years to find it—crossing and intercrossing over 150 cantaloupe varieties before arriving at *Ambrosia*. After that, the new melon was kept "isolated" for another 5 years, to be sure it would perform well over a variety of seasons, and different weather conditions.

Only then were we finally satisfied that we had found what we first started looking for over 15 years ago, and that *Ambrosia* would meet the high standards we set for everything sold by Burpee.

So plant *Ambrosia* in your garden with confidence—and, only 86 days later, expect a bumper crop of what it took Burpee more than 10 years to accomplish—"A food for the gods."

Available only in Burpee's 1975 Catalog

You won't find *Ambrosia* sold in anyone else's catalog. Only Burpee has it. You'll find it on page 92 in the new 1975 Burpee Garden Catalog. That's also where you'll find many other outstanding Burpee breeding achievements.

So order Burpee seeds now for a bountiful harvest. We *guarantee complete satisfaction, or we'll give you a full cash refund.*

Burpee is America's leading breeder of flowers and vegetables for the home gardener

For nearly a century Burpee has been continually developing new vegetable varieties that are easier to grow and produce more bountiful yields in less space, as well as newer and better flowers. As a result Burpee is America's leading breeder of flowers and vegetables for the home gardener. Many new varieties and famous favorites are available only from Burpee.

If you haven't already received Burpee's 1975 Catalog, write to the nearest address below.

W. ATLEE BURPEE CO. — Quality and service since 1876

5185 Burpee Building • Warminster, Pennsylvania 18974 • Clinton, Iowa 52732 • Riverside, California 92502.

This page *Three examples of typography which makes it impossible to read the copy, and one which makes it easy to read.*

Below and right *The headlines and copy in these advertisements would be easier to read if they had been set* under *the illustration,* instead of *on* it.

marching forward. Make some of them interrogative, to excite curiosity in the next run of copy.

5   When I was a boy, it was common practice to *square up* paragraphs. It is now known that widows – short lines – increase readership.

6   Set key paragraphs in bold face or italic.

7   Help the reader into your paragraphs with arrowheads, bullets, asterisks and marginal marks.

8   If you have a lot of unrelated facts to recite, don't use cumbersome connectives. Simply *number* them – as I am doing here.

Vivre comme Dieu en France.

Oder:
Leben wie Gott in Frankreich. Ein deutscher Ausspruch, in dem immer wieder die Sehnsucht nach der Lebensart unseres französischen Nachbarn schwingt. Zeit und Muße, ein herrliches Essen, ein gutes Glas Wein zu genießen. Zeit und Muße, auch mal über die unwichtigen Dinge des Tages zu reden. Kommen Sie. Essen und trinken Sie ein paar Tage oder Wochen wie Gott in Frankreich. Im Herbst, wenn im nördlichsten Weingebiet, der Champagne, sich die sanften Hügel rot-gelb färben. Und die Weinbauern die reifen Reben für den König edler Getränke ernten, Champagner. Oder kommen Sie hin, wo die Weinbauern fruchtig, trockene Weine nach französischer Art machen und lieben. Wo diese herrlichen Weine nach der Rebsorte benannt werden und die Weinhauptstadt Colmar heißt: im Elsaß. Die trockenen, kräftigen Weine haben alle einen reinen, klaren Geschmack. Zum Beispiel der Riesling, der Sylvaner und der Gewürztraminer. Aber nun verraten wir eigentlich schon fast zuviel. Denn diese, nennen wir sie ruhig Werbeanzeige für Weine aus Frankreich, ist die erste von vielen. In den noch kommenden Anzeigen, die Sie im Laufe des Jahres in dieser Zeitschrift lesen können, schreiben wir über die unterschiedlichsten Weingebiete. Über das Land, das Essen, aber vor allem über die Weine. Wie sie beschaffen sind. Z.B. die aus dem Loire-Tal. Ob trocken oder süßer. Rot, weiß oder rosé. Ob leichter oder schwer. Ob elegant oder rustikal. Wann man sie trinkt, wie man sie trinkt, und vor allem, zu welchem Essen man sie trinkt. Übrigens, bei uns in Deutschland, in den Weingeschäften und den Weinabteilungen der Kaufhäuser finden Sie sehr viele französische Weine. Von den preiswerten Landweinen (Vins de Pays) bis zu den edelsten Tropfen. Und damit Sie sich bald noch besser auskennen, werden wir Ihnen auch einiges über die Qualitätsstufen der Weine, z.B. der Weine aus Burgund, sagen. Und etwas über die ausdrucksvolle und vielseitige Sprache der Weinetiketten. Über die Menschen, die Landschaften, warum z.B. Weine des Gebietes Mâcon zu den würzig und jungen Rot-und Weißweinen zählen, die Sie probieren sollten. Und warum es richtig sein kann, einen jungen Rotwein, einen Beaujolais, mal kühler zu trinken. Das schöne Bordelaiser Hinterland um Bergerac, an der Dordogne, sollten Sie unbedingt kennenlernen. Es gibt hier verschiedene ausgezeichnete Tischweine. Am besten, wenn Sie Bordeaux besuchen, das wohl größte Weinbaugebiet Frankreichs. Hier wurde eine Kochkunst entwickelt, die zu den berühmten und edlen Bordeaux-Weinen paßt. Vollkommen anders wieder sind die Weine aus dem Rhône-Tal. Sandige, kieselsteinhaltige Böden und das sonnige Klima geben den Weinen ihre spezielle Kraft. Den feurigen, würzigen Châteauneuf-du-Pape sollte sich kein Weinkenner entgehen lassen. Übrigens, verwahren Sie dieses Blatt, Sie wissen dann später, wo in Frankreich, ob im Norden, Süden, Westen oder Osten, nun die einzelnen Weingebiete liegen. Ein kleines, aber nicht unwichtiges Gebiet z.B. liegt hier: Gaillac. Eine reizvolle Landschaft mit schönen, kleinen Städten. Die unerbittliche Sonne gibt den Weinen des Languedoc-Roussillon und der Provence ihren Duft, ihre Kraft und ihre besonderes Feuer. Kommen Sie in das Lieblingsland der Franzosen. Lassen Sie sich verwöhnen. Von Sonne und Natur. Von der guten Küche und dem Weinen, von denen Sie sicher jetzt schon träumen. Hier, auf der Sonnen-Insel Korsika, gibt es herrliche, volle, runde Rosé- und Rotweine.

Weine aus Frankreich. Erst kennen, dann lieben. A votre santé.

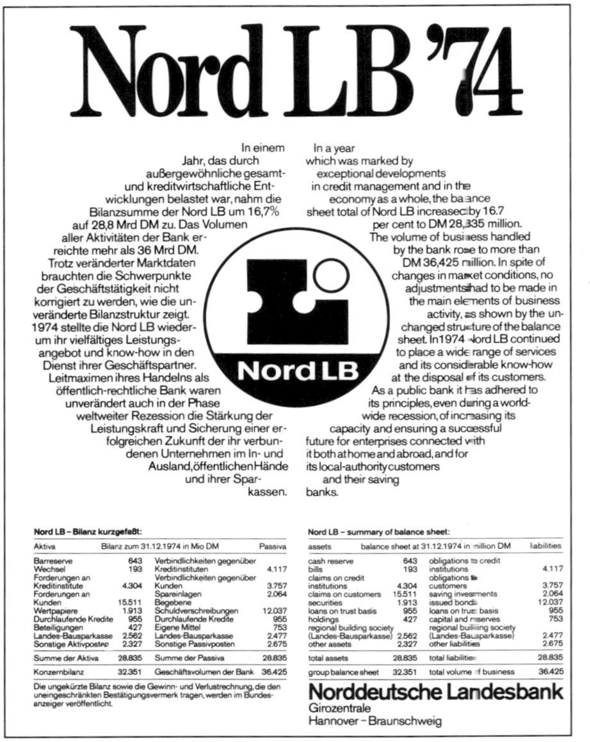

Nord LB '74

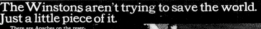

In einem Jahr, das durch außergewöhnliche gesamt- und kreditwirtschaftliche Entwicklungen belastet war, nahm die Bilanzsumme der Nord LB um 16,7% auf 28,8 Mrd DM zu. Das Volumen aller Aktivitäten der Bank erreichte mehr als 36 Mrd DM. Trotz veränderter Marktdaten brauchten die Schwerpunkte der Geschäftstätigkeit nicht korrigiert zu werden, wie die unveränderte Bilanzstruktur zeigt. 1974 stellte die Nord LB wiederum ihr vielfältiges Leistungsangebot und know-how in den Dienst ihrer Geschäftspartner. Leitmaximen ihres Handelns als öffentlich-rechtliche Bank waren unverändert auch in der Phase weltweiter Rezession die Stärkung der Leistungskraft und Sicherung einer erfolgreichen Zukunft der ihr verbundenen Unternehmen im In- und Ausland, öffentlichen Hände und ihrer Sparkassen.

In a year which was marked by exceptional developments in credit management and in the economy as a whole, the balance sheet total of the Nord LB increased by 16.7 per cent to DM 28,335 million. The volume of business handled by the bank rose to more than DM 36,425 million. In spite of changes in market conditions, no adjustments had to be made in the main elements of business activity, as shown by the unchanged structure of the balance sheet. In 1974 Nord LB continued to place a wide range of services and its considerable know-how at the disposal of its customers. As a public bank it has adhered to its principles, even during a world-wide recession, of increasing its capacity and ensuring a successful future for enterprises connected with it both at home and abroad, and for its local-authority customers and their saving banks.

Nord LB – Bilanz kurzgefaßt:

Aktiva	Bilanz zum 31.12.1974 in Mio DM	Passiva	
Barreserve	643	Verbindlichkeiten gegenüber	
Wechsel	193	Kreditinstituten	4.117
Forderungen an		Verbindlichkeiten gegenüber	
Kreditinstitute	4.304	Kunden	3.757
Forderungen an		Spareinlagen	2.064
Kunden	15.511	Begebene	
Wertpapiere	1.913	Schuldverschreibungen	12.037
Durchlaufende Kredite	955	Durchlaufende Kredite	955
Beteiligungen	427	Eigene Mittel	753
Landes-Bausparkasse	2.562	Landes-Bausparkasse	2.477
Sonstige Aktivposten	2.327	Sonstige Passivposten	2.675
Summe der Aktiva	28.835	Summe der Passiva	28.835
Konzernbilanz	32.351	Geschäftsvolumen der Bank	36.425

Die ungekürzte Bilanz sowie die Gewinn- und Verlustrechnung, die den uneingeschränkten Bestätigungsvermerk tragen, werden im Bundesanzeiger veröffentlicht.

Nord LB – summary of balance sheet:

assets	balance sheet at 31.12.1974 in million DM	liabilities	
cash reserve	643	obligations to credit	
bills	193	institutions	4.117
claims on credit		obligations to	
institutions	4.304	customers	3.757
claims on customers	15.511	saving investments	2.064
securities	1.913	issued bonds	12.037
loans on trust basis	955	loans on trust basis	955
holdings	427	capital and reserves	753
regional building society		regional building society	
(Landes-Bausparkasse)	2.562	(Landes-Bausparkasse)	2.477
other assets	2.327	other liabilities	2.675
total assets	28.835	total liabilities	28.835
group balance sheet	32.351	total volume of business	36.425

Norddeutsche Landesbank
Girozentrale
Hannover – Braunschweig

The Winstons aren't trying to save the world. Just a little piece of it.

There are Apaches on the reservation in Clear Fork, Arizona, who can remember the last, hopeless Apache uprising in 1900. But for Della Alakay, a seven-year-old Apache, the enemy is not the U.S. Cavalry.

She and her people are fighting another kind of war. This time the enemies are poverty, disease and despair. And for the first time in generations, there's a chance that the Apaches might win: thanks to the courageous efforts of her own people and other Americans like the Winstons.

Anne and Stan Winston and their two daughters live in a New York suburb 2,000 miles from the reservation. But it's another world. The Winstons live in a big, old house and complain about a big, new mortgage. Their girls have a closetful of clothes and "nothing to wear." They have bikes, skates, games, books, records and "nothing to do."

Della and her seven brothers and sisters have none of these problems. Her father spends as much time looking for work as he does working. Sanitary facilities are almost non-existent. Electricity has yet to reach them. Water is hauled by hand. Even the barest necessities are hard to come by.

Through Save The Children Federation, the Winstons are helping Della. The cost is $15.00 a month. It's not a lot of money, but certainly the Winstons could have thought of a lot of other things to do with it. Fortunately they thought of Della first.

To her, these funds make a remarkable difference. She no longer need feel embarrassed about not having shoes, a decent school dress, school supplies, or pocket money.

Some of the pressure, too, is off her parents, who can now begin thinking about making their home a little more livable. Also, and perhaps most important, part of the money is put into a fund from which the village can borrow to start self-help projects, including better housing and a water system.

Already there is a new feeling of hope among the villagers and confidence in their ability to help themselves. Even little Della has volunteered to give some time each week to keep her school playground clean.

That really is what Save The Children is all about. Although contributions are deductible as a charity, the aim is not merely to buy one child a few hot meals or a warm coat. Instead, your contribution is used to give people a little boost to start helping themselves.

Sponsors are desperately needed for other American Indian children as well as children in Appalachia, Korea, Vietnam, Latin America, Africa and Greece.

As a sponsor you will receive a photo and history of the child, progress reports and a chance to correspond.

The Winstons know they can't save the world for $15.00 a month. Only a small corner of it. But maybe that is the way to save the world. If there are enough people who care. How about you?

Save The Children Federation, founded in 1932, is registered with the U.S. State Department Advisory Committee on Voluntary Foreign Aid, and is a member of the International Union of Child Welfare. Financial statements and annual reports available on request.

National Sponsors (partial list): Claude Arpels, Faith Baldwin, Hon. James A. Farley, Andy Griffith, Gene Kelly, Mrs. Eli Lilly, Paul Newman, Mrs. J.C. Penney, Norman Rockwell, Frank Sinatra

Save The Children Federation
NORWALK, CONNECTICUT 06852
☐ I WISH TO CONTRIBUTE $180 ANNUALLY TO HELP A CHILD.
☐ WHERE THE NEED IS GREATEST ☐ LATIN AMERICA
☐ AMERICAN INDIAN ☐ APPALACHIA ☐ KOREA ☐ GREECE
☐ VIETNAM ☐ AFRICA
ENCLOSED IS MY FIRST PAYMENT
☐ $15.00 MONTHLY ☐ $45.00 QUARTERLY
☐ $90.00 SEMI-ANNUALLY ☐ $180.00 ANNUALLY
☐ I CAN'T SPONSOR A CHILD. ENCLOSED IS A CONTRIBUTION OF $____.
☐ PLEASE SEND ME MORE INFORMATION.
NAME ____
ADDRESS ____
CITY ____ STATE ____ ZIP ____
CONTRIBUTIONS ARE INCOME TAX DEDUCTIBLE. SBA 2/21/0

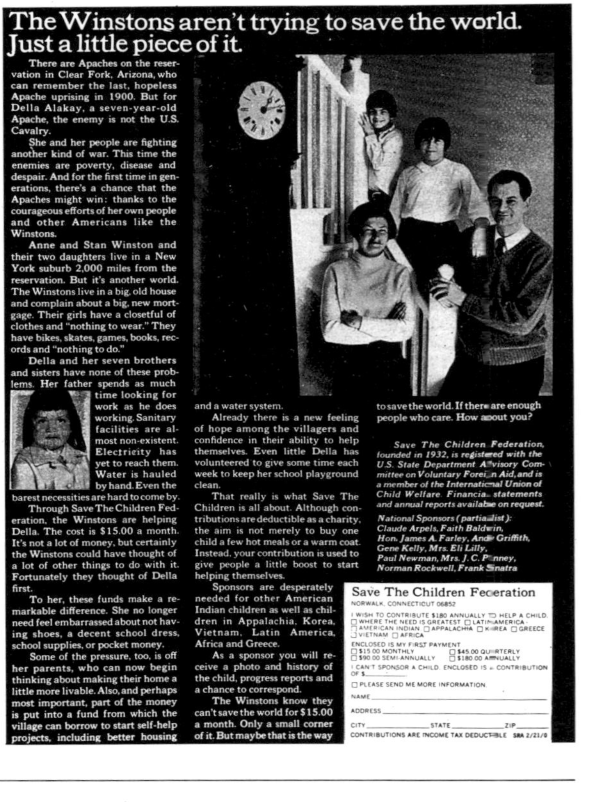

The Winstons aren't trying to save the world. Just a little piece of it.

There are Apaches on the reservation in Clear Fork, Arizona, who can remember the last, hopeless Apache uprising in 1900. But for Della Alakay, a seven-year-old Apache, the enemy is not the U.S. Cavalry.

She and her people are fighting another kind of war. This time the enemies are poverty, disease and despair. And for the first time in generations, there's a chance that the Apaches might win: thanks to the courageous efforts of her own people and other Americans like the Winstons.

Anne and Stan Winston and their two daughters live in a New York suburb 2,000 miles from the reservation. But it's another world. The Winstons live in a big, old house and complain about a big, new mortgage. Their girls have a closetful of clothes and "nothing to wear." They have bikes, skates, games, books, records and "nothing to do."

Della and her seven brothers and sisters have none of these problems. Her father spends as much time looking for work as he does working. Sanitary facilities are almost non-existent. Electricity has yet to reach them. Water is hauled by hand. Even the barest necessities are hard to come by.

Through Save The Children Federation, the Winstons are helping Della. The cost is $15.00 a month. It's not a lot of money, but certainly the Winstons could have thought of a lot of other things to do with it. Fortunately they thought of Della first.

To her, these funds make a remarkable difference. She no longer need feel embarrassed about not having shoes, a decent school dress, school supplies, or pocket money.

Some of the pressure, too, is off her parents, who can now begin thinking about making their home a little more livable. Also, and perhaps most important, part of the money is put into a fund from which the village can borrow to start self-help projects, including better housing and a water system.

Already there is a new feeling of hope among the villagers and confidence in their ability to help themselves. Even little Della has volunteered to give some time each week to keep her school playground clean.

That really is what Save The Children is all about. Although contributions are deductible as a charity, the aim is not merely to buy one child a few hot meals or a warm coat. Instead, your contribution is used to give people a little boost to start helping themselves.

Sponsors are desperately needed for other American Indian children as well as children in Appalachia, Korea, Vietnam, Latin America, Africa and Greece.

As a sponsor you will receive a photo and history of the child, progress reports and a chance to correspond.

The Winstons know they can't save the world for $15.00 a month. Only a small corner of it. But maybe that is the way to save the world. If there are enough people who care. How about you?

Save The Children Federation, founded in 1932, is registered with the U.S. State Department Advisory Committee on Voluntary Foreign Aid, and is a member of the International Union of Child Welfare. Financial statements and annual reports available on request.

National Sponsors (partial list): Claude Arpels, Faith Baldwin, Hon. James A. Farley, Andy Griffith, Gene Kelly, Mrs. Eli Lilly, Paul Newman, Mrs. J.C. Penney, Norman Rockwell, Frank Sinatra

Save The Children Federation
NORWALK, CONNECTICUT 06852
☐ I WISH TO CONTRIBUTE $180 ANNUALLY TO HELP A CHILD.
☐ WHERE THE NEED IS GREATEST ☐ LATIN AMERICA
☐ AMERICAN INDIAN ☐ APPALACHIA ☐ KOREA ☐ GREECE
☐ VIETNAM ☐ AFRICA
ENCLOSED IS MY FIRST PAYMENT
☐ $15.00 MONTHLY ☐ $45.00 QUARTERLY
☐ $90.00 SEMI-ANNUALLY ☐ $180.00 ANNUALLY
☐ I CAN'T SPONSOR A CHILD. ENCLOSED IS A CONTRIBUTION OF $____.
☐ PLEASE SEND ME MORE INFORMATION.
NAME ____
ADDRESS ____
CITY ____ STATE ____ ZIP ____
CONTRIBUTIONS ARE INCOME TAX DEDUCTIBLE. SBA 2/21/0

**This is what happens
when a fly lands on your food.**

**Flies can't eat solid food,
so to soften it up they vomit on it.
Then they stamp the vomit in
until it's a liquid, usually stamping in
a few germs for good measure.
Then when it's good and runny
they suck it all back again, probably
dropping some excrement at the
same time.
And then, when they've finished
eating, it's your turn.**

**This is what happens
when a fly lands on your food.**

**Flies can't eat solid food,
so to soften it up they vomit on it.
Then they stamp the vomit in
until it's a liquid, usually stamping in
a few germs for good measure.
Then when it's good and runny
they suck it all back again, probably
dropping some excrement at the
same time.
And then, when they've finished
eating, it's your turn.**

Top *The prodigious Charles Saatchi wrote this advertisement and had it set in 'reverse' – white type on black background (left). It would have been easier to read in black type on white background (right). Anyway,* bon appetit.

Opposite top left and right *Some art directors use copy as the raw material for designing queer shapes. Don't you think that the copy would have been easier to read if set in columns?*

Opposite left and far left *This charity raised money for starving children by running advertisements set in* reverse – *white type on a black background. When I suggested that they test black type on a white background, they raised twice as much money.*

9 What size type should you use?

This is 5-point, and too small to read.

This is 14-point, and too big.

This is 11-point, and about right.

10 If you use leading (line-spacing) between paragraphs, you increase readership by an average of 12 per cent.

You may think that I exaggerate the importance of good typography. You may ask if I have ever heard a housewife say that she bought a new detergent because the advertisement was set in Caslon. No. But do you think an advertisement can sell if nobody can read it? You can't save souls in an empty church.

As Mies van der Rohe said of architecture, 'God is in the details'.

Michener: Do you know me?

I've written many books about far away places.

But even after five million words, my face often draws a blank.

That's why I finally got the American Express Card.

Now I can get a reception like a page

out of Hawaii.

Anncr: To apply for a Card,

look for this display wherever the Card is welcomed.

Michener: The American Express Card. Don't leave home without it.

8 How to make TV commercials that sell

Everyone who writes about television commercials faces the same insoluble problem: it is impossible to show them on the pages of a book. All I can do is reproduce some storyboards which illustrate my points, and pray that you can decipher them.

In my chapter on *print* advertising, I have relied not only on research, but also on long experience. My experience in television has been more limited. True, I once won an award at the Cannes Festival, but it wasn't a good commercial. So most of this chapter will have to rely on research, and the judgments I have formed while looking at thousands of other people's commercials.

My most valuable source of information is the factor analyses I commission at regular intervals from Mapes & Ross. They measure changes in brand preference. People who register a change in brand preference after seeing a commercial subsequently buy the product three times more than people who don't.

Research organizations also measure the *recall* of commercials, and this method finds favor with many advertisers. But some kinds of television commercials which get high recall scores get low scores on changing brand preference, and there appears to be no correlation between recall and purchasing. I prefer to rely on changes in brand preference.

I will start by telling you about ten kinds of commercial which are found to be *above average* in their ability to change people's brand preference, and three kinds which are *below average*.

Above average

1 *Humor.* Conventional wisdom has always held that people buy products because they believe them to be nutritious, or labor-saving, or good value for money – not because the manufacturer tells jokes on television. Claude Hopkins, the father of modern advertising, thundered, 'People don't buy from clowns.'

I think this was true in Hopkins' day, and I have reason to believe that it remained true until recently, but the latest wave of factor-analysis reveals that humor can now sell. This came as a great relief to me; I had always hated myself for rejecting the funny commercials submitted for my approval.

Left *Testimonials by celebrities are below average in their ability to change brand preference, but American Express has been running commercials like this one since 1975 – with outstanding success. They have a special element of mystery: 'Do you know me?'*

Male: I were no more than knee-high to a grasshopper when I ran away from home

. . . I packed up my marbles . . . me catapults and me Hovis sandwiches and off I went.

I'd just stopped for a bite to eat when up comes a postman . . .

'Am I in London yet?' I asked him.

'Nay lad,' he says, 'and if thou's thinking of legging it down there . . .

thou'll need more Hovis butties than that to keep thee going . . .

. . . (Silent)

. . . come back with me and we'll get your Ma . . .

. . . to make up a suitcaseful!'

Sound: music for three seconds.

2nd male: Hovis still has many times more wheatgerm than ordinary bread. It's as good for you today . . .

. . . as it's always been.

Above *This wrinkled old peasant was cast as the heroine in French commercials for washing machines. She came to be recognized by three out of four people in France, and sales of the product jumped from fourth place to second.*
Left *My favorite from the brilliant series of nostalgic commercials for Hovis bread by the British agency Collett Dickenson Pearce.*

But I must warn you that very, very few writers can write funny commercials which *are* funny. Unless you are one of the few, don't try.

2   *Slice of life.* In these commercials one actor argues with another about the merits of a product, in a setting which roughly approximates real life. In the end, the doubter is converted – your toothpaste really *does* give children healthier teeth.

These playlets have been successful in case after case. Copywriters detest them because most of them are so corny – and because they have been in such wide use for such a long time. But some agencies have succeeded in producing slices which are not only effective at the cash register, but realistic and charming.

3   *Testimonials.* The most effective testimonial commercials are those which show loyal users of your product testifying to its virtues – when they don't know they are being filmed. The interviewer pretends to find fault with the product and the loyal user rises to its defense with far more conviction than if you simply asked him what he thought of it. Here is an example:

> The scene is the forecourt of a Shell station. We see an actor disguised as the man on the pump.
>
> *Announcer:* 'This man is an imposter. He's not really a Shell dealer. He's going to see if he can talk our customers out of buying Super Shell. Let's watch through this hidden camera.'
>
> *Shell dealer:* 'I'll bet you get bad mileage with Super Shell.'
>
> *Mrs. Longo, a customer:* 'It's *good.* I'll tell you where a penny saved is a penny earned.'
>
> *Shell dealer:* 'Aw, come on. What do *you* know about gasoline?'
>
> *Mrs. Longo:* 'You see this little dog I have back here? I bought this little dog because it saves money on food. Now I can save on Super Shell.'
>
> *Shell dealer:* 'Bunk! B-U-N-K.'
>
> *Mrs. Longo:* 'You are absolutely wrong. That is the best gasoline. Why, if I were them, I would *fire* you.'
>
> *Announcer:* 'We'll give him another chance because he got you to say nice things about Super Shell.'

When you pick loyal users to testify, avoid those who would give such polished performances that viewers would think they were professional actors. The more amateurish the performance, the more credible.

A French agency picked an 80-year-old laundress as the heroine in a campaign for washing machines. This keg-shaped, wrinkled old woman came to be recognized by three out of four people in France, and sales of the washing machine went from fourth place to second.

Voice over: Look! We are going to show you the incredible . . .

. . . bonding efficiency of Super Glue 3

Sound: Stopwatch ticking

VO: This sequence was filmed without editing.

Read the instructions. Super Glue 3 also sticks rubber . . . plastic . . . china . . . in just a few seconds.

Left *This French commercial demonstrates how well Super Glue-3 works by applying it to the announcer's shoes and hanging him upside down from the ceiling. Super Glue-3 became the brand-leader and the commercial won First Prize at the Cannes Festival.*

Below *A successful example of using a character to reinforce the authenticity of your product.*

The use of unusual characters increases the power of commercials to change brand preference by a remarkably high percentage.

4 *Demonstrations* which show how well your product performs are above average in their ability to persuade.

Demonstrations don't have to be *dull*. To demonstrate how strong paper-board can be, International Paper spanned a canyon with a bridge made of paper-board – and then drove a heavy truck over it.

The Paris office of Ogilvy & Mather demonstrated the strength of a client's glue by applying it to the soles of the announcer's shoes and

SFX: Natural sounds of wagon moving along road.

Man: (oc) Whoa!!

Timmy! I got some delivery today: Pepperidge Farm Wheat Bread.

Bread like it used to be – baked fresh with no artificial preservatives.

Made with real cracked wheat . . .

. . . molasses, honey, 'n' no artifical preservatives.

Try Pepperidge Farm Wheat Bread.

It's bread like it used to be . . .

SFX: Wagon
VO: . . . 'cause Pepperidge Farm remembers.

hanging him upside down from the ceiling – from which position he delivered his sales pitch.

If you use a demonstration to compare your product with your competitor's, think twice before identifying the competitor by name. It is illegal in Germany, but the US Government encourages it as providing information which will help the consumer make an informed choice. Studies conducted by Ogilvy & Mather found that commercials which name competing brands are *less believable* and *more confusing* than commercials which don't. There is a tendency for viewers to come away with the impression that the brand which you disparage is the hero of your commercial.

5 *Problem solution.* This technique is an old as television. You show the viewer a problem with which he or she is familiar, and then show how your product can solve it.

One of the best problem-solution commercials I have seen was made in Madras for Train matches. It starts by showing a man unable to strike 'ordinary' matches in the muggy climate of southern India. He goes mad with impatience. Then his cool, beautiful wife comes to the rescue with a box of Train matches which strike immediately.

6 *Talking heads.* This is the derisive name given to commercials which consist of a pitchman extolling the virtues of a product. Agency people find them non-creative, and are sick of them, but several advertisers still use them because they are above average in changing brand preference.

Talking heads are particularly appropriate for announcing new products. More than a hundred new brands of cigarette have been introduced in Germany in recent years, and the only one which succeeded was launched by a talking head. Perhaps the most persuasive talking head of all time is John Houseman saying, 'Smith Barney make money the *old-fashioned* way. They *earn* it.'

As a former door-to-door salesman, I shall go to my grave believing that, given two minutes on television, I could sell any product on the face of the earth. Any offers?

7 *Characters.* In some commercials, a 'character' is used to sell your product over a period of years. The character becomes the living symbol of the product – like Titus Moody, the crusty old New England baker who has been extolling the quality of Pepperidge Farm bread for 26 years, or Cora, who sold Maxwell House coffee for seven years.

Provided they are relevant to your product, characters are above average in their ability to change brand-preference.

8 *Reason why.* Commercials which give the viewer a rational reason why they should buy your product are slightly above average. When Maxim Instant Coffee was launched, the commercials said Maxim was superior *because it was freeze-dried.* Nine out of ten advertising people will tell you that consumers don't give a hoot about how products are made. They may be right, but the process of freeze-drying was sufficiently new and interesting to persuade many viewers to try the coffee.

'Even when they have news to tell, which is all too rare, some copywriters underplay it, or leave it out altogether. They should be boiled in oil.'

9 *News.* Commercials which contain news are above average. But even when they have news to tell, which is all too rare, some copywriters underplay it, or leave it out altogether. They should be boiled in oil. Products, like human beings, attract most attention when they are first born.

For an old product, you can *create* news by advertising a new way to use it, like using baking soda to keep refrigerators smelling sweet.

10 *Emotion.* Researchers have not yet found a way to quantify the effectiveness of emotion, but I have come to believe that commercials with a large content of nostalgia, charm and even sentimentality can be enormously effective. The commercials for Hovis bread in Great Britain and Blitz-Weinhard beer in Oregon strike me as among the most persuasive I have seen. (See pages 104, 114-115.)

Emotion can be just as effective as any *rational* appeal, particularly when there is nothing unique to say about your product. 'But,' says my partner Hal Riney, 'here is where things get sticky. Most clients – and I'm afraid most agency people – think the rational appeals for their products are much more important than the consumer thinks they are. If your advertising is going to be successful, if it is going to stand out from the clutter, you must be *objective* about the benefits of your product. What exactly are the "benefits" of candy bars, cigarettes, soda pop and beer?'

I hasten to add that consumers also need a *rational excuse* to justify their emotional decisions. So always include one. Above all, don't attempt emotion unless you can deliver it.

Below average

1 *Testimonials by celebrities.* These are below average in their ability to change brand preference. Viewers guess that the celebrity has been bought, and they are right. To get Farrah Fawcett for three years, Fabergé is reported to have paid $2,000,000. Bob Hope, Gregory Peck, Candice Bergen and Dean Martin charge about $1,000,000 each. The spokesman everyone wants is Walter Cronkite, but he isn't available at *any* price. However, for a beggarly $10,000 you can get Ronald Biggs who escaped from jail after being convicted for his part in England's Great Train Robbery. He lives in Brazil.

Viewers have a way of remembering the celebrity while forgetting the product. I did not know this when I paid Eleanor Roosevelt $35,000 to make a commercial for margarine. She reported that her mail was equally divided. 'One half was *sad* because I had damaged my reputation. The other half was *happy* because I had damaged my reputation.' Not one of my proudest memories.

2 *Cartoons* can sell things to children, but they are below average in selling to grown-ups. They don't hold the viewer as well as live action, and they are less persuasive.

Two commercials were made for a fabric-softener. One used live action, the other used cartoons. The cartoon commercial had no effect on the downward trend in sales. The live-action commercial reversed it.

I paid Mrs. Roosevelt $35,000 to make a commercial for margarine. Here she is telling viewers, 'The new Good Luck margarine really tastes delicious*'. In those days I did not know that it is a mistake to use celebrities. They are remembered but the product is forgotten.*

Open on funeral procession of limousines each containing the beneficiaries of a will.
Male voice over: I, Maxwell E. Snavely, being of sound mind and body do bequeath the following:

To my wife Rose, who spent money like there was no tomorrow, I leave $100 and a calendar . . .
To my sons Rodney and Victor, who spent every dime I ever gave them on fancy cars and fast women . . . I leave $50 in dimes . . .

To my business partner, Jules, whose motto was 'spend, spend, spend' I leave nothing, nothing, nothing.
And to my other friends and relatives who also never learned the value of a dollar, I leave . . . a dollar.

Finally, to my nephew, Harold, who oft time said: 'A penny saved is a penny earned.' And who also oft time said: 'Gee Uncle Max, it sure pays to own a Volkswagen' . . . I leave my entire fortune of one hundred billion dollars.

3 *Musical vignettes,* with a parade of fleeting impressions, were once fashionable, but are on their way out. Entertaining, perhaps, but impotent if you want to sell.

Sixteen tips

1 *Brand identification.* Research has demonstrated that a shocking percentage of viewers remember your commercial, but forget the name of your product. All too often they attribute your commercial to a competing brand.

Many copywriters think it crass to belabor the name of the product. However, for the benefit of those who are more interested in selling than entertaining, here are two ways to register your brand name:

○   Use the name within the first ten seconds. I have seen a brilliant commercial which repeated the brand name twenty times in 340 seconds, without irritating anyone.

The funniest commercial I have ever seen, by Doyle Dane Bernbach for Volkswagen. I used to reject funny commercials on the grounds that people don't buy from clowns. Now research shows that humor sells as efficiently as other techniques.

○ Play games with the name. Spell it. Veterans will remember Alex Templeton, the blind pianist, spelling out the name C.R.E.S.T.A. B.L.A.N.C.A. to the accompaniment of pizzicato strings.

When you advertise a new product, you have to teach people its name on television.

2 *Show the package.* Commercials which end by showing the package are more effective in changing brand preference than commercials which don't.

3 *Food in motion.* In commercials for food, the more appetizing ·you make it look, the more you sell. It has been found that *food in motion* looks particularly appetizing. Show chocolate sauce in the act of being poured over your ice cream, or syrup over your pancakes.

4 *Close-ups.* It is a good thing to use close-ups when your product is the hero of your commercial. The closer you get on the candy bar, the more you make people's mouths water.

5 *Open with the fire.* You have only 30 seconds. If you grab attention in the first frame with a visual surprise, you stand a better chance of holding the viewer.

People screen out a lot of commercials because they open with something *dull. You* know that great things are about to happen, but the viewer doesn't. She will *never* know; she has gone to the bathroom.

When you advertise fire-extinguishers, open with the fire.

6 *When you have nothing to say, sing it.* There have been some successful commercials·which sang the sales pitch, but jingles are below average in changing brand preference.

Never use a jingle without trying it on people who have not read your script. If they cannot decipher the words, don't put your jingle on the air.

If you went into a store and asked a salesman to show you a refrigerator, how would you react if he started singing at you? Yet some clients feel short-changed if you don't give them a jingle.

Many people use music as background – emotional shorthand. Research shows that this is neither a positive nor a negative factor. It does no harm and it does no measurable good. Do great preachers allow organists to play background music under their sermons? Do advertising agencies play background music under their pitch to prospective clients?

7 *Sound effects.* While music does not add to the selling power of commercials, *sound effects* – such as sausages sizzling in a frying-pan – can make a positive difference.

A commercial for Maxwell House was constructed around the sound of coffee percolating. It worked well enough to run for five years.

8 *Voice-over or on-camera?* Research shows that it is more difficult to hold your audience if you use voice-over. It is better to have the actors talk *on camera.*

A manufacturer made two commercials, identical in every respect except that one used voice-over and the other used on-camera voice. When he tested them, the voice-on-camera version sold more of his product.

9 *Supers*. It pays to reinforce your promise by setting it in type and superimposing it over the video, while your soundtrack speaks the words.

But make sure that the words in your supers are *exactly the same as your spoken words*. Any divergence confuses the viewer.

Many people in agencies resist the use of supers. If you tell them that they increase sales, as they do, the stupid buggers turn a deaf ear.

10 *Avoid visual banality.* If you want the viewer to pay attention to your commercial, *show her something she has never seen before*. You won't have much success if you show her sunsets and happy families at the dinner table.

The average American family has the television turned on for six hours a day, and is exposed to 30,000 commercials a year. Most of them slide off the memory like water off a duck's back. For this reason you should give your commercials a touch of singularity, a visual burr that will stick in the viewer's mind. One such burr was the herd of bulls thundering towards the camera, with the superimposed title: 'Merrill Lynch is *bullish* on America.'

11 *Changes of scene*. Hal Riney uses a great many scenes without confusing people, but I can't, and I bet you can't either. On the *average*, commercials with a plethora of short scenes are below average in changing brand preference.

12 *Mnemonics*. This unpronounceable word is used to describe a visual device repeated over a long period. It can increase brand identification, and remind people of your promise. Example: the car driving through the paper barrier in Shell commercials.

13 *Show the product in use*. It pays to show the product being used, and, if possible, the end-result of using it. Show how your diapers (nappies) keep the baby dry. In a commercial for motor oil, show how the pistons look after 50,000 miles.

14 *Everything is possible on TV.* The technicians can produce anything you want. *The only limit is your imagination.*

15 *Miscomprehension*. In 1979 Professor Jacoby of Purdue University studied the 'miscomprehension' of 25 typical television commercials. He found that *all* of them were miscomprehended, some by as many as 40 per cent of viewers, none by fewer than 19 per cent.

If you want to avoid your television commercials being misunderstood, you had better make them *crystal clear*. I cannot understand more than half the commercials I see.

16 *The great scandal*. Television programs cost about $4 a second to produce, but commercials cost $2,000 a second. Which is $60,000 for a 30-second commercial.

This obscene extravagance is largely the fault of the agencies. Says Hooper White, 'Production dollars are typed into the commercial by the copywriter and drawn into the commercial by the art director.' Miner Raymond of Procter & Gamble tells the story of an art director who objected to a table on the set. The client pointed out that it was covered by a cloth and thus invisible. 'But *I* would know what's under the cloth,' said the art director, 'and it just wouldn't be right.' So another table was found and the delay cost the client $5,000.*

The easiest way to reduce the cost of a commercial is to cut actors out of the storyboard. Every actor you cut will save you between $350 and $10,000, depending on how long you run the commercial.

Copywriters specify that a commercial should be shot in Bali when it could equally well be shot in a studio for half the price. They insert expensive animation into live-action commercials. They insist that original music be composed for background purposes, as if there were nothing suitable in the whole repertoire of existing music. Worst of all, they use expensive celebrities when an unknown actor would sell more of the product.

I have no research to prove it, but I suspect that there is a negative correlation between the money spent on producing commercials and their power to sell products. My partner Al Eicoff was asked by a client to remake a $15,000 commercial for $100,000. Sales went *down*.

Radio – the Cinderella medium

Once upon a time, I spent six months studying radio at the feet of John Royal, the pioneering head of programming at NBC. In those days every family in America tuned in to Jack Benny, Edgar Bergen and Charlie McCarthy, Fred Allen, Amos and Andy, Burns and Allen. Some of us also listened to Roy Larsen's marvellous *March of Time*, and Toscanini conducting the NBC Symphony Orchestra.

All this was swept away by television.

For most people radio has become no more than a security blanket, a reassuring noise in the background.

Radio has become the Cinderella of advertising media, representing only 6 per cent of total advertising in the United States. There is no research to measure the efficacy of the commercials, so nobody knows what works. A pilot study I commissioned suggests four positive factors:

1 Identify your brand early in the commercial.

2 Identify it often.

3 Promise the listener a benefit early in the commercial.

4 Repeat it often.

Ninety commercials out of a hundred do none of these things.
In my opinion – and it is nothing more than that – the first thing your

* For more information about what goes on during the filming of commercials, read Michael Arlen's book, *Thirty Seconds*, Farrah, Straus & Giroux, 1980

radio commercial has to do is to get people to *listen*. Surprise them. Arouse their curiosity. Wake them up. Once they are awake, talk to them as one human being to another. Involve them. Charm them. Make them laugh. Here is the script of a radio commercial in a series which increased the sale of Red, White and Blue Beer by 60 per cent:

ANNOUNCER: And now, another inflation-fighting message from Mr Harmon R. Whittle.

This beer commercial, written by my partner Hal Riney, is the best example I know of the use of emotion in advertising.

WHITTLE: One of the biggest strains on our budget is the foreign aid program. Each year, we send billions of dollars worth of planes, computers, tractors and things to foreign

1 **Ottley:** My grandfather came to Harney County, oh around 1882 . . .

2 **ANN'CR:** Howard Ottley is a rancher in South-eastern Oregon.
Ottley: Harney County is still ranching country – pretty much the way it was . . .

5 We believe that's the best way for living and brewing beer.

6 That's why Blitz-Weinhard is brewed only with natural ingredients in the traditional way.

countries . . . Then we pay technical advisers to train them how to use it all. This is expensive.

A more responsive form of foreign aid would be to send them *beer*. American-made Red, White and Blue beer.

Red, White and Blue is less expensive than planes or computers. So we'd save a bundle, right off. It costs less than other premium-quality beer, so we'd save on that. And Red, White and Blue is easier to teach people to use than a computer. So we'd save on technical advisers, too.

And if there's any doubt whether our international

3   . . . My dad was born here on the ranch and my family's been here since . . .

4   **ANN'CR:** His way of doing things is still the natural way.

7   **Ottley:** I haven't been to too many places in the country . . . but I don't think there'd be many like this, anymore . . .

8   **ANN'CR:** Blitz country. . . natural country. . . natural beer.

popularity would increase, ask yourself this: if you lived in one of those hot, dusty countries, what would you rather have? A computer, or an ice-cold, Red, White and Blue? It's an honest beer. At an honest price.

ANNOUNCER: Mr Whittle's comments do not necessarily reflect the views of this station. They do however, reflect the views of the RWB Brewing Company, Milwaukee.

Because radio is a high-frequency medium, people quickly get tired of hearing the same commercial. So make several. Compared with television, radio commercials cost almost nothing to produce.

In some developing countries radio still reaches more people than television. Yet even there nobody really knows what kind of commercials make the cash register ring. Isn't it time somebody tried to find out?

9 Advertising corporations

'With public opinion on its side, nothing can fail'
– Abraham Lincoln

Once upon a time, the head of a big corporation went into Cartier's and ordered a diamond bracelet for his wife. 'Send the bill to my office,' said he. Nothing doing – Cartier had never heard of his corporation. The next morning he instructed his agency to prepare a corporate advertising campaign.

Eighty-one out of the hundred biggest American corporations advertise their corporations as distinct from their products, and spend about $500,000,000 a year in the process. Most of them make a hash of it. However, if well planned and executed, corporate advertising can be a profitable investment. Opinion Research Corporation has found that people who know a company well are five times more likely to have a favorable opinion of it.

Corporate advertising can improve the morale of your employees; who wants to work for an outfit that nobody has ever heard of? It can also make it easier to recruit better people, at all levels. And, I believe, it can make your corporation a more seductive suitor in takeover bids. Discretion stops me naming a rich corporation which has recently failed in several takeover bids because its image is unattractive.

Can corporate advertising make a good impression on the investment community? Yes it can, and this is the unspoken purpose of most such campaigns. A study conducted at Northwestern University examined the stock performance of 731 corporations, and found that corporate advertising had an average positive influence of 2 per cent on the price of their stock. If you think this trivial, reflect that if a corporation has a market value of forty billion dollars – and some do – that extra 2 per cent adds up to $800,000,000. Not to be sneezed at.

DuPont has run corporate advertising for 47 years, General Electric for 62 years, American Telephone for 75 years, US Steel for 46 years, and Container Corporation for 50 years. But the majority of corporate advertising campaigns are aborted too soon to achieve any measurable objective.

You cannot rely on *short-term* advertising to turn the tide of hostile public opinion in your favor, to boost the price of your stock or to put a halo around your reputation. In 1941, when Texaco was accused of selling oil to the Nazis, they assumed sponsorship of the Metropolitan

Right *This advertisement summarizes the case for corporate advertising.*

"*I don't know who you are.*
I don't know your company.
I don't know your company's product.
I don't know what your company stands for.
I don't know your company's customers.
I don't know your company's record.
I don't know your company's reputation.
Now—what was it you wanted to sell me?"

MORAL: Sales start **before** your salesman calls—with business publication advertising.

McGRAW-HILL MAGAZINES
BUSINESS•PROFESSIONAL•TECHNICAL

Opera on radio, but it took a long time for this lovely antidote to exorcize their bad publicity.

Most corporate campaigns are short-lived because they don't start with any clear objective, and because research is not used to track their progress. A glowing exception is DuPont, who for many years measured progress after each television program.

Corporate campaigns seldom have more than one supporter – the Chief Executive Officer. He alone has the vision to recognize its long-term value. His marketing executives regard any diversion of advertising dollars from their products as a frivolous waste of money, and his financial officers cast greedy eyes on the appropriation whenever there is a short-fall in earnings.

Right *Sears devotes most of its gigantic advertising budget to price-off merchandise, but in 1961 I persuaded them to add a campaign which would burnish their corporate image by promulgating their policies. Some of their executives thought it was a pansy waste of money because it did not directly sell merchandise, but Chairman Kelstadt took a longer view. When Joe Cushman succeeded Kelstadt, he told me, 'my father was ashamed when I went to work for Sears. Today, nobody is ashamed to work for Sears.* Thank you.'

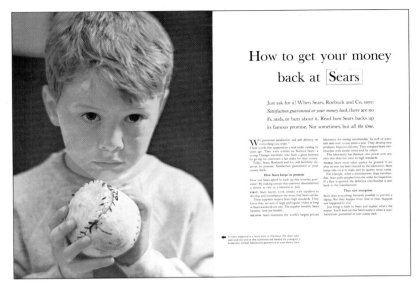

The copy in most corporate advertisements is distinguished by a self-serving, flatulent pomposity which defies reading, and agencies waste endless hours concocting slogans of incredible fatuity. Consider these beauties:

Diamond Shamrock: *The resourceful company.*

Honeywell: *The automation company.*

Boise Cascade: *A company worth looking at.*

Georgia Pacific: *The growth company.*

Dravo: *A company of uncommon enterprise.*

Textron: *THE company. (sic)*

General Motors: *People building transportation to serve PEOPLE.*

Toyota: *Serving PEOPLE'S needs in a hundred basic ways.*

Firestone: *As long as Firestone keeps thinking about PEOPLE, PEOPLE will keep thinking about Firestone.*

Siemens: *Siemens turns ideas into PEOPLE.*

ITT: *The best ideas are the ideas that help PEOPLE.*

General Electric: *100 years of progress for PEOPLE.*

Western Electric: *We make things that bring PEOPLE closer.*

US Steel: *We're involved.*

Crown Zellerbach: *We help make it happen.*

Sperry Rand: *We understand how important it is to listen.*

Rockwell International: *Where science gets down to business.*

You can see mink (from $199 to $799) at 241 of the 740 Sears stores and in the Sears catalog. Any Sears store will order mink for you—and you can always charge it. The natural mink cape above costs $575

How to buy mink at Sears for Christmas

IS THERE any woman in the world who wouldn't like this mink for Christmas?

Look again at the picture. This is a *natural* mink cape. It is made from as many as twenty-four matched skins. And lined in pure silk. You can see why it is called a *bubble* cape. Notice the set-back collar. It is extravagantly *deep*—and *luxurious*. In Paris, this style is called the *Blouson* effect.

This mink costs $575, plus the federal tax of ten percent. Any fur expert will tell you this represents fantastic value. He'll wonder how Sears does it.

The answer is knowing *how* to buy mink and *whom* to buy from.

Sears, Roebuck and Co. is one of the biggest sellers of mink in the United States. Its buyers purchase mink coats, jackets, stoles, capes and scarfs in *quantity* from a few selected suppliers.

These people respect Sears high standards. They know they are sure to get large and regular orders as long as they meet these standards. This helps them cut costs. They pass the savings on to Sears—and Sears passes them on to you.

This is the Sears way of doing business. It's why every department at Sears can offer you more value for your money—whether it is tires, diamond rings or denim pants. Or mink for Christmas.

Satisfaction guaranteed or your money back

J. C. Penney: *We know what you're looking for.*

Chemetron: *We're basic to success.*

Notice that all these bromides are interchangeable – any company could use any of them. They generally appear at the *bottom* of advertisements, where nobody reads them, and, by cluttering up the layout, they reduce readership of the copy.

Many corporate campaigns fail because they are under-funded. Companies which spend millions on advertising their brand names are curiously stingy when it comes to their corporate campaigns. The most sensible way to set the budget is to 'analyse the task.' How much will it cost to achieve a specific goal among a specific audience?

Another common mistake is to confine the campaign to magazines and newspapers. When you add television, tracking studies record a dramatic increase in penetration.

A word of warning to Chief Executive Officers: if you appear in your own commercials, you will be recognized wherever you go and thus become an easier target for kidnappers. More serious, you may not say your lines as well as a professional announcer.

Alphabet soup

Whatever you do, for goodness sake, don't change the name of your corporation to *initials*. Everybody knows what IBM, ITT, CBS and NBC are, but how many of the following can *you* identify: AC, ADP, AFIA, AIG, AM, AMP, BBC (Brown Boveri *and* British Broadcasting), CBI, CF, CNA, CPT, CEX, DHL, FMC, GA, GE, GM, GMAC, GMC, GTE, HCA, IM, INA, IU, JVC, MCI, NIB, NCP, NCR, NDS, NEC, NLT, NT, OPIC (not to be confused with OPEC), TIE, TRW, UBS. Yet this is how 37 corporations sign their advertisements. It will take them many years and many millions of dollars to teach their initials to their publics. What a waste of money.

Can advertising influence legislation?

William H. Vanderbilt, the railroad tycoon, used to say, 'The public be damned.' Abraham Lincoln thought otherwise: 'With public opinion on its side, nothing can fail. With public opinion against it, nothing can succeed.'

Where do people get their information on public issues? Largely from television, and less from the newscasts than from folk heroes like Robert Blake and Jane Fonda. Ms. Fonda says things like this on television:

> 'You'd better get the guts to stand up to the black shadow of oil before it spills across your desk, oozes into your campaign coffers, seals your ears and blackens your hearts. Because if you do not hear our cries now, you will harvest the grapes of wrath.'

Just try writing advertisements which can deal with this kind of rhetoric.

In recent years corporations have been using advertising in

Left *More image-building for Sears. Who would expect Sears to sell* mink?

attempts to influence public opinion on such issues as energy, nationalization and foreign imports. The trouble is that very few readers believe what corporations say. In 1979-80, the Media Institute studied the image of businessmen as they are portrayed in television programs. Two out of three are portrayed as foolish, greedy or criminal. They are seldom shown doing anything socially useful. (I know many businessmen who devote so much time to 'socially useful' things, it's a wonder their stockholders put up with it.)

Most senior executives are curiously unaware of what goes on in the liberal community. As a recent article in the *Harvard Business Review* said, 'While businessmen were minding their own business, intellectuals were busy developing a powerful case against capitalism.' Political and social naïveté can be a handicap when companies run into political difficulty.

Some advertising campaigns seem to have been successful in influencing legislation. Bethlehem Steel, for example, used advertising to win public support for their position on imported steel. I am told that it helped the passage of a bill protecting the steel industry.

When the forest industry was under attack by environmentalists for being irresponsible in its use of national resources, Weyerhaeuser used television advertising to demonstrate that they are *highly* responsible. Research indicated that the advertising worked. The attacks abated.

Below *This campaign emphasized IBM's involvement in people's daily lives – in this case, how IBM helped speed up traffic in New York's rush hour.*

John Babyak at the Traffic Center "situation board," which reflects the status of every traffic light under computer control.

Computerized signal lights keep traffic moving along Northern Boulevard. (Telephoto view shows a six-block section of the Boulevard.)

Giving New York drivers the green light where traffic once crawled.

Every morning New York City must digest a breakfast of three million cars, trucks and buses. But on five main arteries, drivers now average one quarter as many stops. John Babyak's story is another example of how IBM, its people or products often play a part in tackling today's problems.

"Just over a year ago," relates IBM's John Babyak, "a Traffic Department study showed it took 45 to 50 minutes to travel eleven miles of Northern Boulevard in the morning rush hour.

"Along the way, you'd average 23 stops."

"Today, the figures show you can make the trip in 25 to 30 minutes, and average just 7 stops."

The difference is New York's new computerized traffic system which began on Northern Boulevard, in the borough of Queens, and has since been extended to four other main arteries there.

John Babyak, the IBM Systems Engineer assigned to the project, has been working on the application of computers to traffic problems for about ten years.

"In late 1968," says Mr. Babyak, "the City embarked on a program with IBM to develop a system for

Queens. By May 1969 we were officially in operation.

"Right now, the system controls over three hundred intersections along thirty-five miles of the busiest roads in the New York area. Overhead sensors provide continuous traffic flow data to the computer. The system then responds to changing traffic patterns.

"These roads carry 130,000 cars a day.

"The Department estimates it has saved drivers up to fourteen hours a month in travel time.

"What's more, traffic engineers point to the fact that fewer stops mean fewer accidents. Especially the rear-end variety.

"As it now stands, the Queens installation is already the largest computerized traffic control system in the country.

"Even so, it's just a beginning."

IBM

Bethlehem Steel is looking for a fight. A *fair* fight.

Name a foreign steel producer. We'll get in the commercial ring with him and battle it out for America's steel market. And if we both fight by the same rules, we're confident we'll hold our own.

But that isn't the way this "competition" works. When a Japanese or European steelmaker climbs into the ring, his government almost always climbs in with him. That's bending the rules of "free" trade, and we don't think it's fair.

How they fight

Most foreign steelmakers are either owned, subsidized, financed, aided and/or protected in one way or another by their governments. They don't have the same pressure we do to operate profitably or generate capital.

We believe that much of the steel imported into the U.S. is being "dumped"—that is, sold at prices lower than those charged in the producer's own country, and usually below that foreign steelmaker's full costs of production. Dumping is illegal, but it has been hard to prove.

Why they do it

During periods of slack demand at home, foreign steelmakers push to maintain high production rates and high employment. Result: a worldwide glut of steel...16.3 million tons of steel exported to America in 1976, priced to sell...thousands of American steelworkers laid off or working short hours.

Free trade, yes. But fair!

We're looking for a fight, yes. But a *fair* fight, where all opponents in the international arena are bound by the same rules. Bethlehem Steel and the American steel industry are not "protectionist." We are not looking for permanent trade barriers against foreign steel coming into our home markets. All we're asking is a chance to compete on fair and equal terms here in our own country.

Washington must help

We urge the U.S. Government to insist on fair trading practices in steel, especially that steel imports be priced to at least cover their full costs of production and sale...to arrange for prompt temporary relief from the current excessive flow of steel imports... and to press for international governmental negotiations leading to an effective international agreement on steel trade.

If you agree with us about the seriousness of this problem, please write your representatives in Washington and tell them so.

A free folder..."Foreign Steel: Unfair Competition?"...explains our answer to that question. Write: Public Affairs Dept., Rm. 476 MT, Bethlehem Steel Corp., Bethlehem, PA 18016.

Bethlehem

Above *Ads like this helped pass a bill protecting the industry against the dumping of foreign steel.*

Below *This corporate campaign was created to please the governments of countries in which Esso did business.*

A few years ago, the British Labour Party announced their intention to nationalize the banks. Six months of well argued advertising produced good research numbers, and the banks have not been nationalized.

For three years Eli Lilly used television advertising to argue the case against legislation that would have required doctors to prescribe generic medicines. It is thought that the campaign may have helped to head off this threat to their bread and butter.

Advertising whose purpose is to influence public opinion is more likely to be successful if it follows these principles:

If the issue is complicated, and it almost always is, simplify it as much as you reasonably can. For example, the consumer is bombarded with confusing information about what food is nutritious, or even safe. In 1981 General Foods ran a series of advertisements which gave people *simple* advice on the subject.

A classic example of simplifying a complicated issue was the headline on a Chesapeake and Ohio advertisement: 'A Hog Can Cross the Country Without Changing Trains – But YOU Can't!'

But watch out. Simplistic *distortion* can insult people's intelligence and do you more harm than good.

Present your case in terms of the reader's self-interest. For some years Mobil has been trying to influence public opinion by running exceptionally

EWING KRAININ

JAPAN

The bata-bata and
the moon-watching platform

THE Japanese have a wonderful way with words. What we call a back porch they call a moon-watching platform. A fountain pen is a ten-thousand-year brush.

Their name for a motorcycle truck is *bata-bata*—because that is the noise it makes. And do you know a word in any other language that sighs good-bye as wistfully as *sayonara?*

Even official honors reveal a touch of the poet. A Japanese genius and his work can be declared a *mukei-bunkazai*—an *intangible cultural treasure*. At the last count, Japan had half-a-million practising poets, all striving to become suitably intangible.

Then there are the gentle rhythms of Japanese life. Serving tea is a formal art. So is arranging flowers. So are good manners. You will find a hostess on every bus who calls out the stops, helps old people alight, and tells the driver how he is doing on difficult turns.

And there's a charming festival called Seven-Five-Three Day—when parents visit their shrines to seek blessings for children who are seven, five and three years old. Our photograph shows the ancient Inari Shrine in Kyoto.

Yet, despite her engaging sensibility, Japan is no nation of lotus-eaters. She builds more ships than any other country on earth. She has a higher percentage of electrified homes than we do. And Tokyo has recently passed London and New York to become the world's largest city.

The Jersey Standard affiliate that operates in Japan is understandably eager that anybody we send over should see the country at cherry blossom time. We do our best to oblige. We might lose a businessman, but we could gain a poet.

Published in the interests of international friendship by Standard Oil Company (New Jersey)

Right *In the author's judgment, this is the best corporate campaign by any retailer. The copy was written by Leslie Pearl, and appeared in the* New York Times *three times a week for 26 years. Woven into the copy was the idea that Wallachs not only sold superior clothes, but also gave unusually attentive, personal and friendly service. Before the campaign started, a survey was conducted to see how men rated the men's clothing stores in New York. Wallachs came in last. Ten years later Wallachs headed the list.*

Below *This may well be the best advertisement about a public issue that has ever appeared.*

---

did you say button?

Every year or so we ask our store managers to keep count, over a four week period, of the special services we perform.

The most recent check (Mar 4-Mar 30) has just been tabulated and shows a total of 1153 assists. Among other things we sewed on 334 buttons, supplied 295 collar stays and buttons, donated 166 pairs of shoe laces, cleaned up ₂₀₀ spots and punched new holes in 56 belts. And we made 86 special office deliveries.

These, you understand, were all emergency repairs and services, provided on a while-you-wait basis, made without charge and not limited to Wallachs regular customers or to clothes originally bought at Wallachs.

The next time you need sartorial first aid of any kind, go straight to any Wallachs store and don't be bashful about asking for help. We welcome every opportunity to be of service. We'd like to beat that figure of 1153 as soon as possible.

---

what size does he wear?

"He's about your height, perhaps a little heavier, has brown hair and graduated two years ago. What size shirt do you think I ought to get for him?"

Questions like that are routine to any salesman in any men's wear store. For although women are expected to know what size clothes are worn by their husbands, sons, fathers, brothers or beaus, the feat is obviously impossible. Every man wears an assortment of garments requiring a dozen different sizes and half the time he can't remember them all himself.

This problem gets worse for the ladies as Christmas gets nearer, so Wallachs has finally done something about it. We have had a card printed that is just right for a lady's purse. It lists all the things that a man wears and has space for you to fill in the sizes.

Stop at any Wallachs the next time you are shopping and ask for as many cards as you can use. Or we will gladly mail you a few with our compliments.

A Hog Can Cross the Country Without Changing Trains—But YOU Can't!

The Chesapeake & Ohio Railway and the Nickel Plate Road are again proposing to give human beings a break!

It's hard to believe, but it's true.

If you want to ship a hog from coast to coast, he can make the entire trip without changing cars. You can't. It is impossible for you to pass through Chicago, St. Louis, or New Orleans without breaking your trip!

There is an invisible barrier down the middle of the United States which you cannot cross without inconvenience, lost time, and trouble.

560,000 Victims in 1945!

If you want to board a sleeper on one coast and ride through to the other, you must make double Pullman reservations, pack and transfer your baggage, often change stations, and wait around for connections.

It's the same sad story if you make a relatively short trip. You can't cross that mysterious line! To go from Fort Wayne to Milwaukee or from Cleveland to Des Moines, you must also stop and change trains.

Last year alone, more than 560,000 people were forced to make annoying, time-wasting stopovers at the phantom Chinese wall which splits America in half!

End the Secrecy!

Why should travel be less convenient for people than it is for pigs? Why should Americans be denied the benefits of through train service? No one has yet been able to explain it.

Canada has this service . . . with a choice of two routes. Canada isn't split down the middle. Why should we be? No reasonable answer has yet been given. Passengers still have to stop off at Chicago, St. Louis, and New Orleans—although they can ride right through other important rail centers.

It's time to pry the lid off this mystery. It's time for action to end this inconvenience to the travelling public . . . NOW!

Many railroads could cooperate to provide this needed through service. To date, the Chesapeake & Ohio and the Nickel Plate ALONE have made a public offer to do so.

How about it!

Once more we would like to go on record with this specific proposal:

The Chesapeake & Ohio, whose western passenger terminus is Cincinnati, stands ready now to join with any combination of other railroads to set up connecting transcontinental and intermediate service through Chicago and St. Louis, on practical schedules and routes.

The Nickel Plate Road, which runs to Chicago and St. Louis, also stands ready now to join with any combination of roads to set up the same kind of connecting service through these two cities.

Through railroad service can't be blocked forever. The public wants it. It's bound to come. Again, we invite the support of the public, of railroad people and railroad investors—for this vitally needed improvement in rail transportation!

Chesapeake & Ohio Railway · Nickel Plate Road

Terminal Tower, Cleveland 1, Ohio

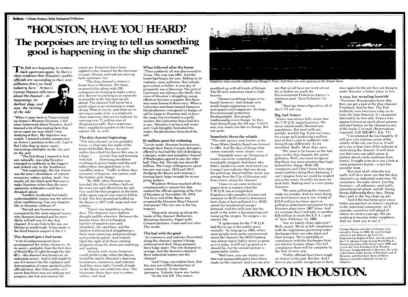

Above *A corporate advertisement in a series by Ogilvy & Mather for General Foods. A complicated subject expounded with simplicity.*

Above right *ARMCO used corporate advertising to tell the people in Houston what they were doing about pollution in the ship channel.*

Below *Mobil seeks to influence public opinion in advertisements which are remarkable for their no-holds-barred copy. They appeal to the educated minority.*

trenchant advertisements. The head of Mobil says that they have produced positive results, but I have reason to think that they work better with the well-educated minority than with the public at large. The advertisements make little or no appeal to the ordinary citizen's self-interest.

Disarm with candor. ARMCO had a reputation as the worst polluter in Houston. They tackled the problem with advertising that told how they had changed their ways. It produced a measurable improvement in their reputation.

Give both sides of the issue. In confronting the anti-highway and anti-strip-mining pressure groups, Caterpillar Tractor gave *both* sides of the issue.

Know who your target is. You can reach Congressmen and others in the Federal Government with a campaign that need not cost more than $800,000 a year, but it won't do you much good. Unless legislators know that you are talking to their *constituents*, they turn a deaf ear. As Ralph Nader is reported to have said, 'If you are weak on the streets, you are weak.'

When Congress was considering a windfall profits tax on oil companies, several of them ran argumentative advertisements directed to Congressmen. But social and political pressures were so great, and demagoguery so rampant, that the bill was enacted. The campaign might have worked if it had started earlier, if it had been addressed to the general public, and if it had been written with more balance.

Many corporations have told me that they need only reach 'thought-leaders' – the people who influence other people. This sounds sensible, and not too expensive. The problem is that nobody really knows who the thought-leaders are. Bishops? Bartenders? Political

Container Corporation started advertising in 1937. The campaign was a succès d'estime *among highbrow laymen, but I denounced it as an exercise in pretension. Forty-five years later the campaign is still running, and I have come to think it is one of the best corporate campaigns that has ever appeared. Even when I don't read the copy, I recognize the sponsor – like recognizing a man who dresses unlike other men. He* looks *different, so he* must *be different. There lies the secret; the campaign has* differentiated *Container Corporation.*

busybodies? Garrulous taxi-drivers? Thought-leaders are spread throughout the population.

In most cases your only hope of making a dent on public opinion is to advertise to the public at large – *and to use television.* Television is the battleground on which public opinion is formed.

Bad news

If your purpose is to affect legislation, the Internal Revenue Service does not allow the cost of your advertising to be treated as a business expense. Worse still, the television networks will not accept 'advocacy' advertising. So you have to use local spots, market by market. You will probably end up with a combination of local television, the *Washington Post,* the *New York Times,* and some upper-crust magazines.

* * * * *

Most advocacy campaigns are too little and too late. They are addressed to the wrong audience, lack a defined purpose, don't go on long enough, are weak in craftsmanship, and advocate a hopeless cause. So they fail.

Advocacy advertising is not a job for beginners.

10 How to advertise foreign travel

I am supposed to be the Grand Panjandrum of travel advertising, because of my campaigns for Come to Britain, Come to France, Come to the United States, and Come to Puerto Rico. I have also done advertising for various carriers, including Cunard, P&O and KLM. And for American Express, who provide the financial oil that keeps international travel going.

When you undertake to advertise a foreign country, you have to be prepared for a lot of political flak. Research told me that what American tourists most wanted to see in Britain was history and tradition – Westminster Abbey, the Tower of London, Changing the Guard at Buckingham Palace, Oxford, that kind of thing. So that is what I featured in the advertisements, only to be slaughtered in the British press for projecting an image of a country living in the past. Why did I not project a progressive industrial society? Why did I not feature the nuclear power stations which the British had just invented? Because our research had shown that American tourists had no desire to see such things, that's why.

When our campaign started, Britain was the fifth most visited European country among American tourists. Today it is *first*.

Not long ago, a Labour Government decreed that the 'Come to Britain' advertisements should feature only those areas of Britain which were economically depressed, the idea being that foreign tourists would cure unemployment. I had to point out that Birmingham, Liverpool and Wigan could not compete with Venice, Paris and Amsterdam.

When we started advertising the United States in Europe, we used research to find out what the Europeans would most like to see. The answer was Manhattan, Grand Canyon, San Francisco, Niagara Falls and cowboys. So these were the attractions we featured in the advertisements – until the US Travel Service instructed us to feature scenes of South Dakota. One of the Senators from that State was on the Senate Committee which voted the advertising budget.

When we took over the French Government's tourism advertising in the United States, the French politician who was our client was not on speaking terms with the brilliant cabinet minister who was his boss, and we got caught in the middle.

For 24 countries, foreign tourists represent one of the three biggest sources of foreign exchange, but the majority of foreign governments fail to give their departments of tourism enough money to advertise. This is true of Germany, Italy, Holland, Spain, Belgium, Scandinavia and scores of others. The exceptions are Canada, Britain, Greece, Ireland and some of the Caribbean islands. For a few years Congress voted a niggardly appropriation for the US Travel Service, but before long even that dried up.

Sometimes you will find it advisable to change the image of the country you advertise. My beloved Puerto Rico had the most unfortunate image of all. Research revealed that Americans who had never been there believed it to be dirty, ugly and squalid. When our advertisements showed it as it really is, beautiful and romantic, the tourists arrived in droves.

While most advertising for countries should be designed to plant a *long-term image* in the reader's mind, there are occasions when it can be used *ad hoc*, to solve *temporary* problems. In 1974 American newspapers were full of reports of shortages of electricity in Britain, enough to discourage Americans who did not relish spending their vacation in the dark. The end of the shortage was not reported in the press, but it was announced in our advertisements, and research showed a satisfactory decrease in anxiety among prospective visitors. At another period it was learned from research that Americans were concerned about high prices

Below *When you advertise countries which are little known, it pays to give the reader a lot of specific information – as in this newspaper ad for Singapore.*

Right *One of a series for the Peruvian airline, Faucett. They pulled 20,000 requests for a brochure offered at the end of the copy.*

Below right *When American tourists got worried about high prices in Britain, this newspaper ad published some* actual *prices.*

Below *In 1974 American tourists were discouraged from visiting Britain by newspaper reports of an acute shortage of electricity. This ad announced the end of the shortage.*

Discuss the weather with a friendly Indian whose father was a headhunter–in Faucett's Peru

You turn to your guide: what has this man dressed in grass and feathers said to you "He says, 'It looks like rain.'" Somehow, it seemed much more.

With a skill passed down from his father, your new-found friend lifts a six-foot blowgun to his mouth. A leaf 200 feet away is impaled by a tiny dart. "Not long ago," you think, "that leaf could have been me." Now, he offers the blowgun to you with a smile.

This is just a part of your adventure, in the valley of the Amazon, in Peru.

Before you leave, you might also be visiting a 2500-year-old "airfield," rediscovering Machu Picchu, lost city of the Incas; seeing animals that simply don't exist in your world.

It can cost less than you think. Visit the Amazon for under $500, including air-fare, a guide and four days in an Amazon jungle camp. Tours of all three of Peru's regions, with airfare, guided tours and deluxe hotels start at under $1000.

While there, you'll save money. Alpaca sweaters and rugs can cost under $20; gold and silver jewelry is a fraction of what you'd pay here.

Faucett Airlines knows Peru best. We've written a 40-page guide filled with figures, facts, photographs and maps. It's free. Write Faucett Peruvian Airlines, 1095 N.W. 77th Avenue, Miami, Florida 33122, or call 1-800-327-3368 and ask for Penny Manning. Or contact your travel consultant.

IN MIAMI CALL 592-7516. IN FLORIDA CALL 1-800-432-3218

Britain is ablaze with lights again!

11.15 p.m. last Sunday evening, March 24. The lights are back on on Piccadilly Circus. And all over Britain.

Hallelujah! The good times are back!
Even more exciting news awaits people going to Britain.

As you can see in this picture of Piccadilly Circus (taken last Sunday evening, Britain is aglow once again. Lights are back on all over the land.

Pubs are roaring, theatres are jammed and stores are bustling.

It's a perfect time to visit Britain.

1. No gasoline rationing. Gas is available and it's cheaper than anywhere on the Continent. You can rent a car and drive anywhere you like.

2. Back to normal. The three-day workweek is over. Hotels, restaurants and places of interest and entertainment never were affected.

3. Easy to get around. Buses, subways, taxis and trams are operating normally.

4. Warm and cozy rooms. Hotel rooms never were affected by heating and lighting cuts.

5. Your dollar worth more. The dollar is worth 11% more than it was last summer. You can buy more, see more, do more – for less.

6. Low-cost vacations extended. Special 8-day vacation packages to Britain have been extended through April 30. Only $360?

Surprisingly moderate prices.

Prices are still surprisingly moderate in Britain. Especially for Americans, since the dollar has increased so much in value in the last year.

For example, a snug country inn with breakfast included, $10 a night.

Pork-pie lunch on an oak-beamed pub beside a crackling fire, $1.90.

Comfortable, moderately priced London hotel, $20 to $35 a night for a double, including a delicious breakfast for two.

Transportation, hotels: Business as usual.

British Airways: Two daily 747 no-stop flights from New York to London plus daily VC-10 service to Prestwick and Manchester.

British Caledonian Airways: The airline Americans love. Daily to London's convenient Gatwick Airport. Ask travel agent about wide range of tours.

Avis Rent-A-Car: 80 stations, 5,000 cars in Britain, all available with full gas tanks. Call nearest Avis reservation office for information.

British Rail: Wide range of dollar-priced BritRail passes for fast, convenient and comfortable travel around Britain. Travel agents have details.

London Transport: 'Go As You Please' tickets (4 days, $7.50; 7 days, $10.00) offer comprehensive, reall including sightseeing in London.

British Transport Hotels: Savings up to 50 percent at 31 traditional hotels in cities and resorts throughout England and Scotland.

Grand Metropolitan Hotels: 22 hotels in London, plus eight in England and Scotland. Call 800-621-1015 (toll-free) for reservations.

Rank Hotels: 12 hotels in Britain, including the Royal Garden overlooking Hyde Park, and the Royal Lancaster, close to Marble Arch.

Trust Houses Forte Hotels: Over 200 hotels in the British Isles, from London's Grosvenor House to country inns and motor lodges.

Special 8-day vacation prices extended through April 30. Only $360!

You can choose from '98 different 8- and 14-day vacation packages. For example, a week in London for only $360 including round-trip air-fare, hotel, breakfasts, sightseeing and even theatre tickets.

Other vacation packages can take you around England, Scotland and Wales.

Facts about these vacations are in our free 52-page color brochure, 'Britain '74.'

For a free copy, see your travel agent. Or mail this coupon to the British Tourist Authority, Britain's National Tourist Office.

As of March 8, 1974
Prices are per person based on a double occupancy, including round-trip 14-day Group Inclusive Tour fare from N.Y. for groups of 16 or more, airfares from airports. Tickets must be purchased 21 days in advance, departures. Prices subject to change. Subject to government approval.

British Tourist Authority
Box 4100
Grand Central Station
New York, N.Y. 10017

Gentlemen,
Please rush me a free copy of 'Britain '74.'

Name
Address
City
State

---

525 Castles & Palaces, $15.
Bed & Breakfast, $13.
Changing the Guard, free.
Ploughman's lunch, $1.95.
2 Magna Cartas, free.
That's what makes Britain great.

Night castles for night inns

If you've been saving up for a trip to Britain, here's good news. You can stop saving and start packing. Because you can vacation in Britain for a lot less than you might think. In fact, many of the major attractions in Britain are not just inexpensive, but free.

In addition to its many values, Britain gives you something that money can't buy–2,000 years of history.

Imagine spending the night in a 500-year-old inn (The New Inn, Pembridge, Herefordshire, for example). Or visiting a fortress dating back to 1097 (the Tower of London). Or standing where William the Conqueror stood. Or where Shakespeare wrote. Or where Thomas à Becket worshipped.

Low-cost lodging.

Even in this day and age you can still find decent accommodations in London for as little as $5.5 (double). If you don't mind sharing a bathroom. And that price includes Continental breakfast. Send the coupon at the right for a list of 52 hotels offering these budget accommodations.

If you're travelling through the countryside, you'll find many charming inns. You'll also find B&B. That's Bed & Breakfast. You'll see it on signs outside homes and farmhouses all over Britain. It means that inside you can get a comfortable bed and a good breakfast for about $13 a person.

In Scotland or Wales, you can rent a 3-bedroom furnished cottage for only $175 a week for your whole family. That's less than $25 a night.

Eating inexpensively.

At a typical London pub, a ploughman's lunch of bread, Cheddar cheese and pickled onions will run you about $1.95, including a half pint of beer. The hot dish of the day might cost you a trifle more. For dinner, have a heaping plate of fish and chips for about $4.

In the countryside, the prices are even lower.

Back in London you might want to see a play. Seats can be had for around $5.

Free sights that are priceless.

Changing the Guard, the Houses of Parliament, Portobello Road and Petticoat Lane, the British Museum (which has two of the four existing Magna Cartas, among other wonders), Westminster Abbey, the National and Tate Galleries, Hyde Park. All free.

Of course, some attractions do cost money. Admission to the Royal Botanical Gardens at Kew is 12¢.

Shopping for values.

Shetland pullovers are currently around $15. A Marks and Spencer raincoat is $54.

And at London's famous outdoor markets and flea markets all you need is a little money and a bit of savvy. You can strike a terrific bargain with a peddler on anything from antiques to zithers. The brochures we're offering have lots of shopping hints.

The low cost of getting around.

Travel London by tube (subway). Everybody does. It's quiet, convenient, comfortable and economical. So are the famous double-decker buses. A $3 ticket bought from one of London Transport's offices will take you all over town. For $3.50 you can take a 20-mile sightseeing tour.

British Rail has some great deals on wheels with BritRail Passes. One plan allows you seven days of unlimited economy class travel in England, Scotland and Wales for just $85. Senior citizens can travel first class for the same price.

And if you're thinking of travelling around, by all means buy an 'Open-to-View' ticket from your travel agent. It opens the doors to more than 525 castles, stately homes and historic sites all over Britain. For just $15.

To learn more, send for our free brochures. They're packed with values, and they'll help assure that your visit to Britain adds up to a trip that's memorable and affordable.

Great Britain Great Value

British Tourist Authority,
Box 2900, Grand Central Station,
New York, NY 10017

Please send me your free 'great value' brochures.

Name
Address
City
State   Zip

BRITAIN
ENGLAND SCOTLAND WALES

Opposite *Research revealed that American visitors to Britain wanted to see Westminster Abbey and other historical buildings more than anything else. This powerful advertisement was written by my former partner, Clifford Field.*

Below *When you advertise a foreign country, illustrate things that are* unique *to that country. This marvelous copy was written by Bob Marshall.*

in Britain. This was met by advertising the *actual* prices of hotels and restaurants.

Perhaps the most important factor in the success of tourism advertising is the subjects you choose to illustrate. My advice is to choose things that are unique to the country concerned. People don't go half the way round the world to see things they can equally well see at home. If you want to persuade the Swiss to visit the United States, don't advertise ski resorts. If you want Frenchmen, don't advertise American food.

Some countries are afraid that foreign tourists will mess up their

London's heart beats faster as the Life Guards clatter by

SUDDENLY, sharp against the humdrum roar of traffic, comes the clean clip of hoofbeats. Your eye is caught by the bobbing scarlet of the Life Guards, or by sunlight blinking on the Horse Guards' silver breastplates.

All heads turn as the cavalry troop sweeps by with a brave jingle. London's heart beats faster. Yours will, too.

This is a daily scene from London's passing show. It's part of the ageless pageantry of Britain.

In spring, summer, fall and winter, special red-and-gold days of pomp and circumstance await you. Whether you're here for Trooping the Colour in June—or in November for the Lord Mayor's Show—you will be struck by the British

genius for showmanship in the grand manner and great tradition.

It costs so little, nowadays, o visit this friendly country. You can fly round trip from New York to London for only $453.60 (to Scotland for $27 *less*); or go both ways by ship for $40c—with an *extra* saving of $50 between September and April. Call your travel agent today.

For free color booklet "Royal Britain," see your travel agent or write Box 135, British Travel Association.
In New York—680 Fifth Ave.; In Los Angeles—606 South Hill St.; In Chicago—39 South LaSalle St.; In Canada—90 Adelaide Street West, Toronto.

Henry VII, Elizabeth I and Mary Queen of Scots are buried in this chapel.

Tread softly past the long, long sleep of kings

THIS IS Henry VII's chapel in Westminster Abbey. These windows have filtered the sunlight of five centuries. They have also seen the crowning of twenty-two kings.

Three monarchs rest here now. Henry, Elizabeth and Mary. Such are their names in sleep. No titles. No trumpets. The banners hang battle-heavy and becalmed. But still the royal crown remains. *Honi soit qui mal y pense.*

When you go to Britain, make yourself this promise. Visit at least *one* of the thirty great cathedrals. Their famous names thunder! Durham and Armagh. Or they chime! Lincoln and Canterbury. And sometimes they *whisper*. Winchester, Norwich, Salisbury and Wells. Get a map and make your choice.

Each cathedral transcends the noblest single work of art. It is a pinnacle of faith and an act of centuries. It is an offering of human hands as close to Abraham as it is to Bach. Listen to the soaring choirs at evensong. And, if you can, go at Christmas or Easter.

You will rejoice that you did.

For free illustrated literature, see your travel agent or write Box 690, British Travel Association.
In New York—680 Fifth Ave.; In Los Angeles—612 So. Flower St.; In Chicago—39 So. LaSalle St.; In Canada—151 Bloor St. West, Toronto.

"We sailed to a lovely little Bermuda cove where we were the only couple."

Scott and Karen Austin Carlson talk about their second visit to Bermuda.

"I can't think of
anything you might
want to do that
isn't here."

"It's a different world, quaint and refined.
We love it."

Couldn't you use a little
Bermuda right now?

Bermuda

See your Travel Agent or write Bermuda, Dept. 0431, 630 Fifth Ave., New York,
N.Y. 10111 or Suite 1010, 44 School St., Boston, Mass. 02108 or 300 North State St.,
Chicago, Ill. 60610 or Suite 2008, 235 Peachtree St. N.E., Atlanta, Ga. 30303.

Left *Bermuda advertises scenes designed to appeal to the kind of visitors it wants.*

Below *The biggest obstacle to tourism in Puerto Rico was its image. Research showed that people believed it to be the dirtiest, poorest, most squalid island in the Caribbean. Nothing could have been further from the truth, and this I demonstrated in advertisements. Tourism increased by leaps and bounds.*

cultural environment. Some years ago a prayer was read from the pulpit in every church in Greece, asking the Almighty to spare the Greeks from the 'scourge' of foreign tourism. When I was in Crete not long ago, it was obvious that this prayer had not been answered. Bermuda, which might easily have been turned into another Miami Beach, has had the wisdom to aim its advertising at the kind of Americans they would like to have.

Most people who travel abroad have had at least a smattering of college education and are unashamed culture-vultures – especially the wives. When they go to Europe, they collect museums, cathedrals, chateaux and so on. An exception was the Texan who told me:'The tour operator had us spend *two days* in Venice. What is there to see in Venice? When you've seen the glass factory, there isn't anything else.' A friend of mine was reluctantly persuaded by his family to visit cathedrals all over Europe. A few days after his return to Minneapolis, he felt it his duty to show me his own cathedral. 'Yes,' he said, 'we have the damn things here too.'

People *dream* about visiting foreign countries. The job of your advertising is to convert their dreams into action. This can best be done by combining mouth-watering photographs with specific how-to-do-it information. You show a photograph of an ancient Oxford college, and tell the reader how much it costs to go and see it. When you are advertising *little-known* countries, it is particularly important to give people a lot of information. In a two-page newspaper advertisement for

Girl by a gate
—in old San Juan

TIME STANDS STILL in this Puerto Rican patio. That weathered escutcheon bears the Royal Arms of Spain. You might have stepped back three centuries. In a sense, you have.

You start to wonder. Can this really be the Puerto Rico everybody is talking about? Is this the island where American industry is now expanding at the rate of three new plants a week? Is this truly the scene of a twentieth-century renaissance? Ask any proud Puerto Rican. He will surely answer—yes.

Within minutes from this patio, you will see the signs. Some are spectacular. The new hotels, the four-lane highways, the landscaped apartments. And some are down-to-earth. A tractor in a field, a village clinic, a shop that sells refrigerators. Note all these things. But, above all, *meet the people.*

Renaissance has a way of breeding remarkable men. Men of industry who can also love poetry. Men of courage who can also be tender. Men of vision who can also respect the past. Make a point of talking to these twentieth-century Puerto Ricans.

It won't be long before you appreciate the deeper significance of Puerto Rico's renaissance. You'll begin to understand why men like Pablo Casals and Juan Ramón Jiménez (the Nobel Prize poet) have gone there to live.

© 1958—Commonwealth of Puerto Rico,
666 Fifth Avenue, New York 19, N. Y.

◄ *How to find this patio in old San Juan. Ask for the City Hall. They call it the Ayuntamiento, in Spanish. Walk straight through this 17th Century building and there is your patio. Our photograph was taken by Elliott Erwitt.*

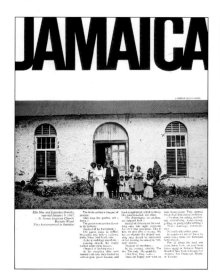

Above and right *To attract tourists to Jamaica, Doyle Dane Bernbach created a campaign which is a classic of travel advertising.*

In Jamaica, we treat our country as though it were one enormous living room. Be our guest.

A homeland is not a house. But, in Jamaica, that's exactly how we treat our country.

We use the outdoors as the place we do most of our living in.

For breakfast, lunch, dinner, cocktails, tea, and snacks, we sit out under arbors, breadfruit trees, trellises, blue sky, moonlight.

We socialize at parties on beaches, at theaters on lawns, at concerts under gazebos.

And we ska, bossa nova, and chachacha open-air.

We also do laundry in rivers, bathe under waterfalls, are married in gardens, get barbered on beaches, and cook under thatched shelters.

Walls and doors are often just air—*nothing* there.

Most rooms are balconied. Terraces are topless.

Movies are roofless. (Look, *real* stars.)

We go to school in buildings that birds can swoop through.

Our fruit stores are mangoes, pawpaw and pineapple spread out on sidewalks.

And our factories are sunlit fields of cane, coffee, spices, and banana.

We live so intimately with the land, the sea, the trees, the flowers that the salt spray of the surf rusts our sewing machines; birds share our breakfast buns; coconut husks stuff our mattresses; bamboo trunks are whittled into our musical instruments; cottonwood trees are carved into our dug-out canoes; and the hibiscus flower is what we use to shine our shoes.

For more about outdoors, indoors, no-doors of Jamaica, see your local travel agent or Jamaica Tourist Board in New York, Miami, San Francisco, Chicago, Los Angeles or Toronto.

Singapore we told readers about what to wear, the weather they could expect, the language, the food, costs, every mortal thing.

For most Americans, cost is the biggest obstacle, followed, I believe, by *fear*. Fear that they won't be able to communicate. Fear that they will lose their money. Fear of the foreigners; research has found that Americans believe the British to be polite, honest and aloof, and the French to be rude, immoral and dirty. Fear of the food.* Do your best to allay these fears.

Patterns of travel are peculiarly subject to *fashion*. The Virgin Islands may be all the rage one year, Hawaii the next. Try to put your country on the map, with headlines like *Suddenly everyone is going to Ruritania.*

Left *The best photograph in the history of travel advertising evokes rural France in masterly fashion. Taken by Elliott Erwitt under the inspiration of Bill Bernbach.*

*Two Frenchmen were driving through the Cotswolds in England. One said to the other, 'You must admit this is a very beautiful country.' 'Yes,' replied his friend, 'it *is* beautiful. Thank God they can't cook it.'

Above *By writing the headline in French – with a translation underneath – I got high readership, and differentiated France from other tourist destinations.*

Tourism advertising works well in magazines, but it can work even better on television. Doyle Dane Bernbach's commercials for France were enchanting. I particularly remember one which sought to persuade American tourists to visit the French provinces. 'When you've seen France, you will never go back to Paris.'

I believe that *charm* works well in tourism advertising. And *differentiation*. If you write your headlines in French, everybody will know you are advertising France.

11

The secrets of success in business-to-business advertising

It used to be called *trade* advertising, or *industrial* advertising, but its practitioners have taken to calling it 'business-to-business,' which sounds classier. It means products that people buy for their companies, not for themselves. I will tell you what I have learned about it, drawing heavily and gratefully on research conducted by McGraw-Hill.

Print
McGraw-Hill tells us that the average salesman's call costs $178, a letter $6.63 and a phone call $6.35, while you can reach a prospect through advertising for only 17 cents.

Admittedly an advertisement, however efficient, can seldom close a sale itself. Its function is to *pave the way* for salesmen, by pre-selling your product and attracting leads.

In industrial companies there are an average of four 'buying influences.' Your sales force is unlikely to know all four. Sixty per cent of 'specifiers' – people who set down the specifications that must be met – read advertisements to learn what's on the market.

By and large, the advertising techniques that work in this kind of advertising are the same as the techniques that work in consumer advertising – like promising the reader a benefit, news, testimonials, and helpful information.

Make sure that what you promise is important to your customer. A supplier of computer software was proud of the size of his company and wanted to make it the feature of his advertising, but research found that his customers were not interested in size. They were looking for responsiveness, support, service – and a good product.

Make your promise specific. Instead of generalities, use percentages, time elapsed, dollars saved. You are talking to engineers.

Testimonials work well, as long as they come from experts in reputable companies. A testimonial from Bud Dacus impresses tugboat engineers because Bud has worked the Mississippi for 25 years – longer than Mark Twain.

Demonstrations are most effective when they compare your product's performance with your competitors'. Try to devise a simple demonstration that your reader can perform himself, like inviting him to scrape the liner of your air-duct with a coin to see how tough it is.

News works well. It appears that readers scan the advertisements in technical journals looking for new products. To my surprise, a McGraw-Hill study found that advertising is twice as effective as an article in the same journal. Be sure to *proclaim* your news, loud and clear.

Information that is useful to the reader in his job can also be effective, provided the information involves your product. For example, you can show the reader how to calculate the amount of money he could save by using your product.

Some copywriters, assuming that the reader will find the product as boring as they do, try to inveigle him into their ads with pictures of babies, beagles and bosoms. This is a mistake. A buyer of flexible pipe for offshore oil rigs is more interested in pipe than anything else in the world. So play it straight.

Layouts should be simple, avoiding the arty devices dear to second-rate art directors – like type which is too big to be readable, eccentric designs and headlines at the bottom of the page. If you make your ads look like editorial pages, you will get more readers. Far more.

A. E. "Bud" Dacus finds Caprinus R Oil 40 helps keep EMD-567C s in top condition. "Works equally well in my Detroit Diesel 6-71 auxiliary diesels," he says.
"I'm impressed–Shell's Caprinus® R Oil 40 keeps my EMD's in better condition than any other oil I've used in 20 years."
Says A. E. "Bud" Dacus, Chief Engineer of the M/V Crescent City since her launching in 1958.
"We've tried a good many engine oils in the Crescent City over the past 20 years," continues Mr. Dacus, veteran engineer for the Sioux City-New Orleans Barge Company of Hartford, Illinois.
Absence of carbon or ash deposits on piston undercrowns demonstrates outstanding stability of Caprinus T and Caprinus R Oils.
"Until recently, we considered Shell's Caprinus*T Oil 40 the best. It kept our EMD's in fine condition. But Caprinus R Oil 40 looks even better."
Mr. Dacus made his comments during a routine teardown of his EMD 16-567Cs after 18,875 hours of service. The engine photographed had been on Shell's Caprinus T Oil and switched to Caprinus R Oil for the last 5,000 hours.
Exceptional Cleanliness
"I never saw an engine look so clean after 5,000 hours on any oil," adds Mr. Dacus. "It looked even cleaner at 18,875 hours than at the 13,000 hour mark. Top decks had just a light oil film. Intake ports were wide open. Practically no sludge in the sump. Minimum wear on rings."
Guards against corrosion
Caprinus R Oil 40 is higher in initial alkalinity than Caprinus T Oil (10.2 TNB-E compared to 7.5) and retains effective alkalinity in extended high-stress service. It neutralizes combustion acids and guards against corrosive wear of rings and liners over long periods.
Filters frequently last longer, too. Caprinus R Oil's dispersant additive system helps keep insolubles in suspension, prevent heavy deposit buildup. Result — the possibility of significantly extended filter service life, an important maintenance saving.
The switch is on to Caprinus R
Top engine performance is why nearly 100 towboats, including ten from the Sioux City-New Orleans Barge Company, have already switched to Shell's Caprinus R Oil. Look into this high alkalinity engine oil for your vessels. It could mean important savings in operating costs for you!
Intake ports for an EMD 16-567C cylinder are completely free of deposits after more than 13,000 hours on Caprinus T Oil and 5,000 hours on Caprinus R.
Send for technical bulletin describing the properties and applications of Caprinus R Oil 40 in medium-speed diesels. Just write: Shell Oil Company, Manager, Commercial Communications, One Shell Plaza, Houston, Texas 77002.
Come to Shell for answers
*Caprinus is a trademark and is used as such in this writing.

Right *Testimonials work well when they come from recognized experts in well-known companies.*

THE LONGEST LINE JUST GOT LONGER.

HERCULES NOW ADDS
TWO NEW GRADES
TO ITS LONG LINE OF
PRO-FAX® COPOLYMERS

First, there's a new "non-blush" grade
that eliminates those costly bruise
marks on injection-molded products like
institutional seating and battery cases.
Second, is a special, new, low-ethylene
random grade, with improved optics for
blow-molded bottles and cast film.
These two new resins join the seven
families of Pro-fax copolymers, all of which
are designed to do a specific job: either
in an application demanding optical superiority; or in a part where toughness
is paramount.
Have we talked about your require-
ment? Send for data on the "longest line"
there is in copolymers.
Hercules Incorporated, Plastic Resins,
910 Market Street, Wilmington, DE 19899.

FOR QUICK
RESPONSE TO
TECHNICAL
AND
APPLICATION
QUESTIONS
CALL
MR. R. COMBS,
TOLL FREE.

800-441-7595

IN DELAWARE, CALL COLLECT: (302) 575-6089.

HERCULES

Reader service No. 4

Above *Some copywriters, assuming that the reader will find the product as boring as they do, try to inveigle him into their ads with pictures of babies, beagles and bosoms. A mistake.*

Headlines get five times the readership of the body copy. If your headline doesn't sell, you have wasted your money. Your headline should promise a benefit, or deliver news, or offer a service, or tell a significant story, or recognize a problem, or quote a satisfied customer.

Body copy is seldom read by more than 10 per cent of the readers of a publication. But that 10 per cent consists of *prospects* – people interested enough in what you are selling to take the trouble to *read* about it. What you say to them determines the success of your advertisement.

When you advertise bubblegum or underwear, there isn't much to say, but a computer or a generator calls for long copy. Don't be afraid to write it. Long copy – more than 350 words – actually attracts *more* readers than short copy.

In business publications four-color ads cost only a third more than black and white, but they attract twice as many readers. Four-color is a good buy.

Captions should appear under all your photographs. Twice as many people read them as read body copy. And use your captions to *sell*. The best captions are mini-advertisements in themselves.

Television
Business-to-business advertisers are turning increasingly to *television*. The audiences for many sports and news programs include a high

It pays to devise a demonstration that your readers can perform for themselves, like this one.

percentage of business people and are therefore efficient buys. The principles that apply to consumer advertising on television are equally valid for business-to-business commercials.

News and *demonstrations* work particularly well. Even humor has its place, as in the hilarious Ally and Gargano commercials for Federal Express. But it is worth noting that the humor in these commercials always supports the powerful end promise: 'Federal Express – when it absolutely has to be there overnight.'

Some products used by business cannot be sold in 30 seconds. In such cases, I advise you to sacrifice frequency to delivering a thorough sales message. For IBM computers we used *three minutes*.

Many small business-to-business advertisers shy away from television because commercials cost so much to produce, but inexpensive commercials can be highly effective – if they come directly to the point and offer something of genuine interest. I have seen a television commercial for an industrial product produce so many inquiries that it had to be taken off the air; the salesmen couldn't handle any more. One commercial for another industrial product produced more inquiries in two months than print advertising had produced in a year. (However, the print advertising produced a higher rate of conversion to sales.)

Differentiating commodity products

Many industrial products are *thought* to be little more than commodities, with no apparent differences between them. How do you differentiate your bolts, washers or machine tools from those of your competitors? But, says Professor Levitt, 'there is no such thing as a commodity. All goods and services are differentiable.'

In a *Harvard Business Review* article, Professor William K. Hall reported on a study of eight industries, from steel to beer. The most successful companies were those that best differentiated their product or service.

According to Professor Hall, the most successful commodity products differentiated themselves in one of two ways: either by low cost or by having the best reputation for quality or service. Advertising can help you spread the news about any *price* advantage you may have, and it can work wonders in creating a reputation for quality or service.

Before 1972, Owens-Corning sold its insulation to builders for use in new homes. In those days insulation was all the same – a commodity. And so the Owens-Corning advertising looked pretty much like its competitors. Later, when fuel prices went up and construction of new homes went down, Owens-Corning differentiated its insulation as the brand of choice for owners of old homes who want to reduce their fuel costs. This was done by latching onto an apparently unimportant feature: the unique *color* of the Owens-Corning product.

Today Owens-Corning Fiberglas has escaped from the 'commodity trap.' It has by far the best reputation for quality among all insulation material, being preferred 3 to 1 over the second brand.

How to stimulate inquiries

McGraw-Hill reports that nearly all inquiries come from people who have a specific need or application in mind; and a substantial percentage of them buy within six months of their inquiry.

Always put a toll-free number in your advertisements, to make the inquiry as fast and as easy as possible. In the United States, seven out of ten readers of trade journals now use such numbers. Include a business reply card *and* a coupon requesting more information. This combination guarantees you the greatest number of productive inquiries.

In addition, *close your body copy* with your offer, your address and phone number. The average business publication is read by three readers besides the subscriber. If the first reader cuts out the coupon, the others cannot respond to the offer without the second address.

Analyse your inquiries

Analyse your inquiries and the action they produce. This will enable you to answer your boss's inevitable question: 'What tangible results am I getting from my advertising?' Here are three ways to analyse inquiries:

1   Survey a sample of inquirers. Do they intend to buy your product? To bide their time until a salesman calls? Or simply to keep your product in mind for the future?

2   Question the sales people who follow up the inquiries. Did the inquiry lead to a sale? Was this account a new prospect? How did the salesman rate this prospect – a one-time sale, a growth account, a dead end? The discovery of a single major sale resulting from an inquiry can do more than anything else to demonstrate the value of your advertising.

3   Relate inquiries to the media that produced them. This can help you fine-tune your media selection. By doing this,

An effective strategy in business advertising is to show the reader how he can calculate the money your product would save him. This advertisement got the highest readership everywhere it ran, and brought hundreds of requests for reprints.

one manufacturer was able to reduce his advertising budget by 25 per cent.

Advertising to top management

Many business purchases require approval from top management as well as the purchasing agent. Top managers may not respond to, or even understand, the details that are important to the specifiers. They are only interested in the broad benefits – particularly cost savings.

It sometimes pays to run separate campaigns – one addressed to top management, the other to the specialists who read trade publications.

12

Direct mail, my first love and secret weapon

With tips on direct advertising in magazines and television

One day a man walked into a London agency and asked to see the boss. He had bought a country house and was about to open it as a hotel. Could the agency help him to get customers? He had $500 to spend. Not surprisingly, the head of the agency turned him over to the office boy, who happened to be the author of this book. I invested his money in penny postcards and mailed them to well-heeled people living in the neighborhood. Six weeks later the hotel opened to a full house. *I had tasted blood.*

From that day on, I have been a voice crying in the wilderness, trying to persuade the advertising establishment to take direct mail more seriously and to stop treating its practitioners as non-commissioned officers. It was my secret weapon in the avalanche of new business acquisitions which made Ogilvy & Mather an instant success.

Today, direct mail has exploded – an explosion caused more than anything by computers. They make it possible to select names from mailing lists by every imaginable demographic classification, by frequency of purchase and by amount of purchase. With a computer you can remove duplication between mailing lists and within a list – a process called 'merge and purge.' You can even avoid mailing to people who don't like receiving mailings.

Computers make it possible for every letter in a mailing of millions to include the name of each addressee, not only in the salutation, but several times in the body of the letter.

Most direct-response buying is now done with a credit card, and the companies that issue the cards know who has bought what. If you have charged a trip to Disney World in Florida, I can send you a mailing for Disneyland in California.

The biggest users of direct mail are magazine publishers in search of subscriptions, catalog houses, food stores, department stores, record clubs and book clubs. It has been estimated that total sales by direct mail in the United States are now more than a hundred billion dollars a year.

Unfortunately, there are a lot of fly-by-night frauds in the direct-mail business, including, say the *New York Times*, ten thousand phoney 'pastors.' In 1980, 1,500,000 consumers complained to the Better

Business Bureau about firms which had failed to deliver the merchandise they had ordered, or had delivered it too late or in damaged condition. In the whole spectrum of marketing, direct mail is where you find the swindlers. That said, the vast bulk of advertising by direct mail is on the level.

Advertisers who distribute their products in the normal way, through wholesalers and retailers, have great difficulty in isolating the results of their advertising from the other factors in their marketing mix, but direct-mail advertisers can measure the results of their mailings to the dollar. This makes it possible for them to test everything they do. *In direct mail, testing is the name of the game.*

You can test every variable in your mailings and determine *exactly* its effect on your sales. But because you can only test one variable at a time, you cannot afford to test them all. So you have to choose which to test. Experienced practitioners always test *some* variables, but seldom those which experience has taught them make little difference in results. Next to the positioning of your product, the most important variables to be tested are pricing, terms of payment, premiums and the format of your mailing.

The price you ask and the terms of payment you offer are critical, and they can be tested by sample mailings. A highbrow magazine tested three terms of payment for subscriptions. In one, the subscriber was asked to pay $65 for 56 issues. In another, $42.50 for 39 issues. In the third, $29.95 for 29 issues. Guess which won? Although it cut the price 40 per cent, the third generated 35 per cent more net revenue.

When collections of Moscow Olympic Games silver, gold and platinum coins were sold by direct mail, a mailing which offered only the *silver* coins led to more sales of the complete collection than a mailing which offered the complete collection itself.

When your profit margin allows, it pays to offer a free premium. Always test different premiums. One of the most effective is cash prizes in sweepstakes. Sweepstakes, premiums, free offers, and low prices will build up your initial response, but the customer who is attracted by these devices is not always the customer who turns into a long-term buyer.

Asking for the full price and cash with the order will reduce the number of people who respond. But it may turn up more customers who are likely to stay with you over the years. Only testing will tell. The more you test, the more profitable your direct mail will become.

Once you have evolved a mailing which produces profitable results, treat it as the 'control' and start testing ways to beat it. Try adding a premium, or putting in an expiration date, or adding enclosures – like a personalized letter from your President. They cost money, but if they increase your *profit*, why worry?

Sometimes an expensive control can be made less expensive without reducing your orders. You can test a smaller mailing piece, or eliminate the personalization, or print your brochure in two colors instead of four, or eliminate the brochure altogether. You may be in for a pleasant surprise. Less can be more.

Innovations, provided you test them, can work wonders.

A solid silver issue
so limited only a fraction of Olympic Coin
collectors can own this edition

Only an extremely limited number of 1980 Olympic Coin Collections will be minted and offered to collectors—so few, in fact, that only a fraction of 1976 Olympic Coin collectors will be able to own them.

For example, only 450,000 of each Coin in Series I Geographic will be minted. 100,000 will be reserved for distribution within the Soviet Union and other related Socialist countries—leaving a total of only 350,000 for the rest of the world. In contrast, the 1976 Montreal Olympic minting was between 650,000 and 1,480,000 of each Coin, depending on the Series.

The 1952 Helsinki issue was 600,000. And the 1964 Innsbruck issue was 2,900,000.

Nearly half a million collectors in the U.S. and Canada purchased Canadian Olympic Coins. Yet, the entire number of 1980 Olympic Coins available to North American collectors is only 20 percent of the Canadian Olympic Coins available in 1976.

In the entire history of Olympic Coinage there has never been an issue quite like this one. These rare and beautiful Coins commemorate the first Olympic Games ever held in the USSR. They are the first Proof Quality Coins ever minted in the Soviet Union. They are legal tender in the USSR, backed for their full face value at the official rate of exchange by the Soviet Authorities.

And because so few 1980 Olympic Coins will be available, their importance is even further enhanced.

Certificate of Authenticity

All Proof Quality 1980 Olympic Coins come with a signed and numbered Certificate of Authenticity, which validates the Proof Quality of the Coins, their precious metal content and their identity as the Official 1980 Olympic Issue by authority of the Chief Manager of the Goznak Mints.

This direct-mail shot for Moscow Olympic Games silver coins worked well.

Prospects for a new Cessna Citation business jet were surprised when we sent them live carrier pigeons, with an invitation to take a free ride in a Citation. The recipient was asked to release our carrier pigeon with his address tied to its leg. Some of the recipients *ate* the pigeons, but several returned alive, and at least one Citation was sold – for $600,000.

My brother Francis wrote a letter in Greek to the headmasters of private schools, selling cooking stoves. When some wrote back that they could not read Greek, he sent them another letter – in Latin. This produced orders.

Successful mailings do not always depend on premiums, brochures and other such paraphernalia. I have seen letters produce satisfactory results all by themselves. But they have to be *long* letters. When Mercedes-Benz were saddled with 1,170 obsolete diesels, we mailed a five-page letter and unloaded the surplus. For Cunard we used an *eight-page* letter with marked success.

'My brother Francis wrote a letter in Greek to the headmasters of private schools, selling cooking stoves. When some wrote back that they could not read Greek, he sent them another letter – in Latin.'

Direct response advertising in magazines and television

So far this chapter has been about direct *mail*. Now I am going to tell you what I have learned about a parallel science – advertisements in magazines and on television which invite people to send their orders direct to you, without going to a store.

In print advertisements, your *headline* is the most important element. The other day I saw one headline produce five times as many orders as another. If your headline promises your strongest and most distinct benefit, you are on your way to success.

Good photographs of your product cost more than bad ones, but they also *sell* more. When you want to show something that cannot be photographed, like cutaways of the inside of your product, use a drawing.

Long copy sells more than short copy, particularly when you are asking the reader to spend a lot of money. Only amateurs use short copy.

Cross-heads give breathing space to your copy, and make it more readable. They should be written in such a way that skimmers get the main points of your sales story.

Testimonials increase credibility – and sales. If one testimonial tests well, try two. But don't use testimonials by *celebrities*, unless they are recognized authorities, like Arnold Palmer on golf clubs.

Winston Churchill said, 'Short words are best, and the old words when short are best of all.' This applies in spades to mail order copy.

Set your copy in black type on white paper. You will already know how much I loathe 'reverse type' – white on black – for the very good reason that it reduces readership. There are only two exceptions. People read theater programs in the dark, holding them up against the light coming from the stage, so they are easier to read when set in reverse. So are slides projected onto a screen.

Readers often skip from the headline to the coupon, to find out what your offer is. So make your coupons mini-ads, complete with brand name, promise and a miniature photograph of your product.

Many readers tell themselves they will mail the coupon 'later,' but never get around to it. One survey showed that twice as much response is lost in this way as is received by the advertiser. Here are four ways to keep your prospects on the hook:

○ 'Limited edition'
○ 'Limited supply'
○ 'Last time at this price'
○ 'Special price for promptness'

It used to be thought that the more cluttered your layout, the more you would sell. My observation has been the opposite. Tidy, well-organized layouts actually increase coupon returns.

Where to advertise

You know exactly how many inquiries, and ultimately how many *orders* you get from each insertion in each publication. One magazine may perform twice as well as another. Such variations can be enough to make the difference between profit and loss.

Watch the media your competitors use, in particular the media they *continue* to use. Watch for editorial changes in magazines. They may attract your kind of reader, or may drive them away.

Go easy on two-page spreads. They cost twice as much as single pages, but seldom produce twice as many orders. Test different units of space, like a page and a business reply card versus a page alone. Although the card may double the cost, it can sometimes generate four times as many orders as the page alone.

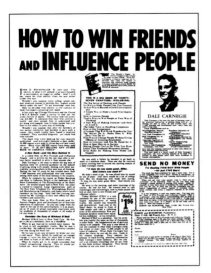

Above *This advertisement, written by Vic Schwab, sold a million books in three years – by mail order. The promise in the headline and the content of the copy were irresistible.*

Right *James Webb Young was the creative head of J. Walter Thompson for 40 years. In his spare time he ran a mail-order business in Santa Fe under the name Webb Young, Trader. This is one of his advertisements, and an object lesson in mail-order advertising. One insertion in* Life *sold 26,000 ties.*

Below right *What parent could resist this British direct-mail advertisement. The copywriter was David Abbott.*

Ogilvy & Mather Direct Response

The advertising agency with the secret weapon

"For forty years, I have been a voice crying in the wilderness, trying to get my fellow advertising practitioners to take direct response seriously. Direct response was my first love. And later, my secret weapon."

David Ogilvy

Forty-two years ago, David Ogilvy, the founder of Ogilvy & Mather, recognised direct response as possibly, the most sophisticated and precise marketing tool available to businessmen. Direct response is effective, cost efficient and accountable.

Today, there are 17 Ogilvy & Mather Direct Response offices around the world, with billings totalling more than US$100 million.

In Singapore, Ogilvy & Mather Direct Response was established in January 1980, by our Managing Director, Peter Stening.

We are the first and only fully computerised direct response company in Singapore, or for that matter, South East Asia.

We offer our clients complete in-house production facilities for every element of their direct response campaigns — from creative planning to media recommendations to computerised mailing.

Our success in our first year prompted Michael Ball, Regional Head of Ogilvy & Mather and a Director of Ogilvy & Mather International, to make the Singapore office the regional coordinating Direct Response centre for South East Asia.

Direct mail — our most powerful tool

Direct mail is the most powerful tool at the disposal of Ogilvy & Mather Direct Response. No other medium can be so precise, yet so flexible.

Unlike print advertising or television commercials, direct mail is not restricted by space or time. There are no limits, except the clients' budget and the creative peoples' imagination.

Direct mail is dependent on selective, constantly updated and deduplicated mailing lists. Effective deduplication can only be achieved on a computer. With-out deduplication, you run the risk of annoying existing or potential customers with repeated mailings. Moreover, each duplicated mailing is money wasted.

The selection of the right prospect list is the most critical point in the direct mail programme. The best creative idea and the soundest copy may go to waste if the right list is not available.

The Singapore office is the only Ogilvy & Mather Direct Response agency in the world to own its own computerised mailing lists. We have direct access to the names, addresses and information of over a million people, companies and organisations in Singapore. So we can reach your target audience with a bull's eye. Everytime!

Our computer bank also provides list storage and processing facilities for our offices in Hong Kong, Bangkok, Kuala Lumpur and Jakarta as part of our regional co-ordination.

Specialists in our own right

Direct response advertising is more than just adding a coupon to an advertisement or writing a letter to a potential consumer.

An agency can produce a magnificent mailing package. Lavish, expensive and beautifully executed. But it will not bring the expected result if the call for action is not correctly emphasised.

Direct response is a specialised form of advertising. There is no such thing as hard sell or soft sell.

It's sell or no sell.

We have seen one direct response advertisement sell *nineteen times* as much of a product as another advertise-ment for the same product. A change in the headline was the only variable. The media rates cost the same for both advertisements.

Direct response requires more specialised skills than, perhaps, any other form of advertising. There are very few people who are adept at the art of direct response advertising . You should not give the job to amateurs.

Anybody can claim they have a direct response capability. But only Ogilvy & Mather Direct Response can prove it. Compared to an average response rate in most western countries of two to three per cent, our direct response advertising in Singapore has yielded average responses of five to seven per cent.

Talk to our clients.
They are our best supporters.

Using our computer, we can reach your target audience individually, with personalised mailings.

Measurable performance

Ogilvy & Mather Direct Response offers you professionals in every aspect: creative, media, production and account management. Because the work we perform for our clients is measurable, our performance is also directly measurable. Ogilvy & Mather Direct Response International has become one of the world's largest direct response agencies because of our professional expertise.

Last year in Singapore, we created more than a million dollars' worth of direct response advertising — in mail and media — for clients big and small.

In the process, we have learnt that direct response advertising can help sell $100,000 cars as well as a $1 jar of baby cream. We have also discovered many other profitable ways to use this most accountable form of advertising as part of our clients' marketing plans. Some of them may be useful to you.

Building sales leads. Direct response has proved to be an extremely effective and economical way to produce highly qualified industrial sales leads.

We created two special mailing packages for Solna, a leading Swedish manufacturer of printing machinery, that provided our client with 850 sales leads.

Building store traffic. A personal letter and an attractive offer can often do wonders for getting customers back into a store.

Our mailing package for Fitzpatrick's Supermarket was highly successful in increasing store traffic.

Getting new business from old customers. It can cost less to sell to your present customers than to acquire new ones. Very often, satisfied customers of one division of a company are ideal prospects for the products and services offered by another division.

Customer communications. More and more companies are rediscovering the bottom-line value of customer goodwill. Direct mail is the most personal and effective way to let your customers know you *care*.

For King & Shaxson Investment Fund Managers, we mail personal letters and news of the latest investment developments to their clients every month. The result? A substantial increase in business.

Our client, American Express, has and will continue to build business through direct mail.

Introducing new products. Direct response can sometimes be an effective way to introduce a new product to key prospects. It can also be used to pre-test the consumer appeal of a new product at only a fraction of normal market test costs.

We helped Aspatra Guan Hoe, agents for Saab cars, launch their Saab Turbo 900 by sending out a mailing package that invited key prospects to come for a test drive. Our client sold three months' stock within the first month!

How to find out more

The true value of direct response advertising is yet to be realised in Asia. In Singapore, we have an ideal direct response market.

Despite the very strong Singapore identity of all our citizens, the population is clearly structured into socio-economic, cultural, language, religious and ethnic groups. Direct response provides a very precise method of reaching these specific groups cost-effectively, particularly when relatively limited advertising or promotional budgets are available.

If you would like to learn more about how direct response advertising can increase your sales and profits, please call Peter Stening or Eric Stanley at 223 8722. Or post the coupon for a copy of our brochure that contains full details of our secret weapon: direct response.

What is direct response?

Direct response advertising refers to any kind of advertising that seeks a direct response — an order or an inquiry- from the consumer.

Direct response can be included in all forms of advertising: press, magazines, television, radio, cinema. Any advertising medium.

Direct response can be direct mail. Information posted to people about whom certain factors are known, eg. income bracket, occupation, interests etc.

Direct response communication can be by telephone. Telephone marketing is a fast growing segment of direct response. Goods and services are being offered over the telephone to obtain orders and inquiries.

Direct response advertising also includes two-way television. This electronic media is already revolutionising the direct marketing fields in Europe and the United States, and is just around the corner for Singapore.

In every instance, the advertisement, mailing piece or telephone call includes a call for action: *A request for a direct response.*

Direct response advertising gives you the ability – unique in advertising – to measure results and returns on investments *precisely*. An irresistible advantage in today's economy.

In addition, you can pinpoint your markets, instead of reaching audiences composed mostly of poor prospects.

When you advertise repeatedly in the same magazine, response rates almost always drop. In some magazines, your ad may make a profit *six* times a year, while you may be able to use other magazines *twelve* times before they become unprofitable.

Television

It may surprise you to know that the right kind of television commercial can persuade people to order products by mail or telephone – mostly telephone. The 'right kind' are those which set up a problem and demonstrate how your product can solve it; give a money-back guarantee; include the price; and ask for the order, explicitly and urgently.

The demonstrations should promise not *one* benefit, but several. (This runs counter to the Procter & Gamble formula.)

My partner Al Eicoff has had more experience than anyone in selling direct on television. He has almost never seen a commercial shorter than two minutes produce profitable sales. These marathon commercials don't seem to irritate people as much as a cluster of short ones – 'like five salesmen knocking on the door, one after another.'

You must allow 20 seconds to give information on *how to order*. This is long enough to give your toll-free telephone number and post office box number, complete with supers; and to repeat the charge-free telephone number at least twice.

'The more people *trust* you, the more they buy from you.'

Most advertisers measure their purchases on television time by cost per thousand viewers reached, but Eicoff measures them by the *number of orders* he receives each time a station broadcasts one of his commercials. He then eliminates the time periods and the stations that don't pay off. The most productive times are early morning, late evening and weekends. January, February and March are the most profitable months.

The better the program on which your commercials appear, the fewer sales you make. When viewers are bored by an old movie, they are more likely to pick up the telephone and order your product than when they are riveted by an episode of *Dallas*.

Remember, there is no correlation between the size of your audience and the number of orders you receive.

*   *   *   *   *

Every chapter in this book is of necessity an over-simplification of a more-or-less complicated subject, and no more so than this one. If you want to know more about direct response, start by reading *Successful Direct Marketing Methods* by Bob Stone, published by Crain Books in Chicago.

13

Advertising for good causes

And raising money for charity

Forty years ago, the advertising establishment in the United States set up the Advertising Council to provide free campaigns for US Savings Bonds, the Red Cross and other good causes. In 1979, the media gave $600,000,000 worth of free time and space to the Council's campaigns, and the agencies charged nothing for their services. In 1980, the Council's campaign to encourage co-operation with the Census received $38,000,000 worth of free time and space.

This admirable system has one drawback: the success of each campaign depends on the generosity of the media, which cannot be predicted. The system in Britain is more controllable: the *government* provides the money.

Here are six examples of advertising for good causes.

World Wildlife Fund
During a period of five years, Ogilvy & Mather begged $6,500,000 worth of free advertising from media for the World Wildlife Fund – in 16 countries.

New York Philharmonic
In 1957 the New York Philharmonic was low in the water. The musicians were demoralized, playing to half-empty houses. My simple solution was to buy a page in the *New York Times* and publish the complete schedule for the coming season, *in advance*. Years later, someone who was in a position to know told me that this had done as much as Leonard Bernstein to put the Philharmonic back on its feet.

United Negro College Fund
A letter was distributed in commuter trains leaving Grand Central Station for the affluent suburbs. It began: 'When this train emerges from the tunnel at 108th Street this evening, *look out of the window.*' What the commuters saw was the black slums of Harlem. In a single evening

Opposite *During a period of five years, Ogilvy & Mather begged $6,500,000 worth of free space for the World Wildlife Fund in 16 countries. The ads produced only modest contributions of cash in the mail, their function being to sensitize the public for more personal methods of fund-raising.*

WWF Kojo Tanaka BCL

The Giant Panda needs your help to survive

ONCE every eighty to a hundred years the bamboo forests in China's Sichuan Province burst into flower and then die off. And that's bad news for the Giant Panda, which depends for its survival on huge amounts of bamboo.

But that's just one of the problems facing the Panda.

To ensure that it has a future it is vital to preserve the complex eco-system in which it lives, to carry out research into its dietary needs and investigate possible alternatives, to discover the reasons for its low repro-duction rate, to study the problem of internal parasites – all these factors and many more which threaten its survival.

Recognition of the urgent need to solve these and other problems has resulted in a unique and historic partnership between WWF and the People's Republic of China.

WWF has agreed to contribute US $1,000,000 towards a total of about US $3,000,000 needed by the Chinese Government to mount a major Panda Conservation Programme. This includes construction of a research and conservation centre in the largest of the Panda reserves – Wolong Natural Reserve in Sichuan Province.

A team from WWF, led by the distinguished ecologist Dr. G. Schaller, is already at work in Wolong together with top Chinese scientists under the leadership of Professor Hu Jinchu.

The Giant Panda is an endangered animal. It is also the symbol of WWF's worldwide conservation efforts to save life on earth.

But WWF needs money – your money.

Please send contributions to the WWF National Organisation in your country or direct to:

WWF International, 1196 Gland, Switzerland.

WWF WORLD WILDLIFE FUND

WWF acknowledges the donation of this space by   *Advertisement prepared as a public service by Ogilvy & Mather.*

Below right *In 1957 the New York Philharmonic was playing to half-empty houses. My simple solution was to buy space in the* New York Times *and publish the complete program for the coming season in advance. This worked.*

Below *To raise money for the United Negro College Fund, I had this letter put on every seat in the commuter trains leaving Grand Central Station for the affluent suburbs. It produced $26,000 in a single evening. The idea came from Bill Phillips, later Chairman of Ogilvy & Mather.*

this letter produced contributions of $26,000 for the United Negro College Fund.

Sierra Club

Howard Gossage, the most articulate rebel in the advertising business, held that advertising was too valuable an instrument to waste on commercial products. He believed that it justified its existence only when it was used for social purposes. One of his advertisements for the Sierra Club, opposing a hydroelectric project in Grand Canyon, pulled 3,000 applications for membership at $14 each.

Teenage alcoholism in Norway

In 1974 the Norwegian Government started an advertising campaign to reduce alcoholism among teenagers. The first advertisements were

aimed at boys and girls between the ages of 14 and 16, with headlines such as 'I vomit almost every time I drink'. Readership was the highest ever recorded in Norway. Later, the campaign was modified to address parents, explaining why children drink and the risks they run, with headlines like: 'The average Norwegian 16/17-year-old drank 155 bottles of alcohol last year. Parents should know what damage their children are risking.' More than 70 per cent of Norwegian parents read these advertisements, and the campaign triggered a massive discussion in the media. Drinking among teenagers decreased for the first time in many years.

Cancer in India

In 1978 a survey in Bombay revealed that knowledge of the causes, symptoms and treatment of cancer was abysmally low. Then the Indian

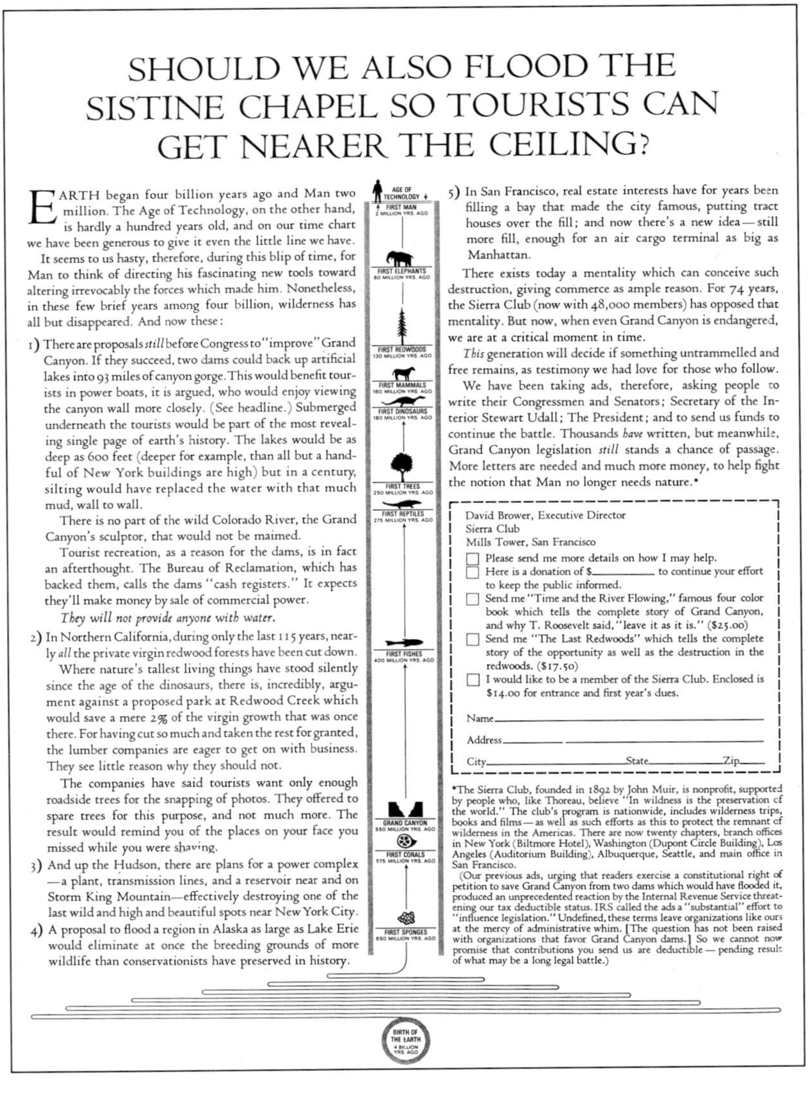
SHOULD WE ALSO FLOOD THE SISTINE CHAPEL SO TOURISTS CAN GET NEARER THE CEILING?
EARTH began four billion years ago and Man two million. The Age of Technology, on the other hand, is hardly a hundred years old, and on our time chart we have been generous to give it even the little line we have.
It seems to us hasty, therefore, during this blip of time, for Man to think of directing his fascinating new tools toward altering irrevocably the forces which made him. Nonetheless, in these few brief years among four billion, wilderness has all but disappeared. And now these:
1) There are proposals *still* before Congress to "improve" Grand Canyon. If they succeed, two dams could back up artificial lakes into 93 miles of canyon gorge. This would benefit tourists in power boats, it is argued, who would enjoy viewing the canyon wall more closely. (See headline.) Submerged underneath the tourists would be part of the most revealing single page of earth's history. The lakes would be as deep as 600 feet (deeper for example, than all but a handful of New York buildings are high) but in a century, silting would have replaced the water with that much mud, wall to wall.
There is no part of the wild Colorado River, the Grand Canyon's sculptor, that would not be maimed.
Tourist recreation, as a reason for the dams, is in fact an afterthought. The Bureau of Reclamation, which has backed them, calls the dams "cash registers." It expects they'll make money by sale of commercial power.
They will not provide anyone with water.
2) In Northern California, during only the last 115 years, nearly *all* the private virgin redwood forests have been cut down.
Where nature's tallest living things have stood silently since the age of the dinosaurs, there is, incredibly, argument against a proposed park at Redwood Creek which would save a mere 2% of the virgin growth that was once there. For having cut so much and taken the rest for granted, the lumber companies are eager to get on with business. They see little reason why they should not.
The companies have said tourists want only enough roadside trees for the snapping of photos. They offered to spare trees for this purpose, and not much more. The result would remind you of the places on your face you missed while you were shaving.
3) And up the Hudson, there are plans for a power complex—a plant, transmission lines, and a reservoir near and on Storm King Mountain—effectively destroying one of the last wild and high and beautiful spots near New York City.
4) A proposal to flood a region in Alaska as large as Lake Erie would eliminate at once the breeding grounds of more wildlife than conservationists have preserved in history.
AGE OF TECHNOLOGY
FIRST MAN 2 MILLION YRS. AGO
FIRST ELEPHANTS 60 MILLION YRS. AGO
FIRST REDWOODS 130 MILLION YRS. AGO
FIRST MAMMALS 160 MILLION YRS. AGO
FIRST DINOSAURS 180 MILLION YRS. AGO
FIRST TREES 250 MILLION YRS. AGO
FIRST REPTILES 275 MILLION YRS. AGO
FIRST FISHES 400 MILLION YRS. AGO
GRAND CANYON 550 MILLION YRS. AGO
FIRST CORALS 575 MILLION YRS. AGO
FIRST SPONGES 650 MILLION YRS. AGO
BIRTH OF THE EARTH 4 BILLION YRS. AGO
5) In San Francisco, real estate interests have for years been filling a bay that made the city famous, putting tract houses over the fill; and now there's a new idea—still more fill, enough for an air cargo terminal as big as Manhattan.
There exists today a mentality which can conceive such destruction, giving commerce as ample reason. For 74 years, the Sierra Club (now with 48,000 members) has opposed that mentality. But now, when even Grand Canyon is endangered, we are at a critical moment in time.
This generation will decide if something untrammelled and free remains, as testimony we had love for those who follow.
We have been taking ads, therefore, asking people to write their Congressmen and Senators; Secretary of the Interior Stewart Udall; The President; and to send us funds to continue the battle. Thousands *have* written, but meanwhile, Grand Canyon legislation *still* stands a chance of passage. More letters are needed and much more money, to help fight the notion that Man no longer needs nature.*
David Brower, Executive Director
Sierra Club
Mills Tower, San Francisco
☐ Please send me more details on how I may help.
☐ Here is a donation of $________ to continue your effort to keep the public informed.
☐ Send me "Time and the River Flowing," famous four color book which tells the complete story of Grand Canyon, and why T. Roosevelt said, "leave it as it is." ($25.00)
☐ Send me "The Last Redwoods" which tells the complete story of the opportunity as well as the destruction in the redwoods. ($17.50)
☐ I would like to be a member of the Sierra Club. Enclosed is $14.00 for entrance and first year's dues.
Name________
Address________
City________State________Zip____
*The Sierra Club, founded in 1892 by John Muir, is nonprofit, supported by people who, like Thoreau, believe "In wildness is the preservation of the world." The club's program is nationwide, includes wilderness trips, books and films—as well as such efforts as this to protect the remnant of wilderness in the Americas. There are now twenty chapters, branch offices in New York (Biltmore Hotel), Washington (Dupont Circle Building), Los Angeles (Auditorium Building), Albuquerque, Seattle, and main office in San Francisco.
(Our previous ads, urging that readers exercise a constitutional right of petition to save Grand Canyon from two dams which would have flooded it, produced an unprecedented reaction by the Internal Revenue Service threatening our tax deductible status. IRS called the ads a "substantial" effort to "influence legislation." Undefined, these terms leave organizations like ours at the mercy of administrative whim. [The question has not been raised with organizations that favor Grand Canyon dams.] So we cannot now promise that contributions you send us are deductible—pending result of what may be a long legal battle.)

Right *In 1966, a group of Arizona Senators proposed a Bill which would have approved the flooding of part of the Grand Canyon for an unnecessary hydroelectric project. Howard Gossage's agency in San Francisco ran a campaign for the conservationist Sierra Club who opposed it. His first ad pulled 3,000 applications for club membership – and the hydroelectric project was scrapped. Gossage believed that advertising justified its existence only when used for social purposes. The most articulate rebel in the advertising business, he said things like this: 'I love the advertising business. I truly do, although it's no business of a grown man. I love it because it's such a lovely Augean stable to clean up.'*

Unni, 14 år:

«Jeg spyr nesten hver gang jeg drikker.»

Hvorfor drikker du likevel?
Ikke fordi det er godt iallfall.
Tåler ikke mye heller, for den
saks skyld. Nesten hver gang
ender det med at jeg må spy.

Men du sier ikke nei til alkohol?
Tør ikke. Vil ikke at de andre
skal fleipe og erte.

Du føler med andre ord et press?
Du kan vel si det. Av og til
skulle jeg ønske at jeg kunne si
nei, så slapp jeg å bli sjuk.

Hvorfor drikker du deg så full?
Det er jo derfor vi drikker. For
å bli fulle. Noen ganger later jeg
forresten som jeg er fullere enn
jeg er, så at de andre skal synes
det er O.K. at jeg ikke drikker
mer.

Vet foreldrene dine noe om dette?
Nei, er du spre!

Har du tenkt over at dine
alkoholvaner kunne skade deg
for livet?
Nei. Sånn tenker vi aldri.
Prater aldri om alkohol. Vi
forteller bare hverandre hvor
mye vi drakk og hvor fulle vi
ble og sånn.

Du synes altså brennevin er
vondt?
Ja, godt er det ikke.

Og likevel drikker du fordi de
andre venter det?
Jo, men det gjør de andre også.

Er ikke dette temmelig tåpelig?
Jo, det er kanskje litt dumt.

Tror du mange har det som deg?
Sikkert.

Hva om dere pratet om det i
gjengen som du vanker i?
Det vil sikkert være lurt, men
jeg tør ikke være den som
begynner.

Alkoholen virker på vårt
likevekts-senter og øyen-
bevegelser. Vår balanse og
avstandsbedømmelse blir
dårligere ved små doser, ved
større doser blir vi kvalme og
kaster opp.

Det krever bare litt mot å si nei.

Send denne kupongen til:
«HOLDNING TIL RUSMIDLER -
ALLES ANSVAR»
Postboks 8152 - Oslo Dep. - Oslo 1,
så sender vi deg opplysningsmateriell
for ungdom ☐ for voksne ☐

Navn: ....
Adr.: ....
Postnr.:............ Poststed: ....

DN 39.74

DEN NORSKE 16/17-ÅRING DRAKK 155 FLASKER I FJOR.

FORELDRE BØR VITE HVILKE ALKOHOLSKADER HAN RISIKERER:

De 155 flaskene som stort sett drikkes på lørdag fordeler seg slik

136 halvflasker øl, 8 halvflasker vin og 11 halvflasker brennevin. Tallene gjelder 16 – 17 år gamle gutters.

gjennomsnittlige forbruk i 1973. 16 – 17 år gamle piker drakk 60 flasker øl, 5 flasker vin og 4 flasker brennevin. Det er liten grunn til å tro at forbruket er mindre i dag.

Overlegen for alkoholomsorgen i Norge, Thorbjørn Kjølstad, sier at alkoholisme kan bli vår alvorligste folkesykdom når disse unge kommer opp i moden alder og har misbrukt alkohol en del år.

SENTRALNERVESYSTEMET er mest utsatt: En lett rus (0,6 – 1,2‰) nedsetter selvkritikk og hemninger, gjør samarbeidet mellom muskler usikkert. Avstandsbedømmelsen svekkes og synsfeltet innskrenkes.

SYNSEVNEN er alltid nedsatt mens man er påvirket av alkohol. I visse tilfeller kan det forekomme varige skader.

HJERTETS rytme forstyrres ofte av alkohol. Misbruk kan også føre til ødeleggelse av hjertemuskelen.

LEVERSKADER oppstår hos kroniske alkoholmisbrukere. Jo tidligere en begynner å misbruke alkohol, jo større sjanse er det for leverskader.

LAMMELSER i armer og ben opptrer hos alkoholmisbrukere som spiser for lite B-vitamin. Lammelsene kan i alvorlige tilfeller bli varige.

MAGEKATARR OG MAGESÅR er hyppig hos alkoholmisbrukere, og skyldes dels alkoholens irriterende virkning på mageslimhinnen, dels nervøse komplikasjoner.

TENÅRINGENE VIL SNAKKE OM DETTE. MEN FORELDRENE MÅ TA INITIATIVET.

Statens edruskapsdirektorat/Statens informasjonstjeneste

Two in a series of advertisements created by the Oslo office of Ogilvy & Mather on the subject of teenage alcoholism. **Left** *The headline quotes a 14-year-old girl: 'I vomit almost every time I drink.' Readership was the highest ever recorded in Norway.* **Right** *The headline reads: 'The Norwegian 16/17-year-old drank 155 bottles of alcohol last year. His parents should know the damage he risks.' More than 70 per cent of Norwegian parents read these advertisements, and drinking among teenagers decreased for the first time in many years.*

Cancer Society asked my Indian partners to mount an advertising campaign. The purpose of the campaign was to change attitudes from ignorance and fatalism to understanding and optimism. Only then could people be persuaded to have regular check-ups at the free clinics of the Society. The theme was one of hope: 'Life after cancer . . . it's worth living'. The advertisements showed real people who had been cured. Within two months, the number of check-ups given by the clinics tripled. (See page 184.)

Raising money

Before you rush off to your favorite charity and volunteer to raise money by running advertisements, I must warn you that it is rare for any advertisement, however powerful, to bring in enough direct contributions to pay for the cost of the space.

What advertising *can* do, is to 'sensitize' the market, thus making it easier to raise money by more personal methods of solicitation. It is difficult to persuade people to give money to a charity unless they know something about it.

14 Competing with Procter & Gamble

Who's afraid of the big bad wolf?

If you are going to advertise disposable diapers, fabric softeners, cleansers, toothpaste, soap or dishwashing liquids, you are going to find yourself up against Procter & Gamble. They have market shares of at least 40 per cent in all these categories, *plus* powerful positions in shampoo, cake mix, coffee, anti-perspirants and home permanents. They spend $700,000,000 a year on advertising, more than any other company, and their sales are $12,000,000,000 a year.

Your chances of competing successfully against this juggernaut will be improved if you understand the reasons for its overwhelming success, so I am going to tell you what my partner Kenneth Roman has learned about them.

First, P&G is *disciplined*. Their guiding philosophy is to plan thoroughly, minimize risk, and stick to their proven principles.

To get a broad trial quickly, they distribute home-delivered samples on a massive scale. In 1977 their Chairman said, 'The largest part of our initial investment is usually in the form of introductory sampling. . . . Only when satisfied customers have had firsthand experience with the product will the elements of the marketing mix, such as advertising and selling, be fully productive.'

They never enter small categories unless they expect them to grow, and they set out to dominate every category they enter. By building huge volume, they achieve lower manufacturing costs than their competitors, and this gives them higher profit margins, or permits them to sell at a lower price.

They often enter more than one brand in a category, and allow each brand to compete with its sibling – with no holds barred.

They use market research to identify consumer needs. Says Ed Harness, their former Chairman, 'We are forever trying to see what lies around the corner. . . . We study the consumer and try to identify new trends in tastes, needs, environment and living habits.'

Most important of all, they have a way of creating products which are superior to their competitors'. And, by blind in-home tests, they make sure that the superiority is apparent to the consumer. Says Harness, 'The key to successful marketing is superior product performance.... If the consumer does not perceive any real benefits in the brand, then no amount of ingenious advertising and selling can save it.'

When they launch new brands, they advertise them *heavily*, and they support their successful brands with large budgets – $29,000,000 for Crest, $24,000,000 for High Point, $19,000,000 for Pampers, $17,000,000 for Tide, and so on.

Their test-marketing is unbelievably thorough – and patient. They tested Folger's regional expansion program for six years before moving into the East. 'Patience,' says their President, 'is one of the virtues of this company.' They would rather be right than first. Only three products in the history of P&G have gone national without being test-marketed for at least six months. Two of them failed.

My admiration for their advertising principles is boundless, not least because they are the same as my own. They use research to determine the most effective strategy, and never change a successful strategy. Their strategies for Tide, Crest, Zest and Ivory Bar have not changed for thirty years.

They always promise the consumer one important benefit. When they perceive that there is an opportunity to increase sales by promising more than one, they sometimes run two campaigns at the same time – often in the same medium.

They believe that the first duty of advertising is to *communicate* effectively, not to be original or entertaining, and they measure communication at three stages: before the copy is written, after the commercials are produced, and in test markets. But, unlike me, they do not believe that testing can measure *persuasion*.

All their commercials include a 'moment of confirmation'. They show a woman *squeezing* the Charmin and attesting to its softness. They show a housewife *observing* that Era gets out grease spots.

In 60 per cent of their commercials they use *demonstrations*, showing how Bounty absorbs more liquid, how Top Job cleans better than straight ammonia, how Zest leaves no film.

Their commercials talk directly to the consumer, using language and situations that are familiar to her. If the product is for use in the bathroom, they show it in a bathroom, not in a laboratory.

They go to great pains to communicate the brand name, verbally and visually. Most of their names are short and simple. They appear within the first ten seconds of the commercial, and an average of three times thereafter.

Their commercials deliver the promise verbally, and reinforce it with supers. And they usually end with a repetition of the promise. They tend to use a lot of words, sometimes more than a hundred in a 30-second commercial.

When Procter & Gamble uses a continuing character to sell a brand, he or she is always an unknown actor or actress, never a celebrity.

'My admiration for their advertising principles is boundless, not least because they are the same as my own.'

Less than half their commercials include a 'reason why'. They have come to think it sufficient to show consumers what the product will do for them, without explaining *why* it does it.

Very often they also show the users of their products deriving some *emotional* benefit. Like 'You'll be more *appreciated* if you use Dash.'

They use television techniques which have been proved to sell – however much their agencies may regard them as old hat. Notably slices of life, user testimonials and talking heads.

Until 1976, Procter & Gamble eschewed music, but they are now using it, albeit in only 10 per cent of their commercials. And they now use a touch of humor in some of their commercials.

While their commercials are often extremely competitive, they do not spend their money *naming* competing brands. They refer to 'the other leading detergent'.

Once they have evolved a campaign that works, they keep it running for a long time, in many cases for ten years or more. But they continually test new *executions* of the ongoing strategy.

Once they establish an advertising budget, they continually test higher levels of expenditure.

Only 30 per cent of their budgets go into prime evening time. The rest is divided between daytime and fringe. Instead of using 30-second spots exclusively, they have been using an increasing number of 45s, finding that the extra 15 seconds allows for better 'situation development' and 'viewer involvement'.

Almost all P&G brands are advertised throughout the year. They have found that this works better than 'flighting' – running them six weeks on, six weeks off. It also provides considerable cost savings.

After competing with P&G in several categories for 30 years, my respect for their acumen knows no bounds. However, they are not infallible. They can be beaten, for all their research and all their testing. Some of their products have failed, including Teel liquid detergent, Drene shampoo, Big Top peanut butter and Certain bathroom tissues.

Their Achilles' heel is their *consistency.* They are always predictable. It helps to win battles when you can anticipate the enemy's strategy.

'The best of all ways to beat P&G is, of course, to market a *better product.*'

The best of all ways to beat P&G is, of course, to market a *better product*. Bell Brand potato chips defeated P&G's Pringles because they tasted better. And Rave overtook Lilt in less than a year because, not containing ammonia, it is a better product. I cannot refrain from adding that both these giant-killers are advertised by guess who?

15   18 Miracles of research

A dvertising people who ignore research are as dangerous as generals who ignore decodes of enemy signals. Before I became a copywriter, I was a researcher. I delivered the first paper on copy-testing in the history of British advertising. Later I ran Dr. Gallup's Audience Research Institute in Princeton, predicting how many people would see movies before they were produced, measuring the ability of the stars to sell tickets at the box office, and so on.

The best fun I ever had was in the early days of Ogilvy & Mather, when I was both Research Director and Creative Director. On Friday afternoons I wrote research reports to the Creative Director. On Monday mornings I changed hats, read my reports and decided what to do about them – if anything. In due course I was able to afford the services of Stanley Canter, a far better researcher. It took Stanley only ten days to get me out of his department. Like I always say, hire people who are better than you are.

Here are 18 of the miracles research can perform for you:

1   It can measure the reputation of your company among consumers, security analysts, government officials, newspaper editors, the academic community.

2   Using mathematical models, research can estimate the sales of new products, and the advertising expenditures required to achieve maximum profits. The Hendry, Assessor, Sprinter, ESP and News models are sufficiently reliable to tell you whether your product warrants the expense of test marketing. (About 60 per cent of new products fail in test markets.)

3   Research can get consumer reactions to a new product when it is still in the conceptual state. After one of our clients had invested $600,000 in developing a line of food products for senior citizens whose digestions were deteriorating, our research found a notable lack of enthusiasm among the old parties concerned. When I reported this disappointing news to the client, I was afraid that, like most executives faced with inconvenient research, he would argue with our methodology. I underestimated him. 'Dry hole', said he, and left the meeting.

Right *This chart from the author's* Continuing Audit of Marquee Values *analysed Ronald Reagan's popularity at the height of his career as a movie-star.*

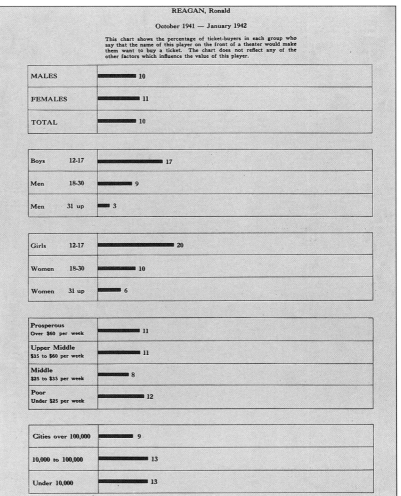

REAGAN, Ronald

October 1941 — January 1942

This chart shows the percentage of ticket-buyers in each group who say that the name of this player on the front of a theater would make them want to buy a ticket. The chart does not reflect any of the other factors which influence the value of this player.

MALES		10
FEMALES		11
TOTAL		10

Boys	12-17		17
Men	18-30		9
Men	31 up		3

Girls	12-17		20
Women	18-30		10
Women	31 up		6

Prosperous Over $60 per week		11
Upper Middle $35 to $60 per week		11
Middle $25 to $35 per week		8
Poor Under $25 per week		12

Cities over 100,000		9
10,000 to 100,000		13
Under 10,000		13

4 Once a product is ready for market, research can tell you how consumers rate it compared with the products they are now buying. If they find your product inferior, send it back to your Research and Development people.

5 Research can tell you what formulation, flavor, fragrance and color will appeal to most consumers.

6 Research can find out which of several package designs will sell best. While you're about it, find out if people can *open* your package. I shall never forget Cornelia Otis Skinner demonstrating to a big food company that she could not open their products without a pair of pliers.

7 Research can help you decide the optimum *positioning* for your product.

8 Research can define your *target audience*. Men or women. Young or old. Rich or poor. Education. Life style. Media habits.

9 It can find out what factors are most important in the purchase decision, and what vocabulary consumers use when talking about your kind of product.

10 Research can determine what 'line extension' is likely to sell best. After Dove carved out a profitable niche in the soap market, Lever Brothers fell to wondering what other products could be marketed under the same name. Research revealed that a liquid for washing dishes stood the best chance, and it was successfully introduced.

11 Research can warn you when consumers show signs of finding an established product less desirable than it once was. Maybe they have noticed that you have been using cheaper ingredients; they usually do.

12 Research can save you time and money by 'reading' your competitor's test markets – even his cost of goods and profit margin. All the information is there to get, if you know where to find it.

13 Research can determine the most persuasive *promise*. 'Promise, large promise is the soul of an advertisement,' said Samuel Johnson. When he auctioned off the contents of the Anchor Brewery he made the following promise: 'We are not here to sell boilers and vats, but *the potentiality of growing rich beyond the dreams of avarice.'*

Dr. Johnson was right 200 years ago, and there is abundant evidence that he is still right today. Advertising which promises no benefit to the consumer does not sell, yet the majority of campaigns contain no promise whatever. (That is the most important sentence in this book. Read it again.)

Only last year Starch reported that advertisements with headlines that promise a benefit are read by an average of *four times* more people than advertisements that don't.

In my experience, the selection of the promise is the most valuable contribution that research can make to the advertising process. One method is to show the consumer a number of promises, telling him or her that each promise is for a new product. The consumer is asked to rate the promises for *importance* and *uniqueness*.

Another technique, which I prefer, is not favored by researchers, perhaps because it is so simple and does not require their services. You write two advertisements for your product, each with a different promise in the headline. At the end of the copy you offer a free sample of the product. You then run the advertisements in a newspaper or magazine, in such a way that half the circulation gets one headline, and the other half gets the other headline. The headline which draws the more applications for a sample wins the test. This technique, which is called *split-run*, was invented by Richard Stanton. Its merit is that it tests promises in the context of advertisements, instead of the unreal context of an interview. But you can only test two headlines at a time.

Try to find a promise which is not only *persuasive*, but also *unique*. For example, 'makes a perfect cup of coffee every time' may get the highest score on persuasion, but it is not unique. You may find that 'gets you clean' is the winning promise for a soap, but I doubt if it is sufficiently unique to make the cash register ring.

'Sometimes you will find that the promise which wins your test is already being used by one of your competitors. Poor you.'

Sometimes you will find that the promise which wins your test is already being used by one of your competitors. Poor you.

14   Research can tell you which of several *premiums* will work best. When thirty-five different premiums were tested by Shell, steak knives won. Different *designs* of steak knives were then tested. When I suggested that packets of shells from Sanibel Island should be offered to motorists who used Shell credit cards, I was coldly informed that shells had been tested and had received a very low score. In France, they were used as the premium without being tested, and flopped.

15   Research can tell you whether your advertising communicates what you want it to communicate. Keep in mind E. B. White's warning, 'When you say something, make sure you have said it. The chances of your having said it are only fair.'

16   Research can tell you which of several television commercials will sell the most.

What is the best technique for pre-testing television commercials? This is the most controversial issue in the advertising business, but there is common agreement among researchers that testing for *recall* is for the birds. Yet, for reasons which escape me, most advertisers still insist on using it. It has four shortcomings:

A   Nobody has been able to demonstrate a relationship between recall and *sales*.

B   Some commercials which score about average on recall, score below average on their ability to change the viewer's brand preference. Celebrity commercials, for example, usually score above average on recall and below average on changing brand preference.

' "When I want a high recall score," says my partner David Scott, "all I have to do is to show a gorilla in a jock strap." '

C   It is too easy for the copywriter to *cheat*. 'When I want a high recall score,' says my partner David Scott, 'all I have to do is to show a gorilla in a jock strap.'

D   It is open to question whether recall tests even measure recall. I believe they measure the viewer's ability to *articulate* what he or she recalls, which is a very different thing.

For all these reasons, I prefer testing methods which measure your commercial's ability to change brand preferences.

Research can measure the *wear-out* of your advertising. For five years, the theme of Shell's commercials was *mileage*, and tracking studies recorded increasingly favorable attitudes to the product. When attitudes finally stopped improving, the advertising was changed from demonstrations of mileage to consumer testimonials, and the upward trend was resumed.

17   Research can tell you how many people *read* your advertisements, and how many *remember* them.

What do grown-ups read in newspapers? The comic strips? The editorials? The weather? The stock market? The sports pages? The

Right *The author and George Gallup.*

main news items? The columnists? Until Gallup came along, editors hadn't the faintest idea who read what.

Gallup invented a method of *measuring* readership. He interviewed representative samples of readers, took them through the newspaper and had them point to the things they had read. It came as a surprise to editors when he reported that more people read the comics then their editorials, and that captions under photographs were read by more people than the articles. When he repeated the same research in Britain, he got the same results. During World War II my brother Francis, then a Wing Commander in the Royal Air Force, slept in the underground bunker which was the center of the high command. He told me that when the Generals, Admirals and Air Marshals came into breakfast, they looked at the comic strips in the *Daily Mirror* before they read the headlines in *The Times*.

When Raymond Rubicam got wind of Gallup's research, he persuaded him to join Young & Rubicam and apply the same method to measuring the readership of advertisements. At about the same time, Daniel Starch started syndicating readership reports to agencies and advertisers, and his successors still do so. The day I spent watching a Starch interviewer at work in the field convinced me that the procedure is reasonably valid.

18 Research can *settle arguments*. When Lord Geddes became Chairman of British Travel, he argued that we should feature *trout fishing* in advertisements – until I pulled out of a chart showing that fishing interested American tourists less than all the 49 other subjects we had tested.

Right *Outside George Gallup's office in Princeton, long ago, the author asks a moviegoer if she would pay money to see* Abe Lincoln in Illinois. *She said she would, but she was kidding herself.*

Armed with this kind of information, it is difficult not to defeat competitors who fly blind. But there are two vital questions that research *cannot* answer:

○ Which campaign will make the biggest contribution to your brand *over a period of years?* Here you still have to rely on judgment.

○ What *price* should you charge for your product? This is one of the most important questions which confront marketers, but, as far as I know, research cannot answer it.

Given sufficient training, any intelligent person can learn to conduct surveys, but getting people to use the results requires salesmanship of a high order. When I did research for the motion picture industry, I had my reports set in type and printed. I found that the Hollywood producers were less likely to argue with printed documents than typewritten memos.

Size of sample

Surveys can produce reliable results with amazingly small samples. If you want to know whether the word *obsolete* is understood by housewives, you don't need an answer which will be statistically reliable within two percentage points. Twenty housewives will suffice. When, however, you are looking for *trends over time*, you had better use larger samples to be sure that any changes are statistically significant. You must also hold the composition of your sample and the wording of your questions rigidly constant.

Pitfalls of research

Some interviewers find it more comfortable to answer questionnaires themselves than to accost strangers. An enterprising London pub used to cater to them by setting aside a private room where they could drink beer while filling out questionnaires.

Respondents do not always tell the truth to interviewers. I used to start my questionnaires by asking, 'Which would you rather hear on the radio tonight – Jack Benny or a Shakespeare play?' If the respondent said Shakespeare, I knew he was a liar and broke off the interview.

When *Gone With the Wind* was a runaway best seller, we asked a cross-section of the adult population whether they had read it The number of *yes* replies was obviously inflated; people did not want to admit that they hadn't read it. The following week we put the question differently: 'Do you *plan* to read *Gone With the Wind?*' It was easy for those who hadn't read it to answer *yes*, they *planned* to read it, while those who had already read it said so. This produced a credible result.

Waiting for a train in Pennsylvania station one evening, I was accosted by an interviewer and asked questions which I had written two days before. They were impossible to answer. I went back to my office and canceled the survey.

A food manufacturer had to decide whether to sell his product in cans or glass jars. He guessed that some housewives would vote for glass because they thought glass sounded more prestigious, so he gave out samples of his product in glass and other samples in cans. Two weeks later he called back and asked the housewives which samples *tasted* better. A large majority declared that the product in the jars tasted better than the same product in the cans. Without knowing it, they were voting for glass.

In a study of the causes of inflation, the French Government cut thousands of cheeses in half and put them on sale. One half were marked 37 centimes, the other 56 centimes. *The higher-priced cheese sold faster.* Consumers judge the quality of a product by its price.

Research among children

If you think that advertising to children is satanic, skip the next two pages. If, on the other hand, you earn your living making toys or breakfast cereals, you may be interested to learn how research can make your advertising produce more sales.

Children understand only the simplest questions, and cannot easily articulate their replies. They also tend to say what they think you

'I was accosted by an interviewer and asked questions which I had written two days before. They were impossible to answer.'

want them to say. Here are three procedures which work reasonably well:

Group dynamics. You show your commercial to a group of children and then get them to play games, like talking to a friend on a play telephone about your commercial. Or you get them to imitate the characters in the commercial. This procedure reveals misunderstandings and negative reactions.

Communication discrepancy. This procedure is for somewhat older children. You show them your commercial and ask them what it told them about the product, and what they *liked* about it. Then you show them the product itself and ask what they like about it. By comparing what they said about the commercial and what they say about the product itself, you find out whether your commercial does your product justice. If it doesn't, you can usually fix it.

Suppose you show a doll commercial. Only 20 per cent of the children say they like the fact that the doll can *walk*. But when they see the doll itself, 60 per cent say they like this. Obviously the commercial has not done justice to the doll.

If, on the other hand, you find that your commercial raises hopes which are disappointed when the children see the doll, I have little doubt that, being an honest person, you will modify the commercial.

Prize pad test. You give children a pad on which four toys are illustrated, including the one you are advertising, and ask them to circle the toy they would like you to give them. Then, after showing them your commercial, you say that some of the children forgot to put their names on the pad, which is probably true. You hand out new pads and again ask them to circle the toy they want. By comparing the votes, you get a measurement of your commercial's persuasion. After doing this with several toys and several commercials, you can relate your score to the norm.

'We are no longer allowed to tell children to importune their mothers to buy our products.'

Gentle reader and fellow parent, if you think it unseemly for researchers to enrol children as guinea-pigs, it will comfort you to know that they are now protected from us admen by ferocious regulations. For example, we are no longer allowed to tell children to importune their mothers to buy our products. Other regulations in force in the United States include these:

○ 'Appeals shall not be used which directly or by implication contend that if children have a product they are better than their peers, or lacking it, will not be accepted by their peers.'

○ 'Material shall not be used which can reasonably be expected to frighten children or provoke anxiety, nor shall material be used which contains·a portrayal of or appeal to violent, dangerous or otherwise anti-social behavior.'

○ 'Advertisements shall not include any dramatizations of any product in a realistic war atmosphere.'

○ 'Advertisements shall include audio and video disclosure when items such as batteries needed to operate a product as demonstrated in the advertising are not included.'

○ 'When a toy is presented in the context of a play environment, the setting and situation shall be that which a child is reasonably capable of reproducing.'

○ 'Advertising shall not employ costumes and props which are not available with the toy as sold, or are not reasonably accessible to the child without additional cost.'

○ 'Each commercial for breakfast-type products shall include at least one audio reference to and one video depiction of the role of the product within the framework of a balanced regimen.'

Just try writing a commercial which obeys *thirty-four* regulations like these.

Where I come out

Few copywriters share my appetite for research. The late and great Bill Bernbach, among many others, thought that it inhibited creativity. My experience has been the opposite. Research has often lead me to good ideas, such as the eyepatch in the Hathaway campaign.

I have seen ideas so wild that nobody in his senses would dare to use them – until research found that they worked. When I had the idea of writing headlines for French tourism *in French*, my partners told me I was nuts – until research revealed that French headlines were more effective than English headlines. Research has also saved me from making some horrendous mistakes.

I admit that research is often misused by agencies and their clients. They have a way of using it to prove they are right. They use research as a drunkard uses a lamppost – not for illumination but for support. On the whole, however, research can be of incalculable help in producing more effective advertising.

'When I had the idea of writing headlines for French tourism *in French*, my partners told me I was nuts.'

16

What little I know about marketing

When they told me I had won the Parlin Award for Marketing, I thought they were kidding. I cannot even understand what the experts write on the subject. Stuff like this from Professor Paul Warshaw of McGill:

> Though use of sample cross-validated correlations is acceptable, the infrequently used squared population cross-validated correlation coefficient ($\hat{P}^2$) is a more precise (although slightly biased) measure (Cattin 1978a, b; Schmitt, Coyle, and Rauschenberger 1977). It utilizes all available data simultaneously rather than bisecting the sample into arbitrary estimation and holdout components. Because of these comparative advantages, $\hat{P}^2$ is used in the present analysis. Though several versions are available, Srinivasan's (1977) formulation of $\hat{P}^2$ is acceptable for models containing fixed predictor variables.*

If *you* can understand this kind of thing, you may find it useful to look up other models of consumer behavior, such as Lavidge and Steiner, Andreason, Nicosia, Engel-Kollat-Blackwell, Howard and Sheth, and Vaughan. All double Dutch to me. However, thirty odd years of rubbing shoulders with marketing practitioners has taught me some things which have helped in my work.

New products
About 35 per cent of supermarket sales come from products which did not exist ten years ago.

You can judge the vitality of a company by the number of new products it brings to market. I have known Chief Executive Officers who made enough profit from the products they inherited from their predecessors to obscure their failure to introduce new ones of their own. It is not uncommon for such men to grudge a measly million dollars for developing a *new* product, but to shell out $100,000,000 to acquire somebody else's product, without turning a hair. Their borrowing-power is greater than their brain-power.

The opposite is seen in the pharmaceutical industry. Merck, for example, spends $200,000,000 a year on new-product research. Years may go by without their discovering anything, then bingo . . . *up comes a miracle drug*. The effect on the share price is lovely to behold.

Why do eight out of ten new consumer products fail? Sometimes because they are *too* new. The first cold cereals were rejected by consumers. More often new products fail because they are not new

*Journal of Marketing Research, May 1980, page 169.

enough. They do not offer any perceptible point of difference – like better quality, better flavor, better value, more convenience or better solutions to problems.

It helps if the point of difference goes hand-in-hand with a chord of familiarity that links the new product to the consumer's past experience – a *disposable* diaper, a *light* beer, a *diet* cola, a *paper* towel.

Naming your product

Finding *any* name which has not already been registered by another company is infernally difficult. There are three kinds of names:

> *Names of men and women* – like FORD, CAMPBELL and VEUVE CLICQUOT. They are memorable, they are difficult to copy and they suggest that your product is the invention of a human being.

> *Meaningless names* like KODAK, KOTEX, and CAMEL. It takes many years and millions of dollars to endow them with any sales appeal.

> *Descriptive names* like 3-IN-ONE OIL, BAND-AID and JANITOR IN A DRUM. Such names *start* with sales appeal. But they are too specific to be used for subsequent line-extensions.

You can use consumer research to find out whether a name says what you think it says, whether it is easily pronounceable, whether it is confused with existing names, and whether it is memorable.

Once I told a computer that I wanted a name for a new brand of coffee, specifying that it had to begin with the letter M and contain no more than seven characters. The computer spewed out *hundreds* of permutations, and I was back where I started.

If it is important that the name appear as big as possible on a package, choose a *short* one like TIDE, and not a long one like SCREAMING YELLOW ZONKERS.

If you want to use the same name in foreign markets, make sure that it does not have an obscene meaning in Turkish or any other language. There have been some nasty accidents.

I have suggested names for dozens of new products, but have not yet had one accepted. Good luck to you.

Sleeping beauties

Some products which sell well without being advertised may sell better, and make more profit, *with* advertising. For 40 years the Lambert Pharmaceutical Company sold modest quantities of a mouthwash called Listerine, without advertising it. When young Jerry Lambert started advertising it – as a remedy for halitosis – sales went through the roof.

Milton S. Hershey built the biggest confectionery business in the world *without* advertising. Some years after his death, his successors asked my partner Bill Weed to find out whether advertising could increase their profits, most of which went to the Hershey orphanage. Bill had commercials made for three of their products and tested them in local markets. One of the products did not respond to advertising, but sales of Hershey Bars went up, and Reese's Peanut Butter Cups went up 66 per cent. By 1980, Hershey was spending $42,000,000 on advertising.

The end of the block-buster brand

It has become prohibitively expensive to launch brands aimed at a dominant share-of-market. Even the manufacturers with the biggest war-chests are finding it more profitable to aim their new brands at narrowly defined segments of the market. The recent launch of a new cigarette cost $100,000,000. The advent of cable television, with 50 or more channels, will make it easier to aim your advertising at special groups of consumers. There may never be another universal giant like Tide or Maxwell House.

'There may never be another universal giant like Tide or Maxwell House.'

Don't waste time on problem babies

Most marketers spend too much time worrying about how to revive products which are in trouble, and too little time worrying about how to make successful products even more successful. It is the mark of a brave man to admit defeat, cut his loss, and move on.

Concentrate your time, your brains, and your advertising money on your *successes*. Back your winners, and abandon your losers.

Don't dawdle

Most young men in big corporations behave as if profit were not a function of time. When Jerry Lambert scored his breakthrough with Listerine, he speeded up the whole process of marketing by dividing time into months. He reviewed progress every 30 days, with the result that he made a fortune in record time.

Promotions

In 1981, US manufacturers spent 60 per cent more on promotions than on advertising, and distributed 1,024,000,000,000 coupons. Bloody fools.

In the long run, the manufacturer who dedicates his advertising to building the most sharply defined image for his product gets the largest share of the market. The manufacturer who finds himself up the creek is the short-sighted opportunist who siphons off his advertising dollars for short-term promotions. Year after year I find myself warning clients about what will happen to their brands if they spend so much on promotion that there is no money left for advertising.

'The manufacturer who finds himself up the creek is the short-sighted opportunist who siphons off all his advertising dollars for short-term promotions.'

Price-off deals and other such hypodermics find favor with sales managers, but their effect is ephemeral, and they can be habit-forming. Said Bev Murphy, who invented Nielsen's technique for measuring consumer purchases and later became President of Campbell Soup Company: *'Sales are a function of product-value and advertising. Promotions cannot produce more than a temporary kink in the sales curve.'*

Says Dr. Ehrenberg: 'A cut-price offer can induce people to try a brand, but they return to their habitual brands as if nothing had happened.'

Don't get me wrong. I am not opposed to all promotions. I would not, for example, think of launching a detergent without sampling to consumers.

Pricing is guesswork

It is usually assumed that marketers use scientific methods to determine the price of their products. Nothing could be further from the truth. In almost every case, the process of decision is one of guesswork.

The higher you price your product, the more desirable it becomes in the eyes of the consumer. Yet when Professor Reisz of the University of Iowa tried to relate the prices of 679 brands of food products to their *quality*, he found that the correlation between quality and price was almost zero.

Most of the marketers I know are afraid of pricing their products above competiton. At a dinner in Europe three years ago, the head of Research and Development in a famous company told me, 'I have never seen my company go to market with the best product I could make. Time after time our marketers force me to give them an inferior product at a lower price.' I was able to tell him that there are now unmistakable signs of a trend in favor of superior products at premium prices. The consumer is not a moron, she is your wife.

Marketing in recession

What should you do in times of recession, when you need every penny to sustain your earnings? Stop advertising?

If you stop advertising a brand which is still in its introductory phase, you will probably kill it – for ever. Studies of the last six recessions have demonstrated that companies which do not cut back their advertising budgets achieve greater increases in profit than companies which do cut back.

In a Morril survey of 40,000 men and women involved in the purchase of 23 industrial products over five years, it was found that share-of-market went up in bad times – *when advertising was continued*.

I have come to regard advertising as part of the product, to be treated as a *production* cost, not a *selling* cost. It follows that it should not be cut back when times are hard, any more than you would stint any other essential ingredient in your product.

During World War II, the British Government prohibited the marketing of margarine under brand names, but Unilever continued to advertise one of their brands during all the years it was not on the retailers' shelves. When the war ended and brands returned, the Unilever brand emerged at the top of the heap.

Keynes might have advised manufacturers not to advertise during boom times, but instead to set aside the money in a reserve for advertising during recessions.

Heavy users

Thirty-two per cent of beer-drinkers drink 80 per cent of all beer. Twenty-three per cent of laxative users consume 80 per cent of all laxatives. Fourteen per cent of the people who drink gin consume 30 per cent of all the gin.

Right *This chart compares sales for companies which cut back their advertising expenditure during the 1974-75 recession with sales for companies that did* not *cut back.*

The companies that did not *cut their advertising budgets did better in every year. By 1977 their sales had more than doubled, while sales had barely gone up 50 per cent fo companies that cut their advertising. 1975 sales were down for the companies that cut their advertising, but up for those that didn't.*

By 1977 the net income of companies that did not cut advertising had more than trebled, while for companies that did cut back during the recession, it had barely doubled.

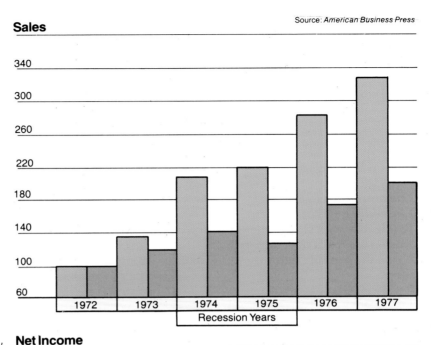

Source: *American Business Press*

Sales

Recession Years

Net Income

Recession Years

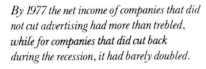

Did not cut in 1974 or 1975   Did cut in both years

In everything you do, keep your eye glued to the heavy users. They are unlike occasional users in their motivations.

Why advertise at all?

Many manufacturers secretly question whether advertising really sells their product, but are vaguely afraid that their competitors might steal a march on them if they stopped. Others – particularly in Great Britain – advertise 'to keep their name before the public'. Others because it helps them to get distribution. Only a minority of marketers advertise because they have found that it *increases their profits*.

On a train journey to California, a friend asked Mr. Wrigley why, with the lion's share of the market, he continued to advertise his chewing gum. 'How fast do you think this train is going?' asked Wrigley. 'I would say about ninety miles an hour.' 'Well,' said Wrigley, *do you suggest we unhitch the engine?'*

Advertising is still the cheapest form of selling. It would cost you $25,000 to have salesmen call on a thousand homes. A television commercial can do it for $4.69. If you spend $10,000,000 a year on advertising, you can now (1983) reach 66 per cent of the population twice a month.

Repertory of brands

A.S.C. Ehrenberg of the London Business School has established that consumers do not buy *one* brand of soap, or coffee, or detergent. They have a repertory of four or five brands, and move from one to another. They almost never buy a brand which has not been admitted to their repertory during its first year on the market.

Dr. Ehrenberg goes on to argue that the only thing you can expect from post-launch advertising is that it will persuade present users to buy your brand more often than the others in their repertory.

If this is true, your launch advertising is a matter of life and death. Spend every penny you can lay your hands on. Now or never. Dr. Ehrenberg writes:

○ 'People have a repertory of brands, each of which they buy fairly regularly ... buying behavior remains broadly characterized as being steady and habitual rather than dynamic.

○ 'Real conversion from virgin ignorance to full-blooded, long-term commitment does not happen often ... sales levels of most brands tend to be fairly steady.

○ 'Consumers mostly ignore advertising for brands they are not already using.'

Dr. John Treasure agrees: 'The task of advertising is not primarily one of conversion but rather of *reinforcement* and *assurance* . . . sales of a given brand may be increased without converting to the brand any *new* consumers, but merely by inducing its existing users, those who already use it at least occasionally, to use it more frequently.'

Sales meetings in the WC

Always hold your sales meetings in rooms too small for the audience, even if it means holding them in the WC. 'Standing room only' creates an atmosphere of success, as in theatres and restaurants, while a half-empty auditorium smells of failure.

Use the absolute minimum of electrical equipment. I have seen the sound systems fail in some of the most elaborately equipped convention centers in the world, including Berlin, where they have 24 operators.

What is marketing?

I once heard Marvin Bower define marketing as *objectivity.* I cannot beat that.

'The codfish lays ten thousand eggs,
The homely hen lays one.
The codfish never cackles
To tell you what she's done –
And so we scorn the codfish
While the humble hen we prize.
It only goes to show you
That it pays to advertise!'
Anonymous

17 Is America still top nation?

The hare and the tortoises

Roughly half of all the advertising in the world is in the United States, and American agencies are paramount in the rest of the world. In West Germany, nine of the top agencies are American. In the United Kingdom and Holland, seven of the top ten. In Canada and Italy, six of the top ten. In 1977 Philip Kleinman, a British observer of the advertising scene, wrote that 'all over the world, admen look to Madison Avenue as Moslems look to Mecca.'*

But things are changing. Alexander Kroll, the president of Young & Rubicam, recently said that 'the best of foreign advertising seems brasher, fresher and more outrageous than ours'.

Remember Aesop's fable of the Hare and the Tortoise?

Britain

The differences between British and American advertising reflect differences in national characteristics. If you question whether those differences are big enough to signify, consider the fact that, on an average Sunday, 42 per cent of Americans go to church, while only 3 per cent go in England.

British commercials tend to be less direct, less competitive, more subtle, more nostalgic, funnier and more entertaining. Techniques which work well in the United States – like talking heads and slice-of-life – are seldom used in Britain. The London agencies produce relatively far-out, trendy commercials. After spending four years in London, my partner Bill Taylor wrote, 'There seems to be a realization in England that maybe, just maybe, the product being sold is *not* the most important thing in the consumer's mind. The decision as to which dishwashing liquid to buy, which beer to drink or which toaster to purchase, is *not* a

*In *Advertising Inside Out*, W.H. Allen, London 1977

One more way Britain can be sure of Shell.

Wouldn't you protest if Shell ran a pipeline through this beautiful countryside?

They already have!

Tom Allen,
Shell Horticulturist:

"When Shell proposed a pipeline from the North East coast of Anglesey to Stanlow refinery, seventy eight miles away in industrial Cheshire, people were worried.

The line would run through part of the Snowdonia National Park and have to pass under rivers Conwy, Elwy, Clwyd and Dee.

What scars would remain?

It is five years since the line was laid, and as I fly along the route today, even I can see no sign of it.

On the ground, the course of the pipe can be followed by a series of small unobtrusive markers. Apart from these, there is nothing to tell you that the top of a pipeline runs one metre beneath your feet.

The sheer invisibility of the line surprises visitors but not me. I was responsible for re-instating the land and well know what unprecedented lengths we went to. Every foot of the way was photographed before digging started, and the vegetation restored the way the record showed it ... even to the exact varieties of grass.

Sometimes, I agreed deviations in the line to avoid disturbing rare trees. In addition, a team of archaeologists preceded pipeline contractors to make sure that the route would avoid cromlechs, barrows, earthworks and other historical sites.

·We are proud of the result, and it shows the way for other conservation projects."

You can be sure of Shell

This British ad for Shell is perhaps the most disarming corporate advertisement ever created.

Above *A superb use of emotion (nostalgia) in an English commercial for Hovis bread.*

life-and-death decision. Realizing this, the British are able to present their product to the consumer in perspective. They joke about it, sing about it, and often underplay it. In short, they have a sense of proportion.' He concludes that, in general, British advertising is the best in the world.

No wonder British copywriters are now in such demand in the United States. The procession which started with Leslie Pearl, Clifford Field and the author is gathering steam. Barry Day, the Creative Head at McCann-Erickson's headquarters in New York is an Englishman, as is Norman Berry, the Creative Head of Ogilvy & Mather in New York.

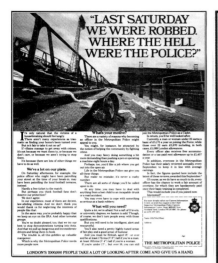

Above and right *British newspaper advertising at its best. Straightforward, direct, never pompous, always interesting. Collett Dickenson Pearce.*

Europe

French advertising is distinguished for its wit, charm and beautiful art direction, qualities which are seen to best advantage in magazine ads and posters. Many French television commercials are equally enchanting, although I often wonder if they appeal to Claudette, my cook. French copywriters and art directors are not subjected to the kind of research which restrains their American and British colleagues from shooting above the heads of the mass audience. They are free to entertain the upper crust.

I find the atmosphere in the better *German* agencies very like New York, but dare I confess that I find some of their advertising rather ugly? German advertisers are bedevilled by an acute shortage of professional staff, and an even more acute shortage of time on television. This obliges them to use magazines more than they would wish.

In *Belgium* and *Sweden*, advertising is not allowed on television. You might suppose that this would result in exceptionally high standards of advertising in magazines and newspapers, but it doesn't.

In the smaller European countries, advertisers cannot afford the kind of research that guides the creative output in North America and the United Kingdom, so they are forced to rely on guesswork, which isn't always accurate. The multinational advertisers have the advantage that they can extrapolate from the results of their research in bigger markets.

The N.I.H. Syndrome

Multinational corporations often wish to use the same advertising campaigns throughout the world, but the managers of their local subsidiaries press their prerogative to commission their own campaigns. The local agencies, even when they belong to the multinational agency which has the parent account, are equally resistant to dictation they argue that their market is different, and point to the danger of being perceived by the local client as the tool of his multinational headquarters.

There is often some weight in these arguments, but the underlying factor is almost always what Professor Levitt of Harvard calls the N.I.H. Syndrome – Not Invented Here. Any campaign not invented in your country is a threat to your self-respect. The best way to settle these arguments is to *test* the international campaign in each country. Only

Opposite top *A beautiful advertisement from the Frankfurt office of TBWA.*

Opposite bottom *Many Germans believed that Club Med resorts were snobbish, that they were for summer only, and that only French was spoken. Ads like this proclaimed otherwise.*

Below *One in a superb series of British advertisements for CIGA Hotels. The agency is TBWA.*

TO BE SURE OF A SEAT ON THE FIRST FLIGHT TO THE MOON, TALK TO THE CONCIERGE AT THE EXCELSIOR, ROME.

In the lobby of one of the world's most famous hotels you'll find the world's most respected concierge. Tommaso Masci.

Tommaso is a bubbling wit. He's also a philosopher, staunchly believing that a concierge's golden keys–in particular his own–can open any door.

This philosophy he continually puts to the test.

He'll proudly tell you that he can get tickets for a sold-out performance of "Tosca". Or arrange a private viewing of the Sistine Chapel. Or even get you an audience with the Pope.

In the past, he's nodded politely to a guest who asked him to walk her pet leopard in the park. And he didn't bat an eyelid when a regular client asked for two seats for the first flight to the moon.

The characters of Signor Masci and the other members of the staff fit in well with the character of the Excelsior.

They're unique and totally original. Indeed, it would be impossible to duplicate the Excelsior in any other part of the world. Even in another part of Rome.

This is because the Excelsior is situated on the throbbing and exuberant Via Veneto–the meeting place of the city–where la dolce vita, "the sweet life", was born.

"La Via Veneto è la dolce vita, è L'Excelsior."

It's here amongst marble fireplaces, echoing halls, intricate plasterwork and priceless carpets that kings stay when they visit Italy.

Kings, queens, princes. And film stars. The guest book of the Excelsior reads like a Who's Who of the arts.

(It's here also that the well-informed and discreet may whisper to you about how some of the most famous love affairs of the century had their beginnings within the hotel's four walls.)

The Excelsior's 394 rooms and 38 suites are attended by an army of chambermaids and porters. It's by no means unusual to stay at a time when staff outnumber the guests.

Or, for that matter, to discover that

a waiter first started work in the restaurant when you were still at school. (Tommaso has been at the Excelsior for over a quarter of a century.)

Such loyalty to a single hotel is easy to understand when that hotel is the Excelsior. There simply isn't a better hotel in Rome to work at.

A team of 140 cooks, chefs and waiters (including one person who changes the flowers every morning) makes the restaurant at the Excelsior one of the finest in Europe.

Indeed, the cuisine is such that it merits its own, very beautiful design of china made specially for the hotel. Break a plate and it takes a year to replace it.

All of this goes to rank the Excelsior amongst the most exclusive and luxurious hotels in Italy. A credential shared by each and every one of the other 21 Cigahotels.

For further information contact your travel agent. Or write directly to Cigahotels, 67 Jermyn Street, London, SW1. (Tel: 01-930 4147).

HOTEL EXCELSIOR ROME

WENN SIE ES UNNÖTIG FINDEN, DASS WIR LEERE HUMMERSCHALEN FLAMBIEREN, IST LACROIX WIRKLICH ZU TEUER FÜR SIE.

Wenn in manchen Restaurants mal wieder die Flammen hochschlagen und die Augen leuchten und einigen Gästen vor Schreck der letzte Bissen aus dem Mund fällt, dann könnte man meinen, Flambieren ist nur ein reiner Showeffekt und sonst gar nichts.

Dabei hat Flambieren sehr wohl etwas mit dem Geschmack zu tun. Nur muß das nicht unbedingt vor großem Publikum passieren, sondern in der Küche tut es das gleiche, und eigentlich gehört es auch dahin. Denn in der Küche wird nun mal der Geschmack der Speisen bestimmt. Am Beispiel unserer Hummersuppe würden wir Ihnen gerne einmal demonstrieren, was Flambieren bedeuten kann.

Wir verarbeiten natürlich frische schottische und irische Hummer. Die Hummer werden gekocht, und das Fleisch wird mit der Hand herausgelöst. Es wird in kleine Stückchen geschnitten und in Butter angeröstet. Dann wird erst einmal das Hummerfleisch flambiert. Der ganz leichte Rösteffekt und ein wenig vom Weinbrand wirken sich hier schon auf den Geschmack aus.

Jetzt kommt aber etwas, das Ihnen wohl am überzeugendsten demonstriert, was Lacroix heißt.

Die leeren Hummerschalen oder Karkassen, wie man die nennt, werden zerkleinert und flambiert. Auch hier tritt ein Rösteffekt ein, und auch hier tut der Weinbrand das seinige. Aber, was soll das Ganze – Sie wollen ja schließlich keine gerösteten Hummerschalen essen.

Geduld, wir sind ja noch nicht fertig. Die Hummerschalen werden jetzt noch einmal gekocht, und der Sud, der dabei entsteht, wird zu der Hummerbrühe gegeben und erzeugt, zusammen mit dem Hummerfleisch, vielen feinen Gewürzen und einem Schuß spritzigen Weißwein, den wohl unnachahmlichen Geschmack unserer Hummersuppe.

Nicht viel anders machen wir es bei unserer Fasanenkraftbrühe. Aber hier sind die Knochen die Karkassen, und die werden nicht mit Weinbrand, sondern mit Gin flambiert. Denn der Wacholdergeschmack von Gin paßt besonders gut zum Hautgout des Fasans. Unsere Fasanen sind übrigens nicht aus irgendwelchen Zuchtfabriken, wie viele andere „wilde" Fasanen heute, sondern haben sich ihr Futter in den weiten Wäldern Polens noch selbst erkämpfen müssen.

Unsere Linsensuppe flambieren wir natürlich nicht, aber wir legen bei ihr genausoviel Wert auf die Auswahl guter Rohstoffe und auf eine schonende Verarbeitung.

Denn wir haben uns vorgenommen, das Lebenswerk unseres Firmengründers Eugen Lacroix in seinem Sinne fortzuführen.

Es gibt ein kleines Gedicht, das sehr schön auf ihn zutrifft: „Der Mensch ist, was er ißt. So lehrt uns die Weise. Sei dankbar drum dem Mann, der uns mit Müh und Fleiß durch seine Kunst erzieht zum kultivierten Esser. Indem er gut uns speist, macht er uns selber besser."

Sein unerschütterlicher Glaube war immer, daß gute Qualität sich durchsetzt und immer Käufer findet, die den Preis dafür zu zahlen gewillt sind. Der Erfolg hat ihm recht gegeben. Und es bleibt uns eigentlich gar nichts anderes übrig, als dieses Prinzip fortzusetzen.

Niemals mit der erreichten Qualität zufrieden zu sein ... und immer auf der Suche nach Perfektion, um das Bessere zu bleiben.

Andernfalls wären unsere Produkte nicht den Namen Lacroix und vor allen Dingen nicht ihren Preis wert.

Im Club kommen Sie manchem auf die Spur. Auch sich

Sprechen wir von Tommi Gundringer und seinem Skiurlaub in „Copper Mountain", Colorado, USA. Denn dorthin zog es unseren Stuttgarter. Einerseits, weil er die Hänge Europas in den letzten Jahren schon leidlich abgefahren hatte. Andererseits, weil er neugierig auf dieses erste amerikanische Clubdorf war. Tommi, Sie merken es, war schon öfter bei uns zu Gast.

So wunderte er sich auch keineswegs über den herzlichen Empfang. Höchstens über sich selbst – wie leicht es ihm in dieser entspannten Atmosphäre immer fiel, locker mit allen Leuten umzugehen. Von der ersten Sekunde an.

Er war mit einem netten New Yorker in einem Zweibettzimmer des Hotels untergebracht, das, wie üblich beim Club, direkt neben der Liftstation lag. Bei der ersten Auffahrt mit Phil, der sich schnell noch Skier im Camp geliehen hatte, zog das ganze Dorfleben an ihm vorbei: Am seichten Hügel, den sie gerade passierten, übten die Anfänger vom Junior-Club in vielen kleinen Gruppen. Weiter oben versuchten die Älteren, die Balance zu halten. Tommi erinnerte sich, wie er einst selbst in den von Club zu Club gleichen Kursen aufgestiegen war. Immer höher ging die Fahrt, vorbei an einigen Langläufern, und dann sahen sie auch schon die Cracks bei ihren Schußfahrten oder irgendwelchen Wettbewerben.

Die Animateure mit ihren Video-Kameras waren auch wieder da, und es fiel ihm ein, daß das nicht nur für die abendliche Gaudi gut war, man lernte so auch schneller.

Von Tommis erster Abfahrt gibt es nur dieses Bild. Schnell und sicher wie eh und je sauste, wedelte oder stemmte er sich durch die Tannen. Und als man ihn später fragte, was ihm denn nun am besten im Club gefallen hatte, sagte er: „Daß die Action hier stimmen würde, das war mir eigentlich schon vorher klar. Nein, das Größte hier sind der Spaß und die vielen Freundschaften und wie du dich selbst irgendwie veränderst. Du machst Sachen, die du dir sonst nie zugetraut hättest, oder nur ganz einfach nur nichts, völlig relaxed ..."

Wenn Sie auf Tommis Spuren wandeln wollen: Im Reisebüro gibt's den Club-Katalog. Oder gegen DM 2,– in Briefmarken direkt von Club Méditerranée: Königsallee 98a, 4000 Düsseldorf 1 Ö.A.M.T.C. Schubertring 1-3, A-1010 Wien Gerbergasse 6, CH-8001 Zürich

Club Méditerranée

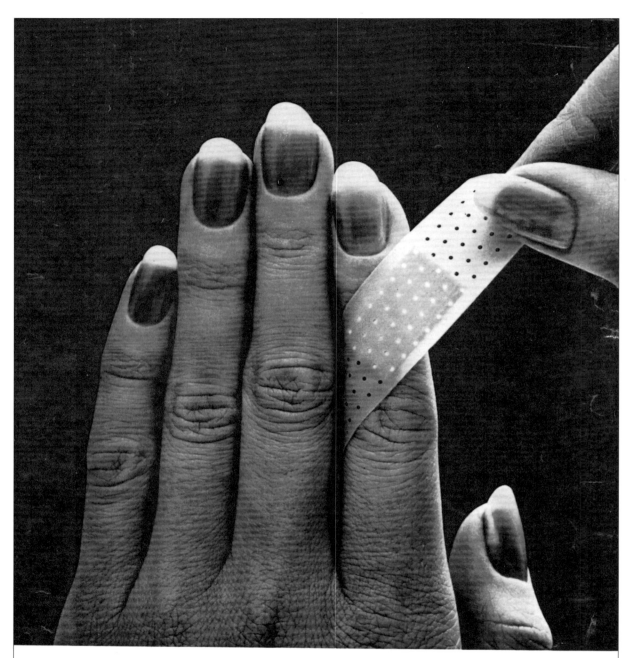

Das bringt Luft an die Wunde. Wunden, die heilen

sollen, brauchen Luft. Je mehr sie davon bekommen, um so besser. Deshalb haben die Pflaster von Hansaplast viele kleine Poren. Und zwar auch dann, wenn man sie gar nicht sieht. Wir von Hansaplast meinen eben, ein Pflaster muß mehr sein als nur Schutz vor Schmutz. Hansaplast. Keiner versteht mehr von Pflastern. Wundversorgung aus den **BDF ●●●●** programmen, Beiersdorf AG, Hamburg

Left *An advertisement by the Frankfurt office of Ogilvy & Mather. Simple and straightforward.*

Below *Shell offers motorists helpful information in booklets about emergency repairs, fire safety and so on. This campaign has worked well in the United States, Sweden, Holland, Germany, France, Canada, Brazil, Australia, Austria and South Africa.*

when the results are positive should it be used locally, and even then it should be modified to fit the local culture. More often than not, campaigns which perform well in the United States perform equally well in other countries. The Esso tiger was a success in 34 countries.

Reader's Digest has found that the *articles* which most interest Americans are the same articles which most interest Frenchmen, Germans, Italians, Dutchmen and Ruritanians. Television commercials which demonstrated the good mileage you get with Shell were equally successful in the United States, Canada, Britain, Germany and Austria.

Advertising in *Latin America* has made big strides in recent years – particularly in Brazil, where José Fontoura is producing some outstanding campaigns.

But the most dramatic improvement of all has been in *South East Asia*. Three years ago, I offered a prize of $10,000 to the Ogilvy & Mather office which created the most brilliant advertising in our world-wide network. Which office won the prize, do you suppose? New

York? Chicago? London? Paris? The prize went to *Bangkok*. Barry Owen, the young Australian Creative Director, was the first to use Thai cultural symbols in Thai advertising, thereby giving the lie to the old charge that multinational agencies impose an alien culture wherever they go. Says Barry, 'What is the significance of a Western jingle to a person who dances beautifully to the sound of a bamboo flute?'

Australian advertising has also improved since I was there four years ago; some of it is now very good indeed. Australian advertising people are the most eclectic in the world, the dominant influence being American rather than British. The most spectacular campaigns are being produced by a new agency called Mojo, with Campaign Palace not far behind. But the fastest growing agency is none other than Ogilvy & Mather, which has a broader range.

New Zealand. Considering that the population is only three million, it is remarkable that New Zealand plays the best Rugby football in the world, produces the best sheep, and one of the two greatest sopranos. The advertising would be better if the best creative people did not, like the Scottish, emigrate to richer pastures.

There is very little advertising in *India* – 37 cents per head per annum, compared with $224 in the United States and $77 in Japan. Indian agency people have an impressive *theoretical* knowledge of advertising, but it seldom shows in their output. The 19-year-old

Below *Some brilliant advertising is now being created in Brazil. The headline on this one says, 'Long before school starts, Mercedes-Benz is already repeating its daily lesson.'*

Muito antes de as escolas abrirem, o Mercedes-Benz já está fazendo a lição do dia.

Para que os estudantes estejam nas escolas
as pessoas no trabalho
os jornais nas bancas
as ruas limpas
as matérias-primas nas fábricas
o leite nas casas
os supermercados abastecidos
as colheitas nas cidades
o peixe fresco nos mercados
os postos de combustível abastecidos
as feiras livres montadas
o lixo recolhido
os materiais de construção nos depósitos
os malotes despachados
as encomendas recebidas
os artigos de consumo nas lojas
as construções mais adiantadas
as novas edições nas livrarias
as padarias abrindo
os consertos de rua prontos
algumas pessoas chegando
outras pessoas partindo.
Para que isso possa repetir-se cada manhã,
o Mercedes-Benz acorda mais cedo todos os dias.

Transportar é tão importante quanto produzir.

Mercedes-Benz do Brasil S.A.

daughter of my Indian partner Mani Ayer calles it 'organized graffiti'. Nevertheless, I have seen a few Indian campaigns, such as that for the Indian Cancer Society, which compare favorably with anything in the West.

Indian advertisers have problems unknown in the West. Their campaigns have to be translated into 12 languages, and the majority of the population cannot read *any* language. The average Indian has an income of $5 a week. Is it fair, do you think, to advertise products which the majority of people will *never* be able to buy?

The population of India has doubled since Independence in 1947. If it doubles again in the next 25 years – to 1,400,000,000 – the consequence will be massive starvation. I came away from India recently with an unshakeable resolve to find out if the skills I have spent

Above *A straight-from-the-shoulder benefit is promised in this African poster.*
Right *In this advertisement, Australian creative director Barry Owen asks, 'What is the significance of a Western jingle to a person who dances beautifully to the sound of a bamboo flute?'*

"Creating in the Asian Image – the Cultural Connection"

By Barry Owen, Creative Director, Ogilvy & Mather Thailand

 Born, educated and trained in Australia, Barry Owen moved to Thailand in the mid-seventies. His work at Ogilvy & Mather has won International acclaim — including two Clio Awards for Singha Beer.
Here he gives a behind the scenes look at how this award and sales winning campaign came to be.

"**M**any Creative Directors in Asia have perceived American advertising as *The International form*. The form that Asian advertising should derive from.
It isn't.
The best American advertising is pure Americana. Its vitality is gained by a cultural connection with specific groups.
The American experience is a potpourri of mostly European and African cultures with two centuries of pioneering spirit.
This in no way resembles the fifty centuries of cultural depth in the Asian consumer.
What is the significance of a Western jingle to a person who dances beautifully to the sound of a bamboo flute?

"Visualizing and verbalizing the Asian experience."

It is an Asian Creative Director's responsibility to conceptualize, visualize, and verbalize the Asian experience.
In Thailand a rather notable experiment in making the cultural connection has been executed over the last seven years for a local beer called Singha.
It is a film campaign in which we do two or three new productions each year.
The refreshment benefit of the product is visualized and verbalized in a way that can only be described as ethnically Thai. Symbolically with the coming of the monsoon. Graphically in the heat of a bronze casting yard. Emotionally with the sound of Thai street vendors.
The music tracks use only Thai instruments. Voice overs are created in a Thai poetic style which is literally untranslatable. Rich with detail, the commercials are usually slow paced and run sixty seconds.
They are executed with love and professional expertise.
They have been honoured with a clutch of international awards: two Clio golds for cinema-photography; a gold, silver and bronze at the New York film awards; a bronze from Cannes.

"Winds like creative and cultural wind a trifle weightier spoken in the same breath as the word advertising. Still, communicating with creative ideas to a group of people with distinct cultural patterns is exactly the business of advertising."

In the local Thai awards, the only place in the world where their content could be truly judged, they have been among the winners every year since the campaign began.

" . . . approach skipped blithely across class barriers . . ."

This ethnic approach skipped blithely across the class barriers that cause so many Thai marketing men to shudder with concern.
It appealed across the board. Sales have trebled.
There are three valuable lessons in this experience:
1. Campaigns can be developed that speak successfully with an authentic Asian tongue;
2. Not an inch of professionalism or style need be surrendered in doing so;
3. This form provides more originality and vitality than a copy of any Western style.
It should be obvious, however, that *there never can be one Asian style*. The pragmatic Hong Kong Chinese is as different from the semi-mystical Thai as the reserved Englishman is from the emotional Latin.
Some countries in Southeast Asia are on the verge of becoming industrialized states. Others will remain for a time, rural based.
The languages are as diverse as the countries themselves; even Chinese changes dialect from country to country.

" . . . something akin to solving Rubik's Cube in the dark."

It is all very complex. Without the right professional assistance, advertising in Asia becomes

something akin to solving Rubik's Cube in the dark.
So we return to the central problem. Identifying and understanding the consumers and creating messages that are both relevant and brilliant enough to jolt them out of their apathy toward advertising clutter.
Why should Ogilvy & Mather — an international agency with a number of expatriate Creative Directors around the region — be the right agency in Asia?
Let's tackle the expatriate question first.
They were originally brought here because of their education, skills and wealth of experience in the craft of communication.

" . . . originators of Asian style."

They stayed to become the originators of the Asian style of advertising, although they certainly won't have the final word on it.
In a recent conversation on the cultural connection topic — and why it seems to originate with expatriates and not locals — a Thai advertising manager commented rather facetiously "The nearer the temple, the further from God."
What he meant was that expatriates aren't necessarily overwhelmed when they enter into the Asian experience.

They may be creatively inspired by the richness and diversity, but they are not overwhelmed.
Whereas the local creative people, who are just as easily inspired, tend to get more excited by influences new to them. Influences from the West.

"Expatriates are in Asia to train."

More importantly, expatriates are in Asia to train. To train by example, and in face to face discussions of practical problems. This involves creating an atmosphere of clear thinking, provoking inquisitiveness, encouraging originality and standing fast for brilliance.
And what of the agency itself?
Ogilvy & Mather is the greatest training agency in the world. This fact alone makes its existence in this part of Asia, where little in the way of formal training exists, significant.
Ogilvy & Mather believes in and instigates many research programmes — especially on consumer attitudes — and uses this research as an invaluable tool in the making of great campaigns.
Ogilvy & Mather believes in advertising that sells. To sell it must work. To work it must be brilliant. To be brilliant it must be relevant, culturally.
It must connect. "

The Ogilvy & Mather Story

Ogilvy & Mather is the largest advertising agency in Southeast Asia. This is the happy accident of striving to be best.
Our agency's founder, David Ogilvy, says "An attitude of divine discontent. Strive for perfection. Settle only for second best."
For more information, please contact the appropriate Ogilvy & Mather office.

Bangkok	Somnidha Tidavadhee (233 5630-7)
Bombay	Mani Ayer (221418)
Hong Kong	Harry Reid (5-690161)
Jakarta	Andrew Kefford (71 4905)
Kuala Lumpur	Roger Winter (986066)
Singapore	Tom Hemming (273 4911)
Tokyo	Bruce Oliver (404 5055)

Ogilvy & Mather
IN ASIA

my life acquiring can help to solve the problem of the birthrate. Says Mani Ayer, 'The elimination of human suffering is too serious to leave to government alone.' The Government of India has been spending less than 10 cents per child-bearing couple per year on family planning.

In *Kenya*, people are lucky to earn $10 a week, and about 70 per cent are illiterate. The principal medium of advertising is radio, and the commercials have to be written in nine languages.

When you advertise cooking fat, you have to make your recipes fit tribal eating habits; don't give the Kikuyu recipes for fried fish – they regard fish as snakes.

There are only 30,000 television sets in a population of fourteen million, but mobile cinemas take entertainment to the rural population. In this environment, *contests* work well. Unilever offers *scholarships* as prizes. When asked to increase the sales of Vaseline, the Nairobi office of Ogilvy & Mather mounted a contest with a *cow* as first prize.

Communist advertising – primitive but not forbidden

Considering the venom with which left-wingers in capitalist countries denounce advertising, you might suppose that Communist countries

Below *In 1978 the Indian Cancer Society used advertising to persuade people to have regular check-ups at its free clinics. The advertisements, by the Bombay office of Ogilvy & Mather, showed real people who had been cured. Within two months the number of check-ups tripled.*

"Sure, I still win at golf sometimes. But the fight I'm most proud of, is the fight I won against cancer!" *says Prahlad Mehta*

Life after cancer...it's worth living

When Prahlad Mehta first noticed the lump on the side of his neck, it was tiny and painless.

"I wasn't prepared for the doctor's diagnosis," he says. "Cancer of the lymph nodes."

Prahlad was treated at the Tata Memorial Hospital in Bombay – one of the most modern cancer centres in the world.

He was lucky. His cancer had been detected early and he recovered very fast.

"In fact," says Prahlad, "I never missed a single day's work or

a single weekend's golf – right through the treatment!"

Prahlad is just one of thousands of Indians who are winning their fight against cancer. But it isn't luck that saves them. It is early treatment.

In recent years, we have developed many effective drugs to control cancer.

Today, most cancers are curable, if treated early. That's why a yearly cancer check-up is so necessary for every adult.

We have several free check-up centres all over Bombay. Find out which is the one closest to you.

Phone 231417 for a free cancer check-up.

Indian Cancer Society
E. Borges Marg, Parel
Bombay 400 012

OBM/3757

"When the doctors told me I had cancer six years ago, my first thought was... who'll take care of my baby. I never knew...it would be me!" *says Ruby Mody*

Life after cancer...it's worth living

Ruby Mody came to our clinic 6 years ago, with what she thought was a minor complaint. A slight thickening of the left breast. Her check-up revealed that it was cancer.

Ruby was lucky. Her cancer was detected early. And her chances of recovery were good.

Ruby was treated at one of the most modern cancer hospitals in the world – the Tata Memorial Hospital in Bombay. Today, she leads a normal, active life.

Ruby is just one of thousands of Indians who are winning their

fight against cancer. But it isn't luck that saves them. It is early detection and treatment.

Yes. In recent years, cancer specialists have developed many effective drugs and techniques to control cancer.

Today, most cancers are curable, if treated early. That's why, a yearly cancer check-up is so necessary for every adult.

We have several free cancer check-up centres all over Bombay. Please find out which is the one closest to you.

Phone: 231417 for a free cancer check-up.

Indian Cancer Society
E. Borges Marg, Parel
Bombay 400 012

OBM 3756

would eschew this capitalist tool. Not so. The Soviet party line was laid down long ago by Anastas Mikoyan, the old Bolshevik who was in charge of foreign and domestic trade under Stalin and Krushchev:

> 'The task of our Soviet advertising is to give people exact information about the goods that are on sale, to help to create new demands, to cultivate new tastes and requirements, to promote the sales of new kinds of goods and to explain their uses to the consumer.'

I could not have said it better myself. However, apart from campaigns for good causes like reducing alcoholism, there is little or no advertising in the USSR, although foreign companies are allowed to advertise their

Above and right *Hungary produces the best advertising in the communist world. There are several agencies and they use not only newspapers and magazines, but also television.*

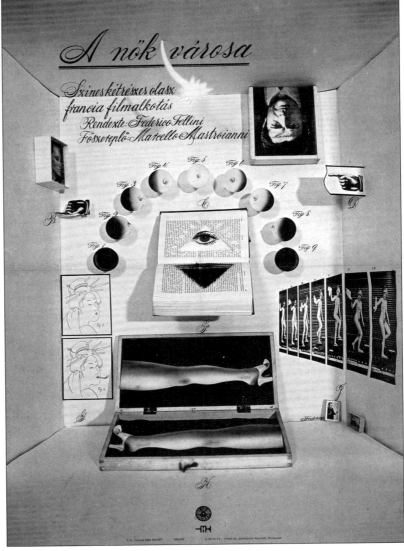

Tu pravou
skotskou
pozná každý

industrial products, and there is a state-owned agency, whose officials are courteous, helpful and efficient.

In *Hungary*, the advertising scene is little different from that in Western Europe. There are several agencies and they advertise in newspapers, magazines and television. There is even a magazine about advertising.

In *Czechoslovakia* there are two agencies, and they advertise in newspapers and magazines as well as on television and radio. There is also an agency in *Poland*, but it has filtered out its creative talent, replacing them with bureaucrats.

There is one agency in *Romania*, and considerable advertising for consumer products. I know nothing about advertising in *East Germany* or *Bulgaria*.

China

Until 1977 advertising in China was considered evil, so there wasn't any. But in 1978 the government endorsed its use. The advertisements look like specification sheets. There are commercials on Chinese television, most of them for industrial products like electric motors; the waste circulation must be astronomic. There is no *need* to advertise consumer products, because most of them are in short supply.

The most important advertising medium in China is radio, the communal speaker system reaching 75 per cent of the population. The commercials are broadcast twice a day, one after another. There are 40 local newspapers, but they consist of only two sheets and their advertising content is less than 25 per cent. There are 160 magazines, mostly devoted to trade and technical subjects, and there are billboards in the big cities.

There are no less than 67 advertising agencies, of which 17 are responsible for advertising Chinese products in foreign countries, and foreign products in China. Dentsu, the Japanese agency, has small offices in Peking and Shanghai, and McCann-Erickson has an office in Peking.

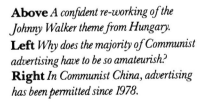

Above *A confident re-working of the Johnny Walker theme from Hungary.*
Left *Why does the majority of Communist advertising have to be so amateurish?*
Right *In Communist China, advertising has been permitted since 1978.*

Above *Young & Rubicam fly their flag on this giant billboard in Shanghai.*

If I knew anything about advertising in *Japan*, I would tell you. But I don't – yet.

* * * * *

In short, while the volume of advertising is still growing in the United States, it is growing faster in the rest of the world, and America is no longer top nation professionally. The tortoises are overtaking the hare.

18

Lasker, Resor, Rubicam, Burnett, Hopkins and Bernbach

Six giants who invented modern advertising

By confining my selection of giants to those who are dead, I avoid the embarrassment of choosing among my partners – and my contemporaries in other agencies.

What, if anything, did these six giants have in common? All six of them were American. All six had other jobs before they went into advertising. At least five were gluttons for work, and uncompromising perfectionists. Four made their reputations as *copywriters*. Only three had university degrees.

ALBERT LASKER 1880-1952

Albert Lasker made more money than anyone in the history of the advertising business. And spent more. *And got his money's worth.*

The son of a prosperous German immigrant, he started his career as a reporter on the *Galveston Morning News*, covering sports, crime, religious services, theater, business and politics. When he was 18 his father got him a job at the Lord & Thomas agency in Chicago. At first he had to clean out the spittoons, but quickly became a champion canvasser for new business, criss-crossing the Midwest by train, buggy and sleigh. When he was 20 he *bought* Lord & Thomas, and remained its head until he retired 44 years later.

Lasker was *more* than an advertising man. In 1918 he came under the influence of Theodore Roosevelt, and this led to his taking four years off as the head of propaganda for the Republican Party and later the chairman of the Shipping Board. In those days he was a militant isolationist, but he lived to become one of Wendell Wilkie's strongest supporters in the One World movement, and did everything he could to advance the foreign policy of Franklin Roosevelt and Harry Truman.

At the age of 65 he started collecting pictures, and died owning

Below *Albert Lasker made more money, spent more and gave more away than anybody in the history of advertising. And he got his money's worth.*

nine Matisses, seventeen Picassos and a hundred other pictures of the first rank. He once bought half a dozen Marie Laurencins to give away as Christmas presents.

He was a brilliant philanthropist, and gave a large part of his fortune to medical research.

But it was as an advertising man that Lasker excelled. When he first joined Lord & Thomas, then the third biggest agency in the country, they employed only one half-time copywriter and paid him $15 a week. Then John E. Kennedy, a Canadian policeman turned copywriter, came into his life and persuaded him that advertising was 'salesmanship in print', a definition that has never been improved. Lasker said later, 'The history of advertising could never be written without first place being given to John E. Kennedy, for every copywriter throughout the length and breadth of this land is today being guided by the principles he laid down.'

'Lasker held that if an agency could write copy which sold the product, nothing else was needed.'

Lasker held that if an agency could write copy which sold the product, nothing else was needed. For years he refused to employ an art director, and when he finally gave in it was only because he had observed that illustrated advertisements were easier to sell to clients. His attitude to research was equally contemptuous. He used to say that he was perfectly able to give his clients advice 'without having to lose six months going out to do research, only to come back and tell us that a jackass has two ears.' He never had what is called today a 'marketing' department. His intuitive genius for marketing can be illustrated in a story he told about the early days of women's sanitary napkins.

> 'When the Kotex people came to us, the business wasn't growing as fast as they thought it should. We didn't have to make investigations among millions of women. Just a few of us talked to our wives and asked them if they used Kotex, and we found they didn't, and in almost every case it was because they didn't like to ask the druggist for it. So we developed the simple idea of putting plain wrapped packages on the dealer's counter so that you could walk into your dealer and walk away with a wrapped package without embarrassment. The business boomed by leaps and bounds.'

By dispensing with marketers, art directors and researchers, Lasker saved so much money that he was able to make a profit of 7 per cent – probably the world's record. If an agency makes more than *1* per cent today, it is exceptional.

He ran Lord & Thomas as a dictatorship. 'As you all know,' he told his staff, 'I am the owner of this business and therefore I decide the policies. Lord & Thomas is the trade name for Albert D. Lasker practicing advertising.' He owned 95 per cent of the shares. After he retired he said that he had never attended a directors' meeting and did not think that one had ever been held.

He hired able men, paid them well and trained them well. He used to say, 'I can get more out of people than they have in them.' But the

'Lasker used to say, "I make my men so good that I can't keep 'em". '

turnover was ferocious. At one point the heads of nine major agencies were Lasker alumni. He used to say, 'I make my men so good that I can't keep 'em.' Before writing his biography of Lasker,* John Gunther asked some of his people what they thought had been his greatest qualities. The consensus was that he combined a sense of detail with a gift for grasping the big picture, and that he had a genius for predicting the reactions of consumers. In addition, his vitality and magnetism were irresistible, and he worked fifteen hours a day. No wonder he made Lord & Thomas the biggest agency in the world – for a time.

He loathed talking on the telephone, and abominated committees. He never belonged to an advertising club, and avoided his competitors. He resigned several huge accounts out of pique, including General Electric, Quaker Oats and RCA, and after his retirement encouraged his successors to resign Lucky Strike.

He had himself driven about in a yellow Rolls-Royce. And, like me, he hated reverse type – 'if it was natural to read that way, the *New York Times* would be printed that way.'

He was not shy about conspicuous consumption. His weekend estate outside Chicago had a staff of fifty. The gardens covered 97 acres, with six miles of clipped hedges – compared with only *one* mile in my garden today. And there was an 18-hole golf course.

He once defined an administrator as 'somebody without brains', but as an administrator himself, he could be ruthless. In the Depression he cut all salaries by 25 per cent when he was taking $3,000,000 a year for himself, and then, at one fell swoop, fired 50 men and women many of whom had been with him for years.

For all his financial acumen, he made at least one major blunder. When his father died, Lasker inherited a lot of Texas real estate. He promptly sold what was to become some of the richest oil land in the world, and a quarter of downtown Houston. That, plus his philanthropies and his extravagance, is why he left only $11,500,000 instead of a billion. He once said, 'I didn't want to make a great fortune. I wanted to show what I could do with my brains.'

His emotional make-up was uncomfortable. Gunther, who knew him well, says that he was sensitive and perceptive, and that he had a bubbling sense of humor. But he could be overbearing, intolerant and arrogant, once being heard to say, 'There is no advertising man in the world but me.' I don't think he was joking. His first wife said that he gave her everything except himself. He could be bad-tempered, demanding and inconsiderate. And he had three prolonged nervous breakdowns.

The best advertisement for Albert Lasker is his widow Mary. She has administered his medical foundation with superb ability, and is one of New York's most constructive citizens. On the one occasion I met her, she told me the story of her husband's abdication. One afternoon, late in 1942, he suddenly said to her, 'Mary, I have decided to get out of the advertising business.' Two days later he gave Lord & Thomas to three of his bright young men (Foote, Cone and Belding), for a token payment of $100,000 – on condition that the name Lord & Thomas should be taken off the masthead. He lived another ten years.

Taken at the Flood (Harper, 1960)

STANLEY RESOR 1879-1962

Stanley Resor was the Brahmin of the advertising business. Austere, dignified, cultured, beautifully mannered and rather donnish.

When he became head of J. Walter Thompson, the agency was billing $3,000,000 a year. When he retired 45 years later, it was the biggest in the world, with billings of $500,000,000.

The secret of his success was his ability to attract exceptionally able men, and to treat them with so much respect that they never left. They included Sam Meek, James Webb Young, Henry Stanton, Ken Hinks and Gilbert Kinney. No other agency has ever had a team of such caliber, or kept it together so long.

'The secret of his success was his ability to attract exceptionally able men, and to treat them with so much respect that they never left.'

Resor was never overbearing like Lasker. He managed by consensus, distrusting what he called Individual Opinion, and thought that brilliance was dangerous.

His agency was structured in the loosest possible way. He detested hierarchies. There were no department heads, and no job descriptions. The agency operated as a partnership, like a big law firm. When he offered me a job, he gave me no inkling what work he had in mind for me. Office boy? Copywriter? His successor? He did not say, and I did not ask him.

Resor worked his way through Yale tutoring other students and selling books, but he also had time to win the James Gordon Bennett prize for economics. He retained a life-long admiration for professors and hired at least three to work at J. Walter Thompson – a psychologist, an economist and a historian. He used to say that his agency was the 'university' of advertising.

Unlike Lasker, he was a fervent believer in research. The economist Arno Johnson was one of his researchers, and another was Virgil Reed, a former Director of the Census. He set up a panel of 5,000 consumers and had them report once a month on everything they purchased. He had a test kitchen in the agency, to invent new recipes for his clients, and he started experiments on television long before it was available for advertising. He also shared my interest in factor-analysis and had a team studying techniques which work and techniques which don't work.

A man of rigid principles, he threw away an opportunity to get the huge Camel account because he would not show speculative advertisements. He never took liquor accounts or patent medicines.

Perhaps his most valuable innovation was to be the first to employ women as copywriters, starting with his wife. They were housed in a separate department and had to wear hats in the office.

Like all the giants, Resor worked long hours. I used to see him on the train that left Grand Central Station shortly before midnight. He was usually reading the Wall Street prices in the evening paper, 20 years before I had any reason to do so.

A few years after I hung out my shingle, I lost my biggest account to J. Walter Thompson, and telephoned Resor to congratulate him. 'David', he said, 'you are a gentleman and a scholar but you are trying to break into the ranks of the big agencies, and that is no longer possible.

Stanley Resor, the Brahmin of the advertising business. He and his copywriter wife made J. Walter Thompson the biggest agency in the world.

The investment is too big. I suggest you give up and join J. Walter Thompson.'

I replied, 'Mr. Resor, I would love to join you, but I couldn't fire a hundred men and women.'

'Oh,' he said, 'times are good. They wouldn't have any difficulty finding other jobs.'

Two years later he repeated the invitation, this time offering to buy my whole agency, like buying a library to get one book. That was the day I met his wife. He had hired her to write copy on the Cincinnati agency where he worked before joining Thompson, and she had become one of the best copywriters in the country. Their partnership, both in business and as a couple, was formidable.

It was Helen Resor who insisted that the agency's offices should be decorated with antique furniture, each executive being allowed to choose the period he liked the best. She was said to believe that if their offices were more attractive than their homes, they would work longer hours.*

In some ways, Helen Resor was *more* than Stanley. She was one of the founders of the planned parenthood movement, and she made use of her experience as a Trustee of the Museum of Modern Art to form an admirable collection of pictures.

Despite the fact that he was married to a copywriter, Resor had a tendency to regard copywriters as idiots. His agency was dominated by its account executives, or 'representatives' as he called them.

Unlike the author, he believed strongly in the selling power of celebrity testimonials. For Lux Toilet Soap he used Hollywood movie stars, and for Ponds he used titled English women; my friend Erskine Childers, who was later to become President of Ireland, had the job of signing them up.

Resor was the first agency chief to start a network of offices outside the United States. This he did in the twenties, at the behest of General Motors.

He looked like Woodrow Wilson, but he was a Republican. He lived in an unostentatious house in Connecticut, where he worked in the garden, and had a ranch in Wyoming. None of Lasker's extravagance.

But Resor made one mistake. He stayed too long. By the time he was 80, his ideas for advertising campaigns had become anachronistic. And partners who would have made good successors retired before he did.

RAYMOND RUBICAM 1892-1978

The day after I arrived in the United States, I called Raymond Rubicam for an appointment, armed with an introduction from Caroline Ruutz-Rees, the famous headmistress of Rosemary Hall.

'State your business,' he barked. 'I want to pick your brains,' I replied.

*This cost JWT the chance to get the Listerine account. Jerry Lambert who owned Listerine told me, 'I would prefer an agency which spends its commissions on service rather than furniture.'

Above *The two best agencies in the world are the lengthened shadows of Raymond Rubicam. He was my conscience for 40 years, teaching me that advertising has a responsibility to behave.*

Opposite *Raymond Rubicam assembled the best team of copywriters and art directors in the history of advertising – like Jack Rosebrook, Roy Whittier, Vaughn Flannery, Henry Lent, George Gribbin, Sid Ward and Norman Robbins. Under Rubicam's inspiration they created advertisements which were read by more people than any other agency's – including this ad for Life Savers.*

The following year, he and George Gallup, who was then his Research Director, hired me to run the Audience Research Institute at Princeton. Rubicam took great interest in our work and treated me with uncommon kindness.

After the war I decided to try my luck in advertising, but I stood in such awe of Young & Rubicam that I did not dare apply to them for a job. As I thought they were the only agency where I would like to work, I had no choice but to start my own. In one of his last letters before he died, Rubicam wrote, 'We *knew* you before you started your agency. How come we missed you?'

By that time we had become great friends. 'Friends' is not the right word. He was my patron, inspiration, counselor, critic and conscience. I was his hero-worshipping disciple. At one stage, long after he retired from Young & Rubicam, he offered to become chairman of Ogilvy & Mather.

If all institutions are 'the lengthened shadow of one man', it can be said that the two best agencies in the world today are the lengthened shadows of Raymond Rubicam.

Next to my grandfather, whom he resembled physically and in many other ways, Rubicam was the most outspoken man I have ever known. He blurted out whatever was on his mind, without considering what effect it might have. One day he would praise one of my campaigns in language which made me blush, and a few weeks later criticize another campaign with a candor which made me wince.

The youngest of eight children in a poor family, he left school when he was 15 and spent the next nine years bumming around the country as a shipping clerk, bellhop, chaperone of cattle, movie projectionist, door-to-door salesman, automobile salesman, and newspaper reporter (at $12 a week). When he was 24 he applied for a job as a copywriter at the now defunct F. Wallis Armstrong agency in Philadelphia. 'I sat in that lobby – on a bench so hard that I can still feel it,' he later recalled. 'At the end of the ninth day, I exploded … I wrote the boss a letter calculated to produce an immediate interview or a couple of black eyes.' The boss stormed into the lobby, waving the letter, and said, 'Those ads you wrote didn't amount to much, but this letter has some stuff in it.'

He stayed with Armstrong for three years, but did not enjoy it. 'Armstrong said that a copywriter was a necessary evil, but an art director was just a goddamned luxury. He lived to outfox everybody.' In 1919 Rubicam moved to N.W. Ayer, then the largest agency in the country. There he wrote campaigns which have been included in every anthology of great advertisements, including 'The Instrument of the Immortals' for Steinway and 'The Priceless Ingredient' for Squibb. Then, after four years with Ayer, he teamed up with an account executive called John Orr Young to start Young & Rubicam, on a shoe-string. Their capital was $5,000 and their first account *was* a shoe-string. Today their agency is either the biggest or second biggest in the world, with billings of about three billion dollars a year.*

*If you lump together the three networks which belong to Interpublic, they come out bigger than Young & Rubicam and its subsidiaries.

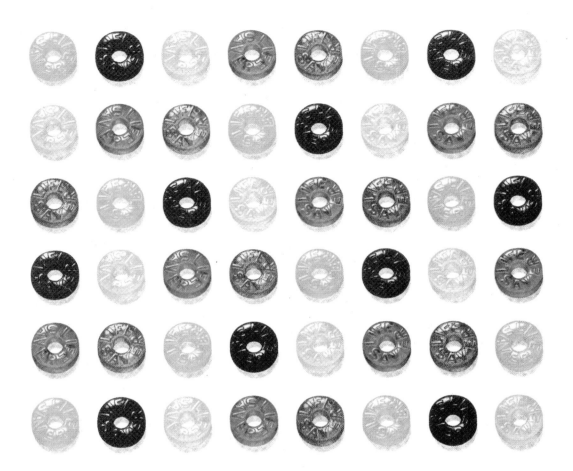

please do not lick this page!

P.S. Get 'em in the handy roll
...everywhere

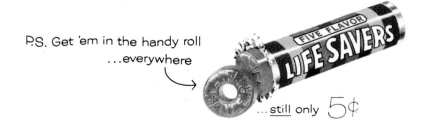

... <u>still</u> only 5¢

'Rubicam used to say, "The way we sell is to get read first". '

He was the first to make research part of the creative process, by bringing in Dr. Gallup from Northwestern University and paying him to measure the readership of advertisements. From this research emerged guidelines which enabled Young & Rubicam to produce advertisements which were read by more people than any other agency's. Rubicam used to say, 'The way we sell is to get read first.'

Observing that the effect of his campaigns was often negated by the marketing incompetence of his clients, he hired first-class sales managers to teach them their business.

During the first year of Young & Rubicam, their advertisements were notable for the excellence of their copy, but their graphics – illustrations, layouts and typography – were as hideous as any other agency's. When this dawned on Rubicam, he hired Vaughn Flannery, the best art director in America. From that day forward, Young & Rubicam's advertisements set a standard of taste which was new in American advertising.

But the achievement of which Rubicam was most proud was a larger one. In old age he told me, 'Advertising has a responsibility to *behave* properly. I proved that you can sell products without bamboozling the American public.' While he had no monopoly on this virtue, he had more right than anyone to boast about it.

His definition of a good advertisement was that 'its public is not only strongly sold by it, but both the public and the advertiser remember it for a long time *as an admirable piece of work.'*

In the eternal battle for power which goes on in agencies between the creative people and the account executives, Rubicam – himself a copywriter – came down heavily on the side of the creative people. He called account executives by the old-fashioned and now pejorative word 'contact men' and insisted that their only function was to get clients to approve the ads.

He taught me to resign accounts when they were spoiling the morale of my staff. He resigned the huge American Tobacco account because he disliked being bullied by the notorious George Washington Hill. His letter is before me:

> 'Young & Rubicam and American Tobacco were both successful companies for some time before our association began. I trust both will continue to be successful companies after our association ceases, *which it is doing as of now.'*

The early success of Young & Rubicam was due more than anything else to the fact that General Foods was their biggest client. One day Rubicam told the head of General Foods that his account had grown too big for any one agency; he should hire a second and later a third. This is how Benton & Bowles got their first major account, and it is why General Foods came to trust every recommendation Rubicam made to them.

At the end of World War II, when I was a Second Secretary at the British Embassy in Washington, I suggested to the Foreign Office in London that they nominate Rubicam to head the public relations function at the fledgling United Nations, only to be told that he should fill out an application form!

Off duty, he was less conservative then Stanley Resor. In 1946 he contributed an article to *McCall's* deploring the dropping of atomic bombs on Japan. He believed that a *demonstration* of the bomb would have convinced the Japanese to surrender, and made the United States the moral leader of the world.

In the early days of radio he proposed that the programs should be paid for by the government and carry no advertising. When he was made a member of the Advertising Hall of Fame in 1974, he said in his acceptance speech, 'The national obsession with television is decreasing the literacy of the nation's children and making the job of the schools much tougher. It is also obsessing the country with crime. Industry and advertising could perform a huge public service if they could induce the television networks to cut down the advertising and cut down the crime.'

During World War II he was a special assistant to the chairman of the War Manpower Commission in Washington, but the environment did not fit him.

Like all the other giants, Rubicam was a perfectionist and had a habit of vetoing advertisements when the account executive was on his way to present them to the client. He used to say, 'The client remembers an outstanding job years after he has forgotten that it was two months late.' He worked non-stop – until he found happiness in his second

Above *This modest ad announced the opening of Young & Rubicam in 1923.*
Below *The ad on the left, written by Raymond Rubicam in 1919, now looks old-fashioned. The ad on the right, written in 1982, has a contemporary look. But which ad is more memorable?*

STEINWAY

The Instrument of the Immortals

There has been but one supreme piano in the history of music. In the days of Liszt and Wagner, of Rubinstein and Berlioz, the pre-eminence of the Steinway was as unquestioned as it is today. It stood then, as it stands now, the chosen instrument of the masters— the inevitable preference wherever great music is understood and esteemed.

STEINWAY & SONS, Steinway Hall, 107-109 E. 14th Street, New York
Subway Express Stations at the Door

177

Fortress Steinway.

So begins the Steinway Grand Piano.
The basic frame, shown here, is so solid, so strong, so well made that even at this early stage of construction—before a note is played—the Steinway takes leave of lesser quality instruments.
Examine the curved rim. While other pianomakers build it in sections, we build it the hard way.
Inner and outer rims are rock maple, laminated in one operation into a rigid arch strong enough to withstand 20 tons of pressure from the strings.
Now take a closer look. The inner rim mount of the Steinway grand is beveled at an 88.5° angle so that the soundboard, when glued in, is forced to arch just enough to increase vibrancy and responsiveness.
Also observe that there are no metal connectors in a Steinway frame. We know they distort the sound and loosen with time.
Instead, the cross braces are joined to the rim with blind wooden dowels, cross-locked for maximum strength.
This homogeneous construction makes the Steinway grand a veritable fortress.
It will take us one full year to complete this piano. But it will last for generations.
For literature about the Steinway, write to John H. Steinway, Dept. 33, 109 West 57th Street, New York, N.Y. 10019.

STEINWAY & SONS

marriage. He then retired, aged 52, and went to live in Arizona, where he speculated in real estate and served as consultant to Campbell Soup Company, a role in which I was to succeed him.

He had been at his agency for only 21 years, compared with Stanley Resor's 45 years at J. Walter Thompson and Albert Lasker's 40 years at Lord & Thomas.

The present President of Young & Rubicam has said that 'Rubicam played a marvelous dirty trick on the rest of us – he didn't leave behind a list of rules.'

He did, however, leave behind an aphorism which appeals to the present generation at Young & Rubicam: *resist the usual*. Or, as his copy chief Roy Whittier put it, 'In advertising, the beginning of greatness is to be different, and the beginning of failure is to be the same.' A point of view which was shared by Bill Bernbach.

I knew Rubicam for 40 years, longer than any of my other giants, and loved him more.

'I knew Rubicam for 40 years, longer than any of my other giants, and loved him more.'

Cooling idea

REMEMBER this picture?

We first used it 6 years ago to remind you how gloriously cool and refreshing a Four-Roses-and-ice-and-soda can be on a warm midsummer afternoon.

We're certain you haven't forgotten, if you tried one. For the keen enjoyment of Four Roses' matchless flavor and mellow smoothness in a highball is something to be long remembered.

Today, as then, there's no other whiskey with quite the distinctive flavor of Four Roses. You'll see how right we are if you'll just make this cooling idea a memorable reality—now! Try a Four-Roses-and-soda—won't you?

* * *

Four Roses is a fine blended whiskey—93.5 proof, 40% straight whiskies 5 years or more old, 60% grain neutral spirits.

FOUR ROSES
A TRULY GREAT **BLENDED WHISKEY**

Frankfort Distillers Corporation, N. Y.

Right *Another elegant and effective ad from the winning Rubicam team.*

LEO BURNETT 1891-1971

The first thing that struck you about Leo Burnett was his extraordinary appearance. Carl Hixon describes it perfectly: 'He was short and slope-shouldered, with a paunch. His lapels were sprinkled with cigarette ash. A large double chin gave him a faintly froggy aspect. When he spoke, his voice was a gruff rumble. But his most memorable feature was his prominent lower lip.'

After working his way through college writing show cards for a department store, Leo landed a job as a reporter on the *Peoria Journal*. Later, he joined the advertising department of Cadillac, from which he went to an agency in Indianapolis. After ten years there, he joined Erwin Wasey as copy chief, and in 1935 set up his own agency in Chicago. But it wasn't until he was 60 that Leo hit his stride. It was as if

he suddenly turned on his after-burners. By the time he died, 20 years later, his agency had become the biggest in the world outside New York.

He was the leader of the 'Chicago school' of advertising – which was his invention. Here is how he told the story:

> 'In the Michigan town where I was raised, you could hear the corn growing on hot nights. I snuck up on Chicago slowly, by way of outlying cities. When I finally got here I was 40 years old and confirmed in my colloquial ways.

> 'People in my home town thought of Chicago as a kind of Rome to which all roads led – beckoning, majestic, maybe a touch or two wicked.

> 'Unlike New York, however, which was a mythical place, Chicago was real. Everyone had an Uncle Charlie or Aunt Mabel living here, in Glen Ellyn or somewhere. Whether people approved of Chicago or not, it was "family", rather like a son who had gone off and made good in an impressive but controversial way. So my little town had a proprietary feeling about Chicago, and when we rubes came flocking in from all quarters of the cornbelt, we recognized each other and knew we were home.

> 'I guess what I'm getting at is that Chicago *is* the Midwest – the heart, soul, brains and bowels of it. Its ad-making ranks are filled with folks whose heads are stocked with prairie-town views and values.

> 'Now I don't intend to argue that Chicago is in any way a worthier city than, say, New York. But I am suggesting that our sod-busting delivery, our loose-limbed stand and our wide-eyed perspective make it easier for us to create ads that talk turkey to the majority of Americans – that's all.

> 'I like to think that we Chicago ad-makers are all working stiffs.' I like to imagine that Chicago copywriters spit on their hands before picking up the big, black pencils. I like to think that the language of our ads has been ventilated in the fresh Chicago breezes and rinsed in the clear waters of Lake Michigan.

> 'It seems to me that Chicago Advertising draws up a lot of nourishment from the richness of American folklore, restores it, and perpetuates it in a keen and lively sense.

> 'I like to think that hereabouts a man can write *ain't* into his copy when *ain't* is precisely what he means. Remember Will Rogers counseled: "A lot of people who don't say *ain't* . . . ain't eatin'!" '

The greatest compliment Leo ever paid me was to tell the *Chicago Tribune* that there was one agency in New York which *belonged* to the Chicago school – Ogilvy & Mather. He suggested we merge.

'Without any doubt, Leo's greatest monument is his campaign for Marlboro.'

His attitude to the creative process can be summed up in three things he said:

1 'There is an inherent drama in every product. Our No. 1 job is to dig for it and capitalize on it.'

2 'When you reach for the stars, you may not quite get one, but you won't come up with a handful of mud either.'

3 'Steep yourself in your subject, work like hell, and love, honor and obey your hunches.'

He set high standards for his copywriters and art directors, and applied them through his Creative Review Committee. He once likened the ordeal of appearing before it to being 'nibbled to death by ducks'. At the end of his life he wrote: 'Looking back over our greatest achievements, I recall that few of them were generated in an atmosphere of sweetness, light and enthusiasm, but rather one of dynamic tension, complicated by off-stage muttering.'

He did not admire originality for its own sake, and used to quote an old boss of his: 'If you insist on being different just for the sake of being different, you can always come down in the morning with a sock in your mouth.'

Instead of assigning a project to one creative group, he had a habit of putting several groups in competition. It was enough, he once said, 'to send strong men staggering to buy a goat farm.'

Without any doubt, Leo's greatest monument is his campaign for Marlboro. It made an obscure brand the biggest-selling cigarette in the world. And it is still running, 25 years after he created it.

Print was always the medium which interested him most. Never having worked in direct response, he did not put much stock in long copy. Most of his ads looked like miniature posters.

He liked earthy, vernacular phrases, and kept a folder on his desk labeled *Corny Language*. 'I do not mean maxims, gags or slang in its ordinary sense, but words, phrases and analogies which convey a feeling of sod-buster honesty and drive home a point. I sometimes run across these phrases in a newspaper story or in a chance conversation. I chuck them into the folder and one of them might show up in an ad years later.'

When he saw somebody on his staff using the product of a competitor, he issued this memo:

'As you well know, your income and mine are derived 100 per cent from the sale of the products of our clients.

'During the 36 years I have been in the agency business I have always been naïvely guided by the principle that if we do not believe in the products we advertise strongly enough to use them ourselves, we are not completely honest with ourselves in advertising them to others.

'I recognize the unconscious spirit of rebellious independence that exists in all of us, and the compulsion you or I may have to demonstrate that we wear no man's yoke. I have always felt, however, that there are better and more rewarding ways of doing this than in conspicuously avoiding or flouting the products of the people who pay our way.

'I guess my feeling is pretty well summed up in the remarks of the vice president of a competitive agency. When asked why he was smoking a not-too-popular brand of cigarette which his company advertised, he replied: "In my book there is no taste or aroma quite like that of bread and butter." '

Leo deplored the tendency of mega-agencies to put their own aggrandizement ahead of service to their clients. Not long before he died, he told his staff:

'Somewhere along the line, after I'm finally off the premises, you may want to take my *name* off the premises, too.

'But let me tell you when I might *demand* that you take my name off the door. That will be the day when you spend more time trying to make money and less time making advertising.

'When your main interest becomes a matter of size just to be big, rather than good, hard, wonderful work.'

I wish I had written that.

He had two sons, a geologist and an architect, and one daughter, a poet. He lived on a farm outside Chicago, but worked 364 days a year, except for occasional visits to the Arlington race-track, where he had a box. He had a passion for wild flowers, trees – and charades.

CLAUDE C. HOPKINS 1867-1932

By exorcizing the pseudo-literary pretentions endemic in British copywriters of my vintage, and concentrating my thoughts on the obligation of advertising to *sell*, Claude Hopkins' book, *Scientific Advertising*, changed the course of my life.

At 17 Hopkins was a lay preacher, but he rebeled against his family's hardshell Baptist brand of religion, and got a job as a bookkeeper. Not long afterwards, he joined the Bissell Carpet Sweeper Company, and invented selling strategies which gave Bissell a virtual monopoly. Then to Swift as Advertising Manager, followed by Dr. Shoop's patent medicine company, where he persuaded his agency to let him write the copy not only for Dr. Shoop's but for Montgomery Ward and Schlitz Beer as well.

When he was 41, he was hired by Albert Lasker to write copy for Lord & Thomas. Lasker paid him $185,000 a year – equivalent to $2,000,000 in today's money. He stayed at Lord & Thomas for 18 years.

Hopkins was a prodigiously hard worker, seldom leaving his office before the early hours of the morning. Sunday was his favorite day, because he could work without interruption.

From his typewriter came campaigns which made many products

Nobody should be allowed to have anything to do with advertising until he has read this book seven times. It changed the course of my life.

famous, including Pepsodent, Palmolive and six different cars. He invented ways to force distribution for new products. He invented test marketing. He invented sampling by coupon. He invented copy research.

He held that nobody with a college education should be allowed to write copy for the mass market. I know what he meant.

He was an uncompromising practitioner of the experimental method, forever testing new ideas in search of better results – even if, as Politz has pointed out, he did not always indicate 'the boundaries between direct findings from experimentation and conclusions arrived at by general observation and reasoning.'

A few of his conclusions have been disproved by later research. We now know, for example, that he was wrong when he said, 'In every ad consider only *new* customers. People using your product are not going to read your ads.' The fact is that users of a product read its advertisements more than non-users.

He was a shy, mousy little man and spoke with a strong lisp. His nickname was Thee-Thee, that being the way he pronounced his initials C.C. But he was a good raconteur and after-dinner speaker. He always wore a fuchsia in his buttonhole, chewed licorice root, and spat profusely on the person he was talking to.

Rich as he became, Hopkins was notoriously stingy, and never paid more than $6 for a pair of shoes. But his second wife persuaded him to buy an ocean-going yacht, to employ an army of gardeners on their estate, and to buy Louis XVI furniture. She filled their house with an endless procession of guests, and played Scarlatti to Hopkins for hours at a time.

He thought illustrations were a waste of space. Perhaps they *were* less important 60 years ago, when magazines and newspapers were thinner, and competition for the reader's attention less severe. But few experienced practitioners of advertising would now argue with these dicta:

> 'Almost any question can be answered, cheaply, quickly and finally, by a test campaign. And that's the way to answer them – not by arguments around the table.'

> 'Ad writers forget they are salesmen and try to be performers. Instead of sales, they seek applause.'

> 'Whenever possible we introduce a personality into our ads. By making a man famous we make his product famous.'

> 'It it not uncommon for a change in headlines to multiply returns from five to ten times over.'

> 'Brief ads are never keyed. Every traced ad tells a complete story.'

Nowadays **Hopkins** is remembered, if at all, as an uncompromising advocate of 'hard sell'. Yet he perceived the importance of brand images – a generation before that term came into use. 'Try to give each advertiser a becoming style. To create the right individuality is a supreme accomplishment.'

Raymond Rubicam abhorred Hopkins, believing that he had devoted his life to cheating the public. He once told me, 'You are Claude Hopkins with a college education.' A backhanded compliment if ever I heard one.

Five years before he died Hopkins wrote, 'My chief work in advertising has been meeting emergencies. Nobody ever called me in when the skies were bright and the seas were calm. Nearly every client quit me when he got into smooth waters.' Sick of rescuing clients from the jaws of bankruptcy and making them richer than himself, he resigned from Lord & Thomas and went into business for himself. Too late.

'Hopkins was interested in *nothing* but advertising.'

Hopkins was interested in *nothing* but advertising. There is macabre pathos in the last sentence of his autobiography: 'The happiest are those who live closest to nature, *an essential to advertising success.*'

BILL BERNBACH 1911-1982

Bill Bernbach and I started our agencies in the same year, and we both made our reputations as copywriters.

He was born 19 years after the youngest of my five other giants. After graduating from New York University with a degree in English Literature, he got a job in the mailroom of Schenley and became the protégé of Grover Whalen, who was the chairman. When Whalen left to run the New York's World Fair, he took Bill with him as his speech writer. After the Fair ended, Bill joined the Weintraub agency, where he worked with Paul Rand, a distinguished art director who was a fugitive from the Bauhaus.

During World War II, he spent two years in the Army, and then went to the Grey agency, where he quickly became creative head. Four years later, with Ned Doyle and Max Dane, he started his own agency, with an investment of $1,200. While his name appeared last on the letterhead, there was never any doubt whose agency it was. Today, Doyle Dane Bernbach is the tenth biggest in the world, with billings of more than a billion dollars.

Bill always created an atmosphere in which talented people blossomed. A woman who wrote deadly dull copy for me wrote brilliant copy for Bill. He was an irresistible salesman of his agency's work, and terrifyingly obstinate. When I was chairman of the United Negro College Fund, he volunteered to make a television commercial for purposes of fund-raising. I dared to warn him that his storyboard, while a work of art, was not calculated to produce cash contributions. Bill replied, 'David, you don't have to worry. There are plenty of other agencies that would be happy to do the job for you.' Bill's commercial ran as presented.

'I am told that he used to carry a card which bore the self-admonition *Maybe he's right.'*

I am told that he used to carry a card which bore the self-admonition *Maybe he's right*. I once actually heard him admit that a client was right. This precedent-shattering event happened at lunch in the White House, when one of President Johnson's assistants criticized

Bill Bernbach – 'a gentleman with brains.'
He worshipped at the altar of originality
and was the hero of the creative fraternity.

an anti-Goldwater commercial that Bill had put on the air the previous night.

He had a genius for integrating copy with illustration, and never made my mistake of subordinating copywriters to art directors.

He held, as I do, that the quality of the idea and the excellence of its execution was the alpha and omega of successful advertising.

He worshipped at the altar of originality, and was never tired of denouncing research as the enemy of creativity. This may have irritated some of his clients, but it made him the hero of the creative fraternity.

Of all his wonderful campaigns, those I most admire are Volkswagen and Avis. He was less successful with package-goods clients who tried to impose orthodox disciplines. I have often wondered if his output would have been less elegant if, like me, he had started as a door-to-door salesman.

He spoke in a quiet voice and looked modest. But he wasn't. The last time I saw him, he and Rosser Reeves were my guests at lunch. Bill lectured Rosser and me as if we were trainees in his agency. When some of his stodgier competitors started raiding his agency in search of swingers, Bill told me, 'They don't realize that these people will be helpless without my guiding hand.' And guide them he did, always insisting that their advertising, however clever and original, should make the product the hero.

He was a philosopher. He lived without ostentation, and organized his time with a self-discipline that is rare among heads of agencies. He once told me that he never stayed in the office after five, never took work home, and never worked at weekends. 'You see, David, I love my family.'

Shortly before he died, Bill was asked what changes he expected in advertising in the eighties. He replied, 'Human nature hasn't changed for a billion years. It won't even vary in the next billion years. Only the superficial things have changed. It is fashionable to talk about *changing* man. A communicator must be concerned with *unchanging* man – what compulsions drive him, what instincts dominate his every action, even though his language too often camouflages what *really* motivates him. For if you know these things about a man, you can touch him at the core of his being. One thing is unchangingly sure. The creative man with an insight into human nature, with the artistry to touch and move people, will succeed. Without them he will fail.'

A gentleman with brains.

*   *   *   *   *

If I had to choose five more giants to complete my All-Time All-American team, they would be three copywriters – James Webb Young of J. Walter Thompson, George Cecil of N. W. Ayer, and Jack Rosebrook of Young & Rubicam; one art director – Vaughn Flannery of Young & Rubicam; and one new business wizard – Ben Duffy of BBDO.

And who would I choose from the living stars? Their names are locked in my safe.

19 What's wrong with advertising?

Toynbee and Galbraith vs. Roosevelt and Churchill

In my *Confessions* I quoted the classic denunciations of advertising by Arnold Toynbee, John Kenneth Galbraith and a galaxy of earlier economists, and wheeled up Franklin Roosevelt and Winston Churchill as witnesses for the defense.

Twenty years later the dons are still tilting at their old windmill. Thus a professor at the New School of Social Research in New York teaches his students that 'advertising is a profoundly subversive force in American life. It is intellectual and moral pollution. It trivializes, manipulates, is insincere and vulgarizes. It is undermining our faith in our nation and in ourselves.'

'Holy smoke, is *that* what I do for a living?'

Holy smoke, is *that* what I do for a living?

Some of the defenders of advertising are equally guilty of overstating their case. Said Leo Burnett, the great Chicago advertising man: 'Advertising is not the noblest creation of man's mind, as so many of its advocates would like the public to think. It does not, single-handedly, sustain the whole structure of capitalism and democracy and the Free World. It is just as nonsensical to suggest that we are superhuman as to accept the indictment that we are subhuman. We are merely human, trying to do a necessary human job with dignity, with decency and with competence.'

My view is that advertising is no more and no less than a reasonably efficient way to sell. Procter & Gamble spends more than $600,000,000 a year on advertising. Howard Morgens, their former president, is quoted as saying, 'We believe that advertising is the most effective and efficient way to sell to the consumer. If we should ever find better methods of selling our type of products to the consumer, we'll leave advertising and turn to these other methods.'

Few of us admen lie awake nights feeling guilty about the way we earn our living. In Churchill's phrase, we just K.B.O.* We don't feel 'subversive' when we write advertisements for toothpaste. If we do it well, children may not have to go to the dentist so often.

*Keep buggering on.

Pablo Casals is coming home – to Puerto Rico

THIS SIMPLE ROOM is in his mother's home at Mayaguez. The first concert Casals ever gave in Puerto Rico was from the balcony of this house last year – just beyond that fanlight.

While his mother's kinsmen listened from the street, Casals played her lullaby, smoked his pipe and wept.

The back of that armchair bears an inscription in Casals' own handwriting. "Este es mi sillón." This is my rocking chair.

Here are gentle thoughts from the world's greatest cellist – on Puerto Rico, the sea and himself:

"The first time I was aware that I was alive, I heard the sound of the sea. Before, I would have said that the most beautiful sea was the one I had in front of my Spanish house. But now I must confess that the sea I am looking at this moment is even more beautiful."

Of his plans for the future, Pablo Casals had this to say:

"The natural thing that occurs to me, is to come back to Puerto Rico and to do for this country everything within my power. I will be back for the festival I have planned for this coming Spring."

PUERTO RICO'S GREAT NEW MUSIC FESTIVAL IN SAN JUAN

The Casals Festival in San Juan opens on April 22nd and will continue through May 8th. Pablo Casals will conduct or perform at each of twelve concerts.

The Festival Orchestra brings together fifty-four of the world's most talented musicians. Principal performers include: Mieczyslaw Horszowski, Eugene Istomin, Milton Katims,

Jesus Maria Sanromá, Alexander Schneider, Rudolf Serkin, Gérard Souzay, Maria Stader, Isaac Stern, Joseph Szigeti.

Two chamber music concerts will feature the Budapest String Quartet.

For further details, write Festival Casals, P. O. Box 2672, San Juan, Puerto Rico; or to 15 West 44th Street, New York 17, N. Y.

© 1957 Commonwealth of Puerto Rico, 579 Fifth Avenue, New York 17, N.Y.

Living room of the house where Casals' mother was born – in Mayaguez, ▷ Puerto Rico's third largest city. Photograph by Elliott Erwitt.

I did not feel 'evil' when I wrote advertisements that attracted tourists and industry to a country which had been living on the edge of starvation for 400 years.

I did not feel 'evil' when I wrote advertisements for Puerto Rico. They helped attract industry and tourists to a country which had been living on the edge of starvation for 400 years.

I do not think that I am 'trivializing' when I write advertisements for the World Wildlife Fund.

My children were grateful when I wrote an advertisement which recovered their dog Teddy from dognappers.

Nobody suggests that the printing press is evil because it is used to print pornography. It is also used to print the Bible. Advertising is only evil when it advertises evil things. Nobody I know in advertising would advertise a brothel, and some refuse to advertise booze or cigarettes.

Left-wing economists, ever eager to snatch the scourge from the hand of God, hold that advertising tempts people to squander money on things they don't need. Who are these élitists to decide what you need? Do you *need* a dishwasher? Do you *need* a deodorant? Do you *need* a trip to Rome? I feel no qualms of conscience about persuading you that you do. What the Calvinistic dons don't seem to know is that buying things can be one of life's more innocent pleasures, whether you need them or not. Remember your euphoria when you bought your first car? Most people enjoy window-shopping the ads, whether for bargains or for luxuries. For 40 years I shopped the ads for country houses, and finally saved up enough money to buy one.

It is not unknown for an advertisement in a newspaper to be read by more people than any news item. When all the New York

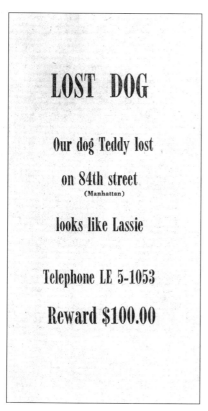

LOST DOG

Our dog Teddy lost

on 84th street
(Manhattan)

looks like Lassie

Telephone LE 5-1053

Reward $100.00

Above *My children were grateful when I wrote this advertisement. It recovered their dog Teddy from dognappers.*

newspapers went on strike for several weeks in 1963, research showed that it was the advertisements which readers missed most.

If advertising were abolished, what would be done with the money? Would it be spent on public works? Or distributed to stock-holders in the form of extra dividends? Or given to the media to compensate them for the loss of their largest source of revenue? Perhaps it could be used to reduce prices to the consumer – *by about 3 per cent.* *

Is advertising a pack of lies?

Introducing me at an Asian Advertising Congress in New Delhi the other day, the Vice-President and former Chief Justice of India said that I had 'mastered what Stephen Leacock called the art of arresting the human intelligence long enough to get money from it.'

If there are still any natural-born liars in advertising, we are under control. Every advertisement we write is scrutinized by lawyers, by the National Association of Broadcasters and other such bodies. The Better Business Bureau and the National Advertising Review Board (in Britain, the Advertising Standards Authority) review suspected violations of the various codes, and the Federal Trade Commission stands ready to prosecute us for deception. *Caveat emptor* has given way to *caveat vendor.*

But how odd that the Commission does not monitor the advertising put out by departments of the US Government. Writes Milton Friedman, 'Anyone who has bought government bonds over the past decade has been taken to the cleaners. The amount he received on maturity would buy less in goods and services than the amount he paid for the bond, and he has to pay taxes on the mislabeled "interest". Yet the Treasury continues to advertise the bonds as "building personal security," and a "gift that keeps on growing".' †

'The dirge of our times'

While very little advertising can be convicted of crimes against humanity, exposure to 30,000 TV commercials every year – the average dosage in American homes – suggests that Wilfrid Sheed had a point when he wrote that 'the sound of selling is the dirge of our times'. When I lived in New York, I did not notice it, either because I was too busy to watch for more than half an hour a day (Walter Cronkite), or because I was corrupted by familiarity. But when I went to live in Europe, I grew accustomed to smaller doses of advertising. Today, when I return to the United States, I am enraged by the barrage to which I am subjected. And this does not apply only to television. On Sundays, the *New York Times* often carries 350 pages of advertisements, and some of the radio stations devote 40 minutes in every hour to commercials. I don't know how all this clutter can ever be brought under control; the profit motive is too strong in those who own the media.

In the average American home, the TV is turned on, if not

*Automobile manufacturers spend 1 per cent of their revenue on advertising. Appliance manufacturers 2 per cent. Soft drinks 4 per cent. Food manufacturers and brewers 5 per cent.

† *Free to Choose*, Harcourt Brace, 1980

Right *The Advertising Standards Authority is the watchdog on British advertising.*

HOW DARE THEY!

If you see an advertisement in the press, in print, on posters or a cinema commercial which makes you angry, write to us at the address below. (TV and radio commercials are dealt with by the I.B.A.)

The Advertising Standards Authority.
If an advertisement is wrong, we're here to put it right.

ASA Ltd., Brook House, Torrington Place, London WC1E 7HN.

watched, for five hours a day, which adds up to 25 years in the average life. But don't blame the *commercials* for this addiction.

Manipulation?

You may have heard it said that advertising is 'manipulation'. I know of only two examples, and neither of them actually happened. In 1957 a market researcher called James Vicary hypothesized that it might be possible to flash commands on television screens so fast that the viewer would not be conscious of seeing them, but his *unconscious* would see them – and obey them. He called this gimmick 'subliminal' advertising, but he never even got around to testing it, and no advertiser has ever used it. Unfortunately word of his hypothesis found its way into the public prints, and provided grist for the mills of the anti-advertising brigade. The British Institute of Practitioners in Advertising solemnly banned the use of subliminal advertising – which did not exist.

'I myself once came near to doing something so diabolical that I hesitate to confess it, even now.'

My only other example of manipulation will make you shudder. I myself once came near to doing something so diabolical that I hesitate to confess it even now, 30 years later. Suspecting that *hypnotism* might be an element in successful advertising, I engaged a professional hypnotist to make a commercial. When I saw it in the projection room, it was so powerful that I had visions of millions of suggestible consumers getting up from their armchairs and rushing like zombies through the traffic on their way to buy the product at the nearest store. Had I invented the *ultimate* advertisement? I burned it, and never told my client how close I had come to landing him in a national scandal.

One way and another, the odds against your being manipulated by advertising are now very long indeed. Even if I wanted to manipulate you, I wouldn't know how to circumvent the legal regulations.

'There is one category of advertising which is totally uncontrolled and flagrantly dishonest: the television commercials for candidates in Presidential elections.'

Hold your horses – I almost forgot. There is one category of advertising which is totally uncontrolled and flagrantly dishonest: the television commercials for candidates in Presidential elections.

Right *Governor Dewey, a scientific demagogue.*

Political chicanery

While statesmen in England, France and Persia have sometimes consulted me, I have never taken political parties as clients of Ogilvy & Mather. First, because they would preoccupy the best brains of the agency, to the detriment of its permanent clients. Second, because they are bad credit risks. Third, because it would be unfair to those people in the agency who pray for the victory of the opposing party. And finally, because it would be difficult to avoid the chicanery which is endemic in all political campaigns.

The first politician to use television was Governor Dewey in his 1950 campaign for the governorship of New York. On one program, Happy Felton, the entertainer, interviewed passers-by under the marquee of the Astor Hotel on 7th Avenue. They would say what interested them in the campaign, and ask questions of the Governor. Dewey watched them on a monitor in the studio, and answered their questions. The day before, his staff had carefully *selected* the passers-by. They had *told* them what they were interested in, and rehearsed their questions. On the last day of the campaign, Dewey was on television from 6 am to midnight. People could telephone the studio. Four women on camera answered the calls and passed along the questions for Dewey to answer. A member of his staff was in a phone booth at the corner drugstore with a pile of nickels.

Dewey, the ex-District Attorney, the battler against corruption, the Governor of the State, thought of himself as an honorable man. It never occurred to him that he was involved in deception. I doubt that it

Right *The bally-hoo of American politics. Should American political advertising have to pass the same scrutiny as commercial advertising?*

would occur to anyone, honorable or dishonorable, to pull such a play today, thirty years later. Times change.

Dewey was a *scientific* demagogue. Before speaking on major issues, he used research to find out which policies had the widest popular support and then put them forward as if he believed in them.

In his book *The Duping of the American Voter*,* my colleague Robert Spero analyzed the commercials used by Kennedy, Johnson, Nixon, Ford and Carter. He concluded that they were 'the most deceptive, misleading, unfair and untruthful of all advertising ... the sky is the limit with regard to what can be said, what can be promised, what accusations can be made, what lies can be told'.

The nine Federal agencies which regulate advertising for products have no say in political advertising. The broadcasting networks, which turn down half the commercials for products submitted to them because they violate their codes, do not apply any code whatever to political commercials. Why not? Because political advertising is considered 'protected speech' under the First Amendment of the US Constitution. The networks are obliged to broadcast every political commercial submitted to them, however dishonest.

In 1964, Johnson's commercials disparaged Senator Goldwater with a cynical dishonesty which would never be tolerated in commercials for toothpaste. They gave voters to understand that Goldwater was an irresponsible, trigger-happy ogre who would start

*The Duping of the American Voter Copyright © 1980 by Robert Spero, Harper & Row, NY

nuclear wars at the drop of a hat. Johnson was presented as a dove of peace.

What had happened was this. Goldwater, one of the most decent men in public life, had been asked by an interviewer to differentiate between the *reliability* and the *accuracy* of guided missiles. He had replied that they were accurate enough 'to lob one into the men's room at the Kremlin'. And he had told another interviewer that it would be *possible* to destroy the forests in North Vietnam by using low-yield atomic weapons. These were no more than theoretical answers to speculative questions. Goldwater did not *recommend* the use of atomic weapons, and Johnson knew this perfectly well.

Nixon's campaigns against Hubert Humphrey and George McGovern were less dishonest, but they too violated the network code for product advertising.

Jimmy Carter's commercials pictured him as an innocent newcomer to politics, with no political organization – a poor farmer with no money. Nothing could have been further from the truth, but the voting public swallowed it. Gerald Ford, his Republican opponent, used commercials which were relatively honest – and lost the election.

Below *In 1964, Barry Goldwater's presidential campaign was effectively scuppered by unscrupulous commercials put out by his opponent, Lyndon Johnson.*

Right *The 'down-home' image of Jimmy Carter's campaign belied the reality – a highly professional, and costly, publicity machine.*

The Kennedys and the Rockefellers have proved that it helps a politician to be *rich*. In his campaign for election to a second term as Democratic Governor of West Virginia, Jay Rockefeller spent $11,000,000 of his own money and defeated his Republican opponent, who spent only $800,000. Rockefeller's commercials were unusually statesmanlike, and a survey found that the people of West Virginia were not shocked by his expenditure. Even his uncle Nelson Rockefeller had not spent so much in his re-election campaign for Governor of New York.

> **'In a period when television commercials are often the decisive factor in deciding who shall be the next President of the United States, dishonest advertising is as evil as stuffing the ballot box.'**

In a period when television commercials are often the decisive factor in deciding who shall be the next President of the United States, dishonest advertising is as evil as stuffing the ballot box. Perhaps the advertising people who have allowed their talents to be prostituted for this villainy are too naïve to understand the complexity of the issues.

The United States is almost the only country which allows political candidates to *buy* commercial time. In England, France and other democracies, the networks allot free time to serious discussion of the issues.

Could political commercials be banned in the United States? Not without violating the US Constitution. Could they be regulated, like every other kind of advertising? That too would be illegal.

Can you imagine Abraham Lincoln hiring an agency to produce 30-second commercials about slavery?

Down with billboards

Highways with billboards have three times as many accidents as highways without billboards. President Eisenhower said, 'I am against those billboards that mar our scenery, but I don't know what I can do about it.' In California, Governor Pat Brown said, 'When a man throws an empty cigarette package from an automobile, he is liable to a fine of $50. When a man throws a billboard across a view, he is richly rewarded.'

Bob Moses, the illustrious Parks Commissioner of New York State, said that 'effrontery and impudence can go no further. The time for compromise with these stubborn and ruthless people is over.' But the majority of legislators are still ready to compromise with them. Here is how a State Senator explains it:

'The billboard lobby shrewdly puts many legislators in its debt by giving them free space during election time. The lobby is savage against the legislator who dares oppose it by favoring anti-billboard laws. It subsidizes his opposition, foments political trouble in his home district, donates billboards to his opponents and sends agents to spread rumours among his constituents.'

Says the *New York Times*, 'the forces of uglification are rampant. The Illinois Democrat and the Florida Republican are united in their determination to protect the financial welfare of the billboard industry at the expense of millions of ordinary tourists who would like to see some scenery as they drive.'

The Highway Beautification Act actually states that it is the purpose of Congress to *promote* outdoor advertising. Some departments

When President Johnson sent the Highway Beautification Bill to Congress, the head of one billboard company claimed that 'There are times when most people would rather look at posters than scenery.'

of the Federal Government are *users* of billboards. The Internal Revenue Service once accepted the free gift of 4,000 empty billboards and used them to urge taxpayers to make honest returns.

One day Monty Spaght, then President of Shell, asked me, 'We get a lot of letters protesting against our use of billboards. Do we *need* billboards?' I replied, 'If you give up billboards, you can still use newspapers and magazines and radio and television. That ought to be enough.' Shell gave up billboards.

Billboards represent less than 2 per cent of total advertising in the United States. I cannot believe that the free-enterprise system would be irreparably damaged if they were abolished. Who is *in favor* of them? Only the people who make money out of them. What kind of people are they? When President Johnson sent the Highway Beautification Bill to Congress, the head of one billboard company protested that Johnson had 'taken a stand in favor of an abstract concept – *beauty*. Some people like scenery and are interested in it. Others can take it or leave it. *There are times when most people would rather look at posters than scenery.*'

The Roadside Business Association has said, 'We do not believe that everyone is for beauty in all things.'

On a Sunday morning in 1958, vigilantes sawed down seven billboards along a highway in New Mexico. Citizens of surrounding areas expressed support for them. One telephone call complained that the vigilantes had not cut down *enough* billboards, and another that they had frustrated the plan of a large group of citizens who had scheduled a mass burning of billboards for later in the month. The vigilantes were never arrested.

In 1961 the Quebec government sent hundreds of men with axes to chop down billboards. In 1963 the head of the New York State Thruway Authority knocked down 53 billboards in a dawn raid; he was sick of legal bickering. But in June 1982, a judge in Oregon overturned an ordinance that required the removal of billboards on the ground that it was *a denial of free speech*. The battle goes on.

Can advertising sell bad products?

It is often charged that advertising can persuade people to buy inferior products. So it can – *once*. But the consumer perceives that the product is inferior and never buys it again. This causes grave financial loss to the manufacturer, whose profits come from *repeat* purchases.

'The best way to increase the sale of a product is to improve the product.'

The best way to increase the sale of a product is to *improve the product*. This is particularly true of food products; the consumer is amazingly quick to notice an improvement in taste and buy the product more often. I have always been irritated by the lack of interest brand managers take in improving their products. One client warned me, 'You are too prone to criticize our products. We could find it easier to accept criticism of our wives.'

Not enough information

Do you think advertising gives you enough information about products? I don't.

Recently, I smashed my car beyond repair and had to buy a new one. For six months I read all the car ads in search of *information*. All I found was fatuous slogans and flatulent generalities. Car manufacturers assume that you are not interested in facts. Indeed, their advertising is not aimed at consumers. Its purpose is to win an ovation when it is projected on the screen at hoopla conventions of dealers. Show-biz commercials have that effect. Sober, factual advertising does not. If their engineering was as incompetent as their advertising, their cars would not run ten miles without a breakdown.

When I advertised Rolls-Royce, I gave the *facts* – no hot air, no adjectives. Later, my partner Hank Bernhard used equally factual advertising for Mercedes. In every case sales went up dramatically – on peppercorn budgets.

I have written factual advertising for a bank, for gasoline, for a stockbroker, margarine, foreign travel and many other products. It *always* sells better than empty advertising.

Before I started writing advertisements, I spent three years selling Aga cooking stoves to Scottish housewives, door to door. All I did was give my customers the facts. It took me 40 minutes to make a sale; about 3,000 words. If the people who write Detroit advertising had started *their* careers as door-to-door salesmen, you and I would be able to find the facts we need in their advertisements.

*   *   *   *   *

Summary

1   Whether economists are right or wrong in proclaiming that advertising is an 'economic' waste, manufacturers do not regard it as a *commercial* waste.

2   Apart from political advertising, which is flagrantly dishonest advertising is now far more honest than consumers realize.

3   The world would be a safer, prettier place without billboards.

4   The majority of campaigns fail to give consumers enough information.

20 I predict 13 changes

I have never been a futurist, and with every passing year my interest in the future declines. However, my publisher insists that I take a shot at predicting the changes that you, gentle reader, will see in the advertising business. So here goes:

1 The quality of research will improve, and this will generate a bigger corpus of knowledge as to what works and what doesn't. Creative people will learn to exploit this knowledge, thereby improving their strike rate at the cash register.

2 There will be a renaissance in print advertising.

3 Advertising will contain more information and less hot air.

4 Billboards will be abolished.

5 The clutter of commercials on television and radio will be brought under control.

6 There will be a vast increase in the use of advertising by governments for purposes of education, particularly *health* education.

7 Advertising will play a part in bringing the population explosion under control.

8 Candidates for political office will stop using dishonest advertising.

9 The quality and efficiency of advertising overseas will continue to improve – at an accelerating rate. More foreign tortoises will overtake the American hare.

10 Several foreign agencies will open offices in the United States, and will prosper.

11 Multinational manufacturers will increase their market-shares all over the non-Communist world, and will market more of their brands internationally. The advertising campaigns for these brands will emanate from the headquarters of multinational agencies, but will be adapted to respect differences in local culture.

12 Direct-response advertising will cease to be a separate speciality, and will be folded into the 'general' agencies.

13 Ways will be found to produce effective television commercials at a more sensible cost.

READING LIST

SCIENTIFIC ADVERTISING by Claude Hopkins. Introduction by David Ogilvy. Bell Publishing, NY.

TESTED ADVERTISING METHODS by John Caples. Foreword by David Ogilvy. Prentice-Hall (Canada) 1975.

REALITY IN ADVERTISING by Rosser Reeves. Alfred Knopf, NY 1961.

MADISON AVENUE by Martin Mayer. Harper & Row, NY 1958.

CONFESSIONS OF AN ADVERTISING MAN by David Ogilvy. Atheneum, NY 1962.

NEW ADVERTISING: TWENTY-ONE SUCCESSFUL CAMPAIGNS FROM AVIS TO VOLKSWAGEN by Robert Glatzer. Citadel Press, NJ 1970.

THE 100 GREATEST ADVERTISEMENTS by Julian Watkins. Dover Publications, NY.

THE ART OF WRITING ADVERTISING by Denis Higgins. Advertising Publications.

HOW TO ADVERTISE by Kenneth Roman and Jane Maas. Foreword by David Ogilvy. St Martin's Press, NY.

ADVERTISING INSIDE OUT by Philip Kleinman. W H Allen, London 1977.

SUCCESSFUL DIRECT MARKETING METHODS by Bob Stone, Crain Books, Chicago 1979.

OR YOUR MONEY BACK by Alvin Eicoff. Crown, NY 1982.

THE ART OF PLAIN TALK by Rudolph Flesch. Collier Macmillan, NY 1962.

WRITING THAT WORKS by Kenneth Roman and Joel Raphaelson. Harper & Row, NY 1981.

THE ELEMENTS OF STYLE by William Strunk and E B White. Collier Macmillan, NY 1979.

THIRTY SECONDS by Michael Arlen. Farrar, Straus & Giroux, NY 1980.

SPEECH CAN CHANGE YOUR LIFE by Dorothy Sarnoff. Doubleday, NY 1970.

THE DUPING OF THE AMERICAN VOTER: DISHONESTY AND DECEPTION IN PRESIDENTIAL TELEVISION ADVERTISING by Robert Spero. Lippincott & Crowell, NY 1980.

OBVIOUS ADAMS by Robert Updegraff. Updegraff Press, Louisville, Kentucky.

Index

PICTURE CREDITS

Doubleday Inc. from *White Collar Zoo* by
Clare Barnes Jr. 58; FCO London 95;
Foote, Cone & Belding 189T; Alan
Hutchison Library 183L, 187B; Keystone
159TL, 210, 212; Pierpoint Morgan
Library 33; Rex Features, 35, 213; Rex
Features/Spia-Press 210B, 211; Frank
Spooner/Gamma 13; J. Walter
Thompson 193; Vision International,
Photo Paolo Koch 214.